U.S. Glasnost

Missing Political Themes in U.S. Media Discourse

The Hampton Press Communication Series
Communication Alternatives
Brenda Dervin, supervisory editor

U.S. Glasnost
Missing Political Themes in U.S. Media Discourse

Johan Vincent Galtung
TRANSCEND: A Peace and Development Network

Richard C. Vincent
Indiana State University

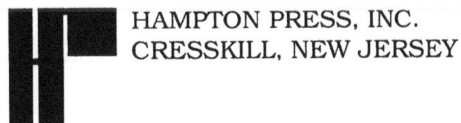
HAMPTON PRESS, INC.
CRESSKILL, NEW JERSEY

Library of Congress Cataloging-in-Publication Data

Galtung, Johan.
    U.S. glasnost : missing political themes in U.S. media discourse / Johan Vincent Galtung, Richard C. Vincent
      p. cm. -- (Hampton Press communication series)
    Includes bibliographic references and indexes.
    ISBN 1-57273-185-0 (cl) -- ISBN 1-57273-186-9 (pbk.)
    1. Mass media--Political aspects--United States. 2. Discourse analysis--Political aspects--United States. 3. United States--Politics and government--1993- I. Title: US glasnost. II. Vincent, Richard C. III. Title. IV. Series

P119.32.U6G35 2003
302.23'0973--dc21

                    2003051110

Hampton Press, Inc.
23 Broadway
Cresskill, NJ 07626

This book is dedicated to the fond memory of a scholar and friend,
Herb Schiller

*   *   *

Herb was an inspiration to activists everywhere. He must also have been a constant source of irritation to the passivists of the world, the mainstream people to whom reality was and is unproblematic, merely a thing producing endless flows of data that can be tapped and distilled and squeezed into publishable career-producing papers and books, an all too common occurrence in our field.

Herb told us that reality was a problematic reality of hegemony, above all by his own country, reducing the material and nonmaterial life chances of others. This perspective he shared with many, probably millions, and should not be trivialized and confused with one tiny line in that spectrum, marxism. New about Herb was that he brought this inquiry into communication studies, particularly as studies of the commodification of culture. He became a leading figure in the media imperialism debate.

Since he wrote his pioneering studies, if anything the situation has deteriorated further. The media have become corporate media, transnationals, and the truths fit to publish are mainly those that serve corporate interests. The passivists fail to imagine what media might have been, and likewise show no alarm that the countless alternative "voices" appearing locally and globally on the Internet demonstrate only a slightly better fulfilling of potential. Just one example of the plight: the reduction of the economy to growth and finance economy with no single mention of distribution, goes unexplored, while real people die, maybe 100,000 a day from mismanaged, distorted, and unreported "economy."

Throughout his life, Herb reacted with revulsion and kept his anger. His perspective will survive when the passivists have receded into a well deserved oblivion. Herb was one of communication's greatest activists, and that is exactly how we shall remember him.

When the unreal is taken for real, then the real becomes unreal;
Where the non-existence is taken for existence, then existence becomes non-existence.

Dream of the Red Chamber
by Tsao Hsueh-Chin
(Doubleday, 1958, p. 7)

Contents

Preface

This book has grown out of a triple frustration.

One is simple: the despair reading, listening to and viewing U.S. media. Here we are in a country reputed to have freedom of the media and yet there are so few signs of that precious commodity. The problem goes far beyond the prominence given to right wing (in the world, not the special U.S. interpretation of that expression) as opposed to left wing views, and the rather obvious tendency for mainstream media to support mainstream politics. In a country with essentially three political currents, again using the world scale-right wing (Clinton, Dukakis), extreme right-wing (Bush, Gingrich, G.W. Bush, Dole) and fascist right-wing (Oliver North and other people behind the Iran-gate and related emanations of their political clout) we would expect a right wing bias.

However, this all-over bias is also shared by much of the rather marginal U.S. left: *the way political issues are cut.* "But that is not the basic problem" is the perennial complaint of so many foreigners in this country, listening to, or reading news commentary in utter disbelief. This is, until they/we learn that *the way the issue is cut is the issue.* Even the basic issue. That the line between reality and virtual reality is not only blurred. The virtual reality constructed by the way the issue is cut is the reality. And this goes far beyond political ideology. Nor does the word *simplification* cover the transformation adequately. No doubt complexity is lost, but some of that is inevitable. The problem is how, why, and with what consequences.

The second source of frustration is more theoretical. Hundreds, perhaps thousands of articles have been published in recent years. The field is blossoming with fascinating material, including some sophisticated theory. It is a beautiful example of how the social sciences today can be inspired by the humanities, just as they were inspired by the natural sciences (the answer is obviously both/and) there is a danger here. In the 1950s and the 1960s social scientists became fascinated with mathematics and statistics for their own sake. Are we now heading for an equally uncritical fascination with literary criticism, with texts, contexts, and sub-texts for their own sake? Only syntax and perhaps semantics, and no pragmatics? Are we going to believe "it is all in the discourse;" is there no external reality "out there" any longer? How are the contact points between discourse analysis, and not only political analysis but also political action going to be articulated? What is going to happen to those fighting for a subjugated discourse, the women, the Blacks, the Iraqis, the Somalis, the Serbs, the suppressed of all kinds, often referred to as *minorities* even when together they constitute a clear majority? They know what discourse involves. They know that discourse control=power=politics, and that discourse critique=power struggle=counter-politics. They know the discourse has to be improved to improve politics. In many ways they=we.

The third source of frustration is more methodological. How is discourse analysis done? A generation or two of social scientists have been sacrificed on the altar of statistical significance tests (for one presentation of counter-arguments, see Johan Galtung, *Theory and Methods of Social Research*, ch. II, 4.4). Some ritualistic sacrifice is still taking place. Is a new generation heading for text analysis is the same sacrificial spirit? At the very least some empirical critical, and also constructive discourse analysis is indispensable as consumer protection. And in the theory, like in any other theory, some minimum of logic makes no harm. Deep intuitions are needed, and so is some basic intellectual craftsmanship of the more artisanal kind. This book is also an effort to offer the reader an elementary introduction to discourse theory; hardly deeper than others have done before, but perhaps solidifying and systematizing the theory construction.

The book is an effort to respond to that triple political-theoretical-methodology challenge, only that the political is also theoretical and the theoretical also political, and both of them have to with methods and vice versa, as usual. The focus is on world politics as communicated in U.S. media, with the hope that one day there may be a USA Glasnost, giving voice, articulating the concerns of Other, not only Self; and not only by interviewing them but by reporting and discussing issues so that their views are accommodated. The book was preceded by the same authors' *Global Glasnost: Toward a New World Information and Communication Order?* which explores the state of world news flow and equity.

Professor Galtung is indebted to James Skelly and Michael Schudson of the University of California, San Diego (where he was visiting Professor Spring 1987), and to Majid Tehranian of the University of Hawai'i (where he was Distinguished Professor of Peace Studies, and lectured in the Department of Communication Spring 1988). His work in the field of communication goes back to 1961 when the first version of "The Structure of Foreign News" was published by the fledgling Peace Research Institute in Oslo. Obviously, the media are a major concern of peace studies. He is presently engaged in getting courses and summer schools in "peace journalism" started in a number of countries and heavily engaged in the activities of TRANSCEND: A Peace and Development Network.

Professor Vincent specializes in media communication and has done previous work on its discourse. He too is grateful to Majid Tehranian, Andrew Arno, and many other colleagues at the University of Hawai'i (where he was an associate professor of Communication), Farrell Corcoran, Paschal Preston, and others at Dublin City University (where he was a Fulbright scholar in international communication), and to colleagues at Indiana State University, where he serves as chairperson of the Department of Communication. They have all encouraged his work on news discourse and in media studies generally.

Needless to say, we are also very grateful to our students for their constructive criticism, and particularly to Carolyn DiPalma, Robert Zimmerman, and Malia Robinson, then at the University of Hawai'i, for research and secretarial assistance, and finally our students and staff at TRANSCEND and Indiana State University for their assistance and support. We particularly wish to acknowledge the contributions made by Pei-Ling Lee.

Johan Vincent Galtung
Versonnex (Ain), France

Richard C. Vincent
Terre Haute, Indiana (USA)

Introduction
What Discourse is All About

—But that is not the basic problem.

It was Fall 1985. One of the present authors was Visiting Professor of World Politics of Peace and War at Princeton University that academic year. The telephone rang one morning. A TV journalist was calling, and the question was one with which anybody working on international politics in general, and peace and war politics in particular, would be rather familiar: "Professor Galtung, the United States has just withdrawn from the World Court in connection with adjudication in the Nicaragua case, the mining of the harbor. I understand you are working in this field and wonder whether we could have an interview?"

The answer was yes, on the premise that the issue was a relatively simple one. The United States had withdrawn, essentially because Washington thought, rightly, that the Court would come up with a conclusion not in Washington's favor.[1] Washington might be subjectively convinced that the Court would be wrong in arriving at such a conclusion, and might also be subjectively convinced that by being present Washington would in fact legitimize the Court's decision through participation. World commentary, except for the most U.S.-influenced and U.S.-loyal press, indicated that Washington might be relatively alone in entertaining this kind of opinion. The journalist was ready for commentary.

The network team arrived and installed its hardware, of considerable size, brightening the room and heating it up to sauna-like conditions. The first question came like a shot: "Professor Galtung, why is the World Court so unpopular around the world?"

Galtung had recently arrived in the United States, 25 years since he last visit as a social science professor, and had no particular illusions about U.S. media ability to handle world issues when the United States is heavily involved. But much had changed since his first long stay as a junior professor at Columbia University in 1957-60; and not for the better. He was taken aback. The answer after the first exclamation, "But that is not the basic problem!", when like this: "I do not think the issue is whether the World Court is unpopular or not; moreover, I doubt that the World Court is unpopular all around the world. Rather, the issue in connection with the U.S. withdrawal is whether the World Court is popular in Washington, which it definitely is not in this case, as the United States probably is heading for a decision not in agreement to the Court."

From this point on they actually had a quite good discussion. The interviewer tried to recapture him in her discourse. He entered it to some extent, then tried to catch her in his discourse, which he felt better reflected the real issue. The end of the story was already in sight: the interview never came on the air. An explanation was given later: "The viewers would not understand it."

No comment. Let us proceed to the second example, which occurred at the University of California, San Diego, in April 1987. A TV "space-bridge" between the Soviet Union and the United States had been set up, in this case with media people in Moscow and San Francisco participating. *Glasnost* and *perestroika* were major themes in both U.S. and Soviet presentations and analyses of the Soviet Union. The space bridge was functioning perfectly, with big audiences in both cities, and the TV audience must also have been considerable. The U.S. editors were probing the extent of freedom in Soviet media, and vice versa.

The basic point in the debate can be summarized roughly as follows. The U.S. side explored whether Soviet journalists have the freedom to inquire into issues related to civil and political human rights. The Soviet journalists answered "yes." The U.S. journalists followed up stating, never doubting the answer, that "your freedom is limited by one important consideration: you cannot criticize the nature of the socialist system that produces so many infractions of civil and political rights, you can only pursue individual cases!" No real answer came from the Soviet side.

The Soviet journalists then did the same for issues related to social and economic human rights in the United States. "To what extent can U.S. media pursue the cases of the thousands of shelterless people lying in the streets, the tens of millions who go hungry to bed?" U.S. media people eagerly denied that there is any restraint in pursuing these issues. The Soviet journalists then followed up insisting, never doubting the answer, that "your freedom is limited by one important consideration: you cannot criticize the nature of the capitalist system that produces so many infractions of social and economic human rights, you can only pursue individual cases!" No real answer came from the U.S. side.

Having witnessed such ping-pong matches between those superpowers and their client-states people in general more times than one might care to remember, and having had the bad fortune of spending the better part of one's life in that waiting room in history euphemistically known as the "Cold War,"[2] waiting for disaster or for somebody to lift the cold curfew, Galtung left the room. He had seen about enough. Outside in the brilliant sunlight, while he was enjoying the reprieve from this miserable debate, a local TV team with an eager journalist approached him: "Professor Galtung, you are working in this field, you just saw a part of the program. Tell us, is there any sign that they are loosening up?" "To be quite frank, I did not see any sign that the last speakers, the U.S. side, were loosening up. It sounded just like the old verbal game of trying to drill the other party into the corner where it supposedly is weakest, and one's own country strongest." "I was thinking of whether the Russians are loosening up!?" "My answer is that I did not see any sign of either side loosening up. This is an old game they have been playing throughout the Cold War, the U.S. side complaining, correctly, about the lack of civil and political rights in the Soviet Union and the Soviets, equally correctly, complaining about the lack of social and economic rights in the United States. It is very easy for me as a person from the Nordic countries to take a 'plague on both your houses' stance, because in our countries we have both types of human rights fairly well established."

The rest of the story was predictable: the interview was never aired. The explanation, already given on the spot, was "our viewers will have difficulty understanding this."

To many U.S. readers the author probably comes through as an unnecessarily difficult person.[3] The legitimacy of the discourses opened up by the interviewers is too deeply internalized to be called into question. Why not answer a straightforward question? If the United States withdraws from the World Court, something must be wrong with the World Court. If anybody in the world has to loosen up, then it should not be the United States, but most definitely the Soviet Union.

In a country where so many inhabitants seem to believe that "no press in the world is as free as ours," a discourse already firmly imprinted on the minds of men, women, children, everybody, is not easily changed. Whether "our viewers don't understand it" or "the journalists don't understand it," both or neither, should be a matter of empirical investigation. However, the journalists are probably at least partly right, as the discourses tend to be not only conventions of speech but also of thought. Thus, an idea like "plague on both your houses"—that both the Soviet Union and the United States might suffer from serious human rights deficits[4]—might not easily be accommodated; and being against U.S. harbor mining might read like being in favor of the Sandinistas, again excluding the third possibility (being skeptical of both). There certainly is an issue here, and more than enough justification for both the title and the subtitle of this book.

This book proceeds as follows.

First, a chapter about why this whole issue is so important, and how it fits into the theory of democracy and censorship.

Second, case studies, twenty of them in a chapter on discourse inadequacy. The reader is at the same time introduced to alternative ways of thinking about a number of issues, many of which are from the Cold War period. A little distance makes us see issues more clearly, among them the "missing themes."

Third, along the same line, twenty more issues, this time taken from a book, *Taking Sides*, showing that in almost all cases the authors of the book are doing exactly that, taking sides, in applying a special U.S. angle to a complex reality. The issues are taken from foreign policy and world politics.

Fourth, a theory of discourse analysis. Based on the preceding chapters, basic tools of discourse analysis are now introduced, such as definitions, classifications and typologies, cartesian products—useful not only for speech, but also for thought—ending up with an identification of such basic dimensions of discourse analysis as narrow versus broad, deep versus shallow, more or less adequate. A basic goal of the book is the definition and exploration of the dimensions of adequacy.

Fifth, a theory of discourse expansion. How do we improve discourses? The general argument of the book is never in terms of one discourse being wrong and other (the authors', for example), being right, but in terms of one discourse being broader, deeper, more adequate than the other. The problem is how to do it.

Sixth, factors impeding discourse expansion. The general solution to the problems discussed is not to rule out any position taken on an issue, but to develop a broader and deeper discourse. Why does that not happen more often, what stands in the way?

Seventh, discourse and meta-discourse, an effort to identify hidden or not-so-hidden codes that steer discourse construction.

Eighth, script and meta-script, an effort to identify some of those hidden or not-so-hidden codes that steer how we construct texts, putting flesh on the discourse bones, so to speak, speaking and writing, not to mention acting and thinking.

Ninth, discourse, script, and new technologies, discussing the impact new communication technologies will have on the construction of news discourses.

Tenth, a conclusion, recapturing the title of the book, the major theme—*glasnost*—and how more of that precious commodity could blossom in the United States. Soviet *glasnost* now belongs to history, but that word caught the imagination of millions. This book is a small contribution to help keep it alive, not merely consigning it to history—however, with full knowledge that this is an uphill struggle.

A few words of warning. This book is about media discourse, discourse theory, and missing political themes in U.S. discourse. It is not about other topics highly relevant to the state of affairs in the U.S. media such as ownership patterns,[5] simple, clear-cut cases of censorship,[6] how consciousness is manufactured,[7] how our minds are managed in general,[8] and by public opinion agencies in particular.[9] The present book focuses more on the non-intended, the non-manufactured, the non-managed, on communication going wrong even when it is not distorted by interests and values.

At no point in this book is there any institution or person who is found particularly guilty of anything. No direct violence is being exercised against our civil and political rights. Talking about structural violence does not make much sense either. What is being discussed is in our minds, in the cognitive section. It is found in that part of the deep culture rather in the social structure, or in the personalities of editors. Cultural violence, yes: the distortions may often serve the important functions of legitimizing direct and structural violence. To identify these distortions and develop some ideas about their removal is not only communication research, but also peace research, and intended as such. However, in no way should that be interpreted to mean that there are not also other, and serious, problems with U.S. media.

NOTES

1. Which it did, in the International Court of Justice judgment of June 27, 1986, not only deciding that the blockade was in violation of international law, but so was U.S. aid to the contras; this was against the votes of the U.S., the U.K., and the Japanese judges.
2. It may be worth remembering that only a part of the Cold War was about borders and freedom in East Europe and East Asia and which system should prevail in the world (and the arms race that came out of this and some other factors). The Cold War was also inside societies: *which side are you on?*—the simple logic being, if you are against one of them then you have to be in favor of the other. Those who were against both of them obviously had some problems, being disliked in both camps (but not in the third camp, the nonaligned movement).
3. As an example of another difficult person, Gore Vidal might serve. He has suffered the same frustrations and more than once, as reported in this article "Cue the Green God, Ted," *The Nation*, August 7/14, 1989. He reports (p. 173) how his answers to a rather important question, "What will the United States do without the Enemy" (use Arabs, the Japanese, and the threat to the ecosphere instead) were prerecorded on the occasion of the famous Gorbachev UN speech of December 7, 1988. "None of this was used, of course, but a man who writes Russians Are Coming thrillers was shown." Evidently Vidal cut the issue the wrong way; and/or "our viewers will not understand it." This made the United States look irrational by entering a discourse of deeper motives in foreign policy.
4. For an elaboration of this theme of flexible human rights agendas, see Johan Galtung, *Human Rights in Another Key* (Cambridge: Policy Press, 1994), "Blue, Red, and Green Generation Rights—and Then What?," pp. 151-154.
5. See the important book by Ben H. Bagdikian, *The Media Monopoly*, Boston, Beacon Press, 1983, 1989, and his article "The Lords of the Global Village," *The Nation*, June 12, 1989. There is also the report attacking ABC's "Nightline" and Ted Koppel for his selection of "guests" (prepared by William Hoynes and David Croteau of the Department of Sociology, Boston College), which includes that the chances of being invited are particularly high if one is a "white, male member of the government, military or corporate Establishment" (*The Honolulu Advertiser*, February 6, 1989)—the ruling class, in other words. Also, see the article by Mark Crispin Miller, "Free the Media," *The Nation*, June 3, 1996, pp. 9-28, with the already famous

"centerfold" (pp. 23-26) showing which great corporations control how much and what: General Electric (NBC), Time Warner (CNN), Disney/Cap Cities (ABC), and Westinghouse (CBS); two of them with heavy defense contracts. The term "corporate media" is an effort to capture this phenomenon, but perhaps insensitive to the free space that strong individuals can create, like CBS' "60 Minutes."

6. Thus, the documentary movie "Coverup," dealing with the Iran-Contra affair, although launched June 24, 1988, was not shown on TV during the entire election campaign of Fall 1989, although it was clearly relevant. *Censored: The News That Didn't Make the News—and Why* has already published its 20th anniversary edition (New York: Seven Stories Press, 1996), featuring Walter Cronkite with a chronology of censorship from 605 B.C. to 1996.

7. See the important books by E.S. Herman and Noam Chomsky, *Manufacturing Consent: The Political Economy of the Mass Media* (New York: Pantheon Books, 1989); Andrew Kreig, *Spiked: How Chain Management Corrupted America's Oldest Newspaper* (Old Saybrook, CT: Peregrine Press); and Mark Hertsgaard, *On Bended Knee: The Press and the Reagan Presidency* (New York: Farrar, Straus, Giroux, 1988).

8. See the classic by the dean of critical communication studies, Herbert I. Schiller, *The Mind Managers* (Boston: Beacon Press, 1973); or, for instance, his article "Information: Important Issue for '88," *The Nation*, July 4-11, 1987.

9. See Johan Carlisle, "Public Relationships: Hill & Knowlton, Robert Gray and the CIA," *CovertAction*, No. 44, Spring 1993, pp. 19-25. For Ruder Finn, the other major agency working for clients in former Yugoslavia, see Nora Beloff, "PR—The Secret Weapon," *Jewish Chronicle*, December 10, 1993, and *Intelligence Digest*, February 4, 1994. Sooner or later PR news management will become a major issue. The revelations after the Kuwait incubator and the Kuwaiti ambassador's daughter scandals left no trace—the system goes on unabated.

1

Democracy and Censorship: a Mini-Theory

MEDIA, IMMEDIA, DEMOCRACY A AND DEMOCRACY B

Why are media so important? Because they mediate. They are in-betweens, go-betweens, between the sectors of society, making one sector visible to the other, being a mirror of social reality. They can do this job well or badly. In small societies relations are immediate, direct; society is based on "immedia," talk and body language, and things. Media are not needed. But in a larger society media become indispensable. And even the smallest village cannot rely on immedia alone, as it is also embedded in districts, countries, regions, and the whole world. Try to think the media away and we are left in the dark. Complain about them, but as there is no way of doing without the media, we might as well try to make the best of the situation.

But there is another reason. If the society is a democracy, which requires accountability, then more than mutual visibility among sectors of society is demanded. We demand transparency—the hidden story, not only a surface reflected in a mirror—because we might act upon the images conveyed by the media. The media still mediate, but now in a very dynamic way. And that answers a question unasked above: what does it mean that the media do the job well, or badly? The answer: they do their job well when they serve democracy.

In the beginning was the word and then not just the single human individual, but human interaction in the small group, the small society. Without gender division people could not procreate, without generation division people could not perpetuate. And without a division between rulers and ruled they probably could not grow. Democracy enters: *rule with rulers having the consent of the ruled.*

That makes democracy an exercise in communication, for how can the ruled know whether they want to give that consent unless they know what the rulers are doing in speech and/or action, and how can the rulers know whether they have that consent unless the ruled communicate their thoughts in speech and/or action. The question is whether that communication is immediate or mediated.

If immediate, then we have direct democracy, or *Democracy A,* the primordial way of obtaining consent through dialogue until there is consensus, like in a kinship or friendship group, an African tribe, a Japanese corporation with "quality circles." Not everybody among the ruled will participate, and some sides of the divides will have more status, some less. There is also a maximum size to the group.

If mediated, then we have indirect democracy, or *Democracy B,* the big-society way of obtaining consent through debate until a vote is called; today this is found in a majority of countries around the world as elections. Not everybody among the ruled will have the right to vote, some sides of the divides having more status, some less. But there is no maximum size (think of Indian Union elections or elections for the European Union Parliament).

The two forms do not exclude each other, as indicated by the examples. But whereas Democracy A can do with immedia as means of communication, Democracy B cannot. Media are indispensable as carriers of signals, messages, and images, like ambassadors in a world without telecommunication. Ideally they have to make the rulers transparent to the ruled, and the ruled transparent to the rulers, both in terms of speech and action, perhaps also thought (intent).

In modern society it seems reasonable to distinguish between rulers of two kinds—those who run the state, and those who run capital. Most of the ruled do not do that, but can be found in civil society, with its countless organizations along the lines of kinship and friendship, vicinity and affinity. Montesquieu's classical division of power[1] into legislature, executive, and judiciary can be located inside the state, capital not having attained such orders of magnitude in his days.

But today it has, and so have the media. They both mediate between the other three (state, capital and civil society) and constitute a fourth power in their own right, whether counted relative to the Montesquieu three or the larger three. And that gives us one image of the four pillars of modern society:[2] The media are supposed to mediate. They are placed in the middle, ideally telling each "pillar" what goes on in the other two, accurately for mirroring, adequately for transparency. There are three clear ways they can go wrong: by being ruled by the political power of state, by the economic power of capital, or by vulgar culture—poor tastes in civil society. The media need to have much power over themselves to steer clear of all three. The best among them do, although most do not.[3]

Democracy is a cybernetic system with feed-back mechanisms, and the media provide these feedback mechanisms. The more unimpeded the communication in all directions, the more democratic potential in the country, other things being equal.

In *direct democracy* there is a direct feedback loop between ruler and ruled. The ruler acts and the ruled reacts in verbal or nonverbal languages. The ruler then responds with re-reactions and so on, in sequences with no beginning and no end. But there is more to democracy than general interaction processes where expectations of how the other party will react are taken into account. The point about democracy is that the ruled in principle have the upper hand, the final say, such as by a referendum.

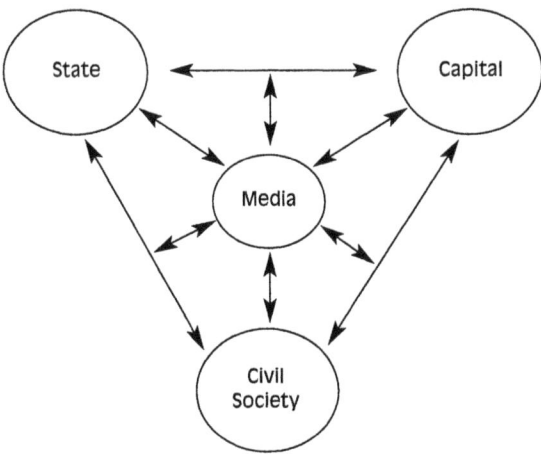

Figure 1.1. Modern society: The four pillars (and powers)

In *indirect democracy* the loops are expanded because the system is too large for ruler and ruled to interact face to face, and for either one to take adequate note of the reactions of the other. With the media inserted we get a triangular ruler-media-ruled loop that may run both ways, yielding six relations.

The ruled provide general instructions through elections to the rulers, but may have difficulties ascertaining exactly what happens as a result. The system is less than transparent. The media, through investigative reporting, should be able to report exactly what happens. But a condition for democracy to function is that the ruled are (a) able to and (b) motivated to use media information to emit the same or new instructions to the rulers, and (c) that the rulers care. The media have to give voice to the ruled, not only to the mediators, journalists, columnists, and editors.

Democracy may easily go wrong along any one of the six links in the loop. The instructions given by the ruled to the rulers may be too vague or too precise; the rulers may make themselves opaque, impenetrable to any investigative reporting; the media may report, but be so cozy with the rulers that no message is conveyed to the ruled; the ruled may fail to use the media or be excluded from them; and the media may be too sophisticated or too crude (or both) for the ruled, and so on. The democratic loop is as strong as its weakest link. Democracy, consequently, is highly vulnerable.

This becomes even more obvious when we bring in Figure 1.1. Civil society communicates with the state by having a "Trojan horse" inside the state—the Legislature—reflecting some particular associations in civil society called parties. And the state, more particularly the executive, communicates with civil society proposing bills and so forth, and in principle makes itself accountable—in a democracy, that is. The two-way link can easily be corrupted, as the legislators often have better contact with the executive than with civil society, their voters. After all, they both live in the head of the social body, the capital of the country.

But this link is a jewel relative to two key missing links in modern society—capital-civil society and capital-state. Of course, capital communicates with the market by providing a supply of goods and services, and with civil society by responding to demand backed up by cash-voting with money. But that communication is primitive. The two parties have to guess intentions rather than having debates and dialogues about empirical and potential products. They do not really relate.[4]

Capital and state do relate, however, but in the form of lobbying and corruption. Moreover, as opposed to the legislature-executive link, even if they may make themselves transparent to each other, that relation remains opaque to civil society in spite of, or because of, the enormous impact on society. Modern society has not yet succeeded in the task of integrating capital in a democratic way. They are like elephants in china shops: huge, threatening.

Figure 1.1 can be read as two triangular ruler-media-ruled loops, one with state and one with capital, with six relations in each. Then there is the state-media-capital loop; a total of eighteen relations, each of them to be made public. And each of them can go astray, including the four pillars themselves.[5]

But there is also a simpler reading. The media have, essentially, six tasks: to report on state, capital and civil society, making them transparent to themselves and to each other; and to report on the relation between them, making communication or non-communication transparent. This should be done in a language sophisticated enough to convey details about reality, yet crude enough to be understood, so that debate and dialogue can have an impact on the three pillars and their relations.

A crucial task for communication theory is to explore the conditions for messages to pass through this cybernetic system. One problem is that any discourse adequate for political *reality* is a discourse of the past, accommodating reports about that which *is*—*empirical* reality—and not political *thinking* about that which *might be*—*potential* reality.[6]

The discourse battle line also runs here. *Status quo*-oriented people will claim that discourses that served them well in the past will also be adequate in the future because future reality will essentially be identical with empirical reality (the meaning of status quo.) Change-oriented people will not only have to fight for changes in reality, but also for changes in speech and thought processes about reality, in other words for discourse change.

If there is a tacit alliance between the rulers and the media because the media have been reporting only empirical reality, the situation becomes even more difficult. People with new ideas will have an uphill fight influencing the rulers by getting their ideas through the media unmolested. They will have to superimpose potential on empirical reality. Media serving democracy will have to steer a middle course between the two.

When media people say "people simply do not understand," this is wrong when referring to people in general, but not when referring to themselves.[7] The media people may "simply not understand," meaning that they may have to be educated, or that alternative media will have to be created. Under censorship regimes, "alternative media" usually means clandestine media, smuggled from one private space to the other. Or it might mean *samizdat*, not exactly clandestine, but not exactly public either. Under more liberal regimes alternative media would be on the margin of society: like small news-sheets; that extra little program slot beamed to "fringe groups"; *The Nation, The Village Voice, Mother Jones, The Utne Reader*, not to mention the legendary I.F. Stone's *Weekly*.[8]

A major implication for democratic theory is that democracy is not only dependent on an open channel of messages shaped as a loop, with signals being initiated at any point in the loop, beamed in either direction, running the loop, correcting and being corrected everywhere. Democracy also means that certain demands have to be placed on this channel. Thus, there should be *channel diversity*: the principle of manifold certainly applies. If one channel fails, as very often happens, there should be others. The channel to fall back upon should not only be direct, the face-to-face immedia, but there should be additional media channels; public *and* private, national *and* local, high-tech *and* low-tech, and so forth.[9]

The channels should have a certain capacity, and a certain velocity. The time lag between action and reaction should not be so long that the actor initiating the action in the meantime forgets what it is about. Moreover, democratic channels will have to be two-way. Rulers have to appear in public, at least in press conferences, even if the media must mediate the reactions of the public. In no way should this exclude the direct, unmediated approach that often made Cuba so fascinating in the early 1960s: Fidel appearing in mass meetings, responding to questions from the audience. Circus to some, Democracy to others, but no substitute for the secret, unimpeded ballot. Nor is the ballot a substitute for direct democracy, and effective steering in a cybernetic mechanism also presupposes variety adequacy, as stipulated by Ashby's Law.[10] The yes/no choice of an election is very small, but the variety of all signals from all ruled would be too high for rulers to act.

Another necessary condition is *content adequacy*, which obviously varies from case to case. Generally, communication should reflect both empirical and potential reality sufficiently well to accommodate empirical, critical, and constructive analysis.

Over and above all of these points, however important they are, looms the problem of *discourse adequacy*. The telegraph lines traversing the countryside during the last century and into this one were channels in a highly visible form. But they would be of no use unless signals could pass, and that presupposed as a minimum an alphabet (Morse) by means of which words can be formed, by means of which sentences can be formed, by means of which texts can be formed. For the received reading not to be too discrepant from the sent reading there has to be a mental framework shared between sender and receiver, between ruled, ruler, and media. Another name for that mental framework is *paradigm*, or *discourse*. The discourse should be adequate to the task, and that is the topic of this book.

To understand better what adequacy means, the reader is now invited into two chapters dealing in different ways with discourse inadequacy, combining examples with some excursions into the discourse theory. The theory will then be presented in chapters 4, 5, and 6 and elaborated further in chapters 7 and 8. But before that, and serving as one more introduction to discourse analysis, communication when democracy has been negated in a repressive society will have to be examined. One negation is anarchic, falling back on immedia. Another negation is repressive, known as censorship.

CENSORSHIP I AND CENSORSHIP II

In any theory of discourse such concepts as more or less "broad," "deep," or generally "adequate" discourse will play a major role. A theory of discourse should not be purely descriptive or predictive; there should also be evaluative or prescriptive elements, otherwise the theory is not very useful. There should be policy implications, even guides for action.

This brings us immediately to a very important problem: what could prevent a discourse from being "broad," "deep," and "adequate," regardless of what precise meaning we give to these terms? As will be seen in chapters 4 and 5, as well as 6, 7, and 8, answers are complex, numerous, often subtle and very different. But one obvious answer is very well known in the history of media: *censorship*. It is direct, intended, like direct violence, not hidden and subtle like structural and cultural violence.[11] It is more similar to the answers to be explored in chapters 4 through 8.

Censorship limits speech, often by controlling discourse. Rules are given dividing *what* can be talked about and *how*, in two or three categories: the "permitted" and the "not permitted," sometimes subdividing the "permitted" into the "prescribed" and the "indifferent," with "not permitted" referred to as "proscribed."

Hence, there are taboos. These taboos are enforced in the sense that there is punishment awaiting whoever transgresses the borderlines and ventures into non-permitted, proscribed territory. People may think whatever they wish, and may even express it in speech as long as this takes place in private space, inside the family, apartment, house, or in such innocent places with status as free intellectual zones (even under very authoritarian regimes), such as churches, mosques, temples, and institutes/academies.[12] The status given to the latter, for instance in ex-socialist Europe, was probably not only due to the expectation, often justified, that academic speech will be incomprehensible to the population at large anyhow. Rather, it is a reflection of the special nature of the people populating such places: clerics, intellectuals, researchers. In the traditional, feudal European class/caste order such people were at the top of the social order, even above the aristocracy. To silence them is a dramatic step indeed, almost impossible—better to isolate them, marginalize them. Specify that they keep their speech within clear, not only social but even spatial limits—inside the dwelling, their working quarters, the academy, the campus. Kill them with silence, not bullets, unless they come out in the public space of citizens in general, with clear words.

What is censored is not speech but *public* speech, even more so in the mass media, because they presumably reach the "masses" and, particularly if accessible to all, are not couched in the jargon of religious, ideological, academic, or professional groups. Public speech, however, is a broader category than mass media, as it would also include addressing audiences or informal meetings, gatherings, crowds, mobs, and so forth, in public space. And even though thoughts are private, like speech in private quarters, today we know how the Stasis in the DDR, like the Nazis before them, also kept an attentive ear on speech in private space, assuming it might go public.

This was the general rule in Eastern European authoritarian regimes. *Glasnost* expanded that freedom far into public space; hitlerism and stalinism limited the freedom even in private space; for example, encouraging children to inform on their parents. No space was any longer considered private.

We shall now define two types of censorship, *Censorship I* and *Censorship II*, and use them as tools to understand why and how there could be a *glasnost* giving voice, in the Soviet Union and why it does not happen in the United States, although it is much needed.

Censorship I is easily understood. The editor has to submit drafts of articles, editorials, and so forth to the state censor, that "little head," the *glavlit*, who might actually have an office in the newspaper itself, or a central office in the city/town for all local mass media to report to. The censor literally speaking draws lines indicating what is permitted and what not, and on what index.

From this point on a complex bargaining game with two players, editor and censor, can be played in many different ways. The two actors operating are clearly distinguishable persons: the editor and the censor, not counting the rest of the staff on both sides (in reality it is, of course, much more complicated). There is also the important distinction between the prescribed and the indifferent. Thus, the editor can gain credit by printing the prescribed, that which the censor would like to see in print even if the editor does not believe a single word, and apply that credit toward the debts he incurs when something proscribed gets into the columns in spite of the censor's keen surveillance.

Further, it might be possible to make another deal: the editor lessens the censor's work burden by guaranteeing that there is some "indifferent" copy he does not have to read, it is clean anyhow. In return the editor is occasionally permitted to print something not quite as it should be. Could that "once in a while" under certain conditions be extended from once a month to once a week until the system becomes an empty shell, ready to be abandoned? In the end something like that evidently happened.

All these are important questions in the life cycle of an editor-censor relationship. But the basic point remains that not only are there issues and perspectives that should be avoided, there are also concrete positions that should be avoided on issues that nevertheless should be articulated. In pre-*glasnost* Soviet Union, productivity was certainly a concern. But the only position along that important dimension to be expressed publicly would be that productivity is increasing, or at least not decreasing. When or if it decreases the censor would prescribe silence, not only for that (stand-)point, but for the whole dimension.

In the classical Soviet model nothing of this was contrary to the emphasis put on the freedom of the press, defined as freedom from any pressure exercised by capital[13]—for instance by (threatening) withdrawal of advertising. Freedom of the press meant freedom from influence by (strong) capital, "capital" in practice meaning capitalists. With capitalists no longer around the syllogism had a neat conclusion: there is freedom of the press, by definition. No doubt this definition picked up one aspect of a free press.

We now contrast Censorship I with Censorship II. Censorship is operating, but there is no assumption that there is any representative from high up, any State *glavlit*, present in the media building, or in a central office downtown, or anywhere else for that matter, except in a limited sense; for example, in connection with sex and violence (particularly the former—for the latter there appears to be no limit), and "very sensitive" national security issues.[14]

As the ex-Soviet Union the United States also has a clear definition of freedom of the press: freedom from any pressure exercised by the state—the state meaning "ministry of information" or "ministry of culture," information meaning "disinformation." As the ex-Soviet Union the United States has implemented its particular type of freedom of the press.[15] The absence of state-appointed censors is taken as evidence that censorship is not present, the way absence of economic pressure from economic organizations was interpreted in the Soviet Union. But the freedom of the Soviet press from capitalists was in a vacuum, because there were no capitalists around. No struggle was needed to ensure a freedom already there. The freedom of the U.S. press from the state is not in a vacuum; there is quite a lot of state around. More control may actually be exercised than most realize, through the FBI or CIA for instance, or by persuading the media to hold a story for a day or two for security reasons. Struggle against Censorship I is also on the agenda in the United States, but that is not the topic of this book.[16] The topic is Censorship II, and the U.S problem is that the Censorship II, *glavlit*, can be said to reside inside the heads of publishers, news directors, and reporters.

There is a collectively shared mass media culture, to a large extent subconscious, although some of it may be very conscious in the minds of certain editors.[17] It is collectively shared in the sense that they all know that the other members of the collectivity also know and write and publish according to roughly speaking the same rules.[18] Of course, this does not mean that positions are prescribed down to a single point, except around July 4 when exalted comments about the United States of America as a social formation in general, and its unique role in the world in particular, are certainly not only permitted but also prescribed. A paper, a radio station, a TV channel that does not come up with a very positive viewpoint in its commentary on that occasion would probably suffer the consequences, unless already marginalized.

What emerges is something implicit, and also in a sense much more insidious: *dimension control* under Censorship II, as opposed to *point control* under Censorship I. An issue is raised. Almost immediately a consensus seems to emerge about how the issue is going to be discussed (chapter 2), meaning more precisely along which dimensions. Along those dimensions any position may be permitted under Censorship II regimes, assuming no Censorship I element. What is not permitted is to venture outside those dimensions, broadening the discourse. Example: terrorism is to be discussed in terms of *consequences*, and possible counter-measures; not in terms of political *causes*, unless these causes can be seen as clearly non-applaudable or non-laudable, such as those originating from "cranky and/or criminal" individuals, and then by psychiatrizing them.

The insidious nature of this latter type of censorship can be most clearly seen when comparing the two models. In Censorship I the control takes place in a *social* system consisting of editor and censor; in Censorship II the control takes place inside the *personal* system of the editor. It is less explicit. There is no counterpart against whom anger and rebelliousness can be acted out. There may not even be awareness that censorship is taking place. Yet almost everybody in the editorial office, in the cacophony of typewriters, computers, teleprinters, fax machines, telephones, and e-mail knows in his or her guts when the thin line is transgressed. Under Censorship I, the censor can punish the editor—for example, by revoking a license. Under Censorship II the editor is at best trained to punish himself by a bad conscience, whether in the form of guilt or anticipated shame. But more realistic is the question: what will the colleagues say!

The neophyte will very quickly be told that "we don't write stuff like that" by the older journalist. The older journalist no longer asks the question—he knows. The editor will tell himself that "we don't print that kind of stuff" because (a) "our readers do not like it" and/or (b) "our readers will not understand it." The young journalist might not agree, having just returned from an interesting interview with some atypical person and trying to adjust his (the journalist's) discourse to reflect those interesting views. But whatever *new* insight a journalist out in the field might get is not easily communicated to the editor in his office, long since out of touch with direct field experience. Yet the ultimate decision is his, or the dreaded "night editor's."[19]

There are substantial advantages to dimension control over point control from a democratic point of view. To be able to express at least two different views, the minimum to constitute a dimension, is far preferable to only one view. To have to express only hagiography, adulation, reporting *in extenso* speeches and communiques from ministries, is not very edifying. The prescribed becomes repetitive and extremely boring, except to the true believer whose lingering faith may need daily reinforcement.

As a little example of hagiography consider this, taken from a sizeable birthday party in the honor of President Ferdinand E. Marcos, in Honolulu, Hawai'i, in Spring 1988:[20]

We praise You Almighty God, our Stronghold and our Shield, for giving us President Ferdinand E. Marcos, Your chosen soldier. We salute this soldier: Cast upon the character of his race, the time of a man who has navigated the sun seventy times with the grace of a warrior, whose seasons of crises and glory have conquered the movement of the winds, wrapped the torrent of the tempests with the flash of that persistent brightness, until the valor in his dreams became the color of our skins. Destiny's choice, from one battlefield into another, across the regions of history, he is the hour of our time, the measure of the length and depth of greatness, the discipline of visions, the splendor of the finest mind that ever dared suffer the most bitter pain of the wounds without blood, the final word for audacity, the purity of our democratic revolution.

There is no report of how the septuagenarian felt about this.

But the counter-argument to arguments favoring Censorship II should also be taken seriously. To have a choice does not mean that the choice is adequate. The dimension, buoyed by consensus, may be the wrong choice. Moreover, people in a country suffering from point control know that the media are wrong and do not believe a single word of what they see, hear, or read, but people in a country suffering from dimension control with different positions expressed may suffer from the illusion that they have freedom. They may even believe that they have the freest press in the world when different ways of fighting drug supply are discussed—for example, police in the streets of the United States versus U.S. military in the countryside of Colombia or Bolivia. Left out is any serious discussion of legalizing such drugs as marijuana, or of what happened to alcohol during and after Prohibition. Also excluded is an analysis of the demand side, of why so many in the United States become drug addicts, an analysis that might easily become very painful.

Under Censorship I deals can be made; under Censorship II the censor is located inside the editor. The two have become one, an amalgamated editor-censor, engaged in permanent, internalized self-censorship. He does not necessarily have a split personality, because of the high level of integration. In short, there is little raw material out of which a deal can be forged.

The basis for the revolt against the censor is absent, because the editors will have to revolt against themselves. This is not impossible, but the collectively shared subconscious among editors in particular and reporters in general will have to be brought into the daylight. The difficult transition from the collective subconscious to conscious has to be made; "pluralistic ignorance"[21] has to be overcome. This occasionally happens—for instance, when grotesque cases of Washington disinformation (Viêt Nam, Watergate, Iran-Contra) are brought to public attention.[22] In that case a collectively shared revolt might take place, the personal risk to the individual editor doing it alone generally being too high.[23]

FROM CENSORSHIP I TO CENSORSHIP II AND BACK AGAIN

It is interesting to speculate on how a system might be oscillating between Censorship I and Censorship II. Imagine the country of Censorship I going through not only a *glasnost* but also a *perestroika*. *Glasnost* is more verbal; new things are supposedly said, given voice. *Perestroika* is more structural; new things are supposedly done, even on a regular basis. For new things to be said some new things have to be done, such as the removal of censors, and there is an outpouring of words. But sooner or later new wrong things will be said. The unspeakable will be spoken, and there will be a call for "responsibility," against "abusing the new freedoms." The new rules will be less explicit than under a Censorship I regime as the system moves toward Censorship II after an interlude of freedom, internalized in the responsible editor rather than institutionalized in a censor-editor relation.

In a similar vein, imagine a collective revolt has taken place abolishing or diminishing some of the Censorship II limitations, as in the post-Viêt Nam United States and in post-Lebanon Israel. After some time the power system will defend itself, as it does in the United States and Israel. When particularly violent foreign policy operations are carried out there may be a news blackout, such as during the Grenada operation of October 1983, the anti-*intifadah* operations of Israel 1987-93, or the Pentagon "pool" system of censorship during the Gulf War because of the "sensitivity" of the operations.[24,25] The road from Censorship I to Censorship II and back again can be short, and the freedom interlude even shorter.

There is also another approach that looks more benign. Whatever comes out of the power system may be pre-censored, such as in the press communiques coming from the power systems running the Falkland/Malvinas, Afghanistan, Gulf Wars, and Kosovo. Pre-censorship does not preclude deals, and some journalists/editors may have better inside access than others. But the access may be used to reinforce Censorship II conditions by communicating to editors in advance, telling them how "critical" this is for "national security," particularly emphasizing how "the lives of our boys" or "extremely sensitive negotiations" will be in danger if the line between permitted and proscribed is transgressed. These were the controls and limited access placed on Gulf War coverage by both sides.

Thus, one plausible hypothesis might be that systems high on activities incompatible with clear daylight, meaning a freely operating press with investigative reporting and the clear right to print what is reported, may oscillate between Censorship I and Censorship II. Moreover, the two forms of censorship do not exclude each other. Censorship I may have been operating long enough for the editors to internalize its rules. They have, in fact, entered the Censorship II phase without knowing it, meaning that Censorship I actually can be lifted. There is sufficient internalized knowledge of what is unspeakable.

But the basic point in the present context is not a theory of fluctuations between censorship systems. Nor are we trying to develop a theory of relatively censorship-free systems that we think can only be obtained in societies where the power system has little to hide—for instance, because the country is too small to harbor big secrets (but that would at most be a necessary condition). More basic is the general level of empowerment of people relative to the system, the establishment—in other words, the level of democracy.

The point explored here is how Censorship II operates. Dimension control has been singled out as the key form, self-censorship as the key mechanism. But to explore how it works, more is needed. *Discourse analysis* may reveal patterns of censorship—not only the control down to *one* point characteristic of Censorship I, but the less obvious control down to *one* dimension, Censorship II. But how is that control exercised? What is the price for speaking the unspeakable points or dimensions under the two reigns of censorship? How can it nevertheless be done with impunity?

The words themselves are not punished—they are only eliminated, erased from the tape, deleted, shredded. It is the word-maker who is punished under Censorship I and/or Censorship II regimes: fines-imprisonment-expulsion-execution under Censorship I; bad conscience and/or inattention-marginalization-isolation-ostracism under Censorship II conditions—guilt versus shame.

However, a general condition for guilt certificates to be issued in connection with the "crime" of speaking the unspeakable or writing the unwritable is that the "crime" was *intended*. If the author can plead, successfully, that the words were not indicative of the true state of his mind, he might be reprieved. And that opens for a host of possibilities—elementary for the people concerned.

COPING WITH CENSORSHIP

First on the list is the possibility so brilliantly portrayed in the movie *The Unbearable Lightness of Being*, based on Milan Kundera's novel: retract the statement. Say it was a *slip*, not really intended, not indicative of any lasting intention. In severe cases retract publicly. Issue a repentance certificate. Sever the ties between yourself and your offensive statement. Say "sorry," the number of times commensurate with the severity of the crime.

The second approach is very different, and more important in other contexts, less political, more emotional: be drunk, or at least pretend to have been inebriated. The assumption is that alcohol dissolves the link between thought and speech, if not completely, at least partially by making the link more blurred. A particular version of this would be to let a child articulate or utter the offensive remark, including the very famous one: "But he has no clothes on!" The child may take the initiative. But the adults may also be pushing the child in front of themselves, according to the Norwegian adage that "truth comes from children and drunk people." From sober adults, being too well disciplined, by themselves and/or others, only lies and half-truths can be expected.

A third approach would be analogical or allegorical, based on *isomorphism*. Most famous in this connection is probably the use of plays that portray a situation (from far-away history, or from far-away places) similar to the situation at hand, even to the point that the reader/spectator can say, or at least think, "this person corresponds to that person; this act to that act."

The message is conveyed. Myths and other metaphors are useful here as are anecdotes, as they may in capsule form convey very dense and significant political messages without a single word touching the concrete situation directly.

The fourth and most important approach is *joking*. At this point the author may even depict and characterize the situation in very precise terms, only injecting an element of humor, even a farcical element, making it possible to say "it was only a joke."

Three countries with "heavy" state policies and tendencies for the state to see itself as above the people, particularly in foreign affairs, all have well-institutionalized joke outlets:[26] in the ex-Soviet Union, *Krokodil'* and Ogonek; in France, *Le Canard Enchaîné*; in the United Kingdom, *Spitting Image*. And in the United States it would be Garry Trudeau's *Doonesbury* and the Art Buchwald column—both superb commentaries, both widely read by the political class.

Using these four outlets authors and editors can very often get away with proscribed speech. The more joke, and the less detailed resemblance with reality, the more easily can the author escape punishment. The court jester has always been confronted with the same professional dilemma testing his survival skills: how to avoid the Scylla of being too close to reality and the Charybdis of being a joker with no message. Real skill is to convey the message to those in power, make them laugh heartily, get the message, and yet pretend they do not.

Thus, those in power are free to make changes in their policies as if these changes had their roots and causes in themselves only, never in any "pressure" from the outside, and least of all from a jester, a joker. Autocrats, in principle feed on auto-causation.[27] To respond to others is seen as weakness. To respond to the people (democracy, in other words) is even seen as the epitome of weakness, submitting to the ordinary, the vulgar, the masses.[28]

One conclusion would be that the more political jokes there are in a country, the more serious the situation in terms of Censorship I and Censorship II. However, we think the curve is A-shaped rather than J-shaped. With increasing censorship the jokes will increase. But then there is probably a point beyond which both Censorship I and Censorship II will take a dim, perhaps highly critical view even of jokes. From that point on publicly circulated jokes will decrease; they become too dangerous. The very act of joking is already indicative of subversion. The jokes recede into the deeper crevices of the social structure, to be consumed far away from public space.[29]

The political situation in most Eastern European countries used to be somewhat less restrictive than in the ex-Soviet Union. The political jokes flourished to an almost incredible extent, growing into a major industry, in general more penetrating, more searching than in the Soviet Union. As the ex-Soviet Union moved further into *glasnost* conditions we would imagine the number of openly circulated jokes to increase. But as a country then moves even further away from any type of censorship the jokes may disappear, or simply be unnecessary. The price paid for freedom from censorship is a certain dullness in political life, such as in Switzerland, the Nordic countries, Canada, and Australia. It is not necessary to express oneself by means of jokes, hence it is not done. There may simply not be sufficient political raw material to process into jokes for the reason mentioned: the smaller the country, the smaller the secrets, the smaller the scandals and so on.[30]

To summarize: from the beginning is the human being, with the spirit (soul) trying to control the mind and the body. Society is this human being writ large, and the problem of control will stay with us at both levels, the rulers trying to control the ruled. Thus, it is not by chance that the people try to get more of a say relative to state and capital at the same time as body and mind try to assert themselves relative to the spirit. Inner dialogue within the person and outer dialogue in society are the best answers we have today. Spirit and state-capital may make decisions, but mind-body and people may reopen the issue. The task of the media is to make the whole process transparent, censored by nobody.

NOTES

1. *The Spirit of Laws* from 1748 is a doctrine about the separation and balance of power of the legislative, executive, and judiciary branches, also inspiring the American Constitution. Today this doctrine is part of an almost universal culture, at least as an ideal. But as societies evolve, separation and balance of power among state, capital, civil society, and the media call for a Montesquieu II. The supreme recent example would be the Italian Silvio Berlusconi, who combined being prime minister

with the command over a number of companies, a major football club (a sure entry into civil society), and TV channels. No doubt communication works in this empire, but only inside the head of Silvio Berlusconi, transparent to anyone else.

2. See Johan Galtung, "Democracy and Development," in D. L. Sheth and Ashis Nandy, eds., *The Multiverse of Democracy* (New Delhi/Thousand Oaks/London: Sage, 1996), pp. 100-115.

3. Everyone will have favorite examples of media steering clear of all three sources of corruption—maybe the best of British press, such as the *Sunday Times*, *The Guardian (Weekly)*, or *The Independent*. In the United States we would have to go to the margin, to the U.S. version of *samizdat* (see later), the major papers like *The New York Times* and the *Washington Post* being too close to the official policy line in foreign affairs for comfort (the *Los Angeles Times* less so). The international paper owned by the two together, the *International Herald Tribune* is less of a voice for Washington, possibly because it wants to be read all over the world (on the other hand, this argument would also apply to CNN, which speaks on world affairs with an unmistakable Washington accent). In Germany *Der Spiegel* is independent of all three, but marred by a certain tendency to be against absolutely everybody, with the exception of itself.

4. It is too similar to the twin saying "voting with the feet," when the ruled leave a dictatorship, like Eastern Germany, during the Cold War. In both cases we are talking about failures to achieve democratic accountability.

5. Thus, if the state collapses the result is anarchy (but also, possibly, growth of local rule); if capital collapses (not the same as the state running capital) the result is economic collapse (but also, possibly, growth of local economies); if civil society collapses the result is anomie/atomie (normlessness and atomization, deculturation/ destructuration) with heavy violence (but also, possibly, growth of a heavy state); and if the media collapse the result is the Internet (but also, possibly, the control by heavy state and heavy capital). All four processes are currently going on in the United States.

6. For more on this distinction, see Johan Galtung, "Empiricism, Criticism, Constructivism: Three Aspects of Scientific Activity," chapter 2 in *Methodology and Ideology* (Copenhagen: Ejlers, 1977), particularly pp. 68-69.

7. Just as for all other categories of people there are journalists and journalists, as anybody having had his or her fair share of interviews will know. There are those who know the issue and those who do not; among the latter there are those who know they do not know and those who do not; among the latter there are those who pretend they know and those who do not; among

the latter there are those who learn during the interview and those who do not; among the latter there are those who are charming and those who are not; among the latter there are those who blame the interviewee and the readers and those who do not. . . . And so on, and so forth.

8. Stone's method: ". . . reading himself blind in the files of the Congressional Record, and the reports of practically every committee of every government department that produced statistics and hard facts" (Obituary: I.F. Stone, in *The Guardian Weekly*, July 1989). Thus, Stone rebutted "Edward Teller's claim that underground atomic weapons tests couldn't be detected more than 200 miles away by simply going to the Geodetic Survey section of the Department of Commerce. . . ." This, however, is only the intelligent search for facts within an established discourse. More important from the point of view of identifying missing dimensions was his general advice on how to read such documents: "Read them like a radical, with a sense of history and a sense of class forces."—one recipe for identifying missing dimensions, out of many.

9. See Majid Tehranian, *Technologies of Power: Information Machines and Democratic Prospects* (Norwood, NJ: Ablex, 1990).

10. Basically, not only should the variety be "neither too high, nor too low," but the variety should also be relatively uniform for the whole democratic cycle. Thus, nothing is gained by having the electorate issue very detailed instructions to the executive if the executive only produces the same ritualistic output regardless of circumstances. Conversely, a standardized output from the ruled, because there is only one party or political platform available, obviously exercises no steering on the rulers. The latter is usually held to be non-democratic, the former not. According to the vision of democracy sketched here both are non-democratic. The point about Ashby's Law is that the steering obtained depends on the variety available in the channel, and that channel, like any chain, is as weak as the weakest link—the channel with a variety of only two, or, worse still, one.

11. For a presentation of these terms, see Johan Galtung, *Peace By Peaceful Means* (London, Thousand Oaks, New Delhi: Sage, 1996), part IV, ch. 1.

12. For example, Israeli citizens were for a long time not permitted to meet with Palestinians, except in academic conferences.

13. For a theory of the freedom of the press in the Soviet Union, see Frederick S. Siebert, Theodora Peterson, and Wilbur Schramm, *Four Theories of the Press* (Urbana: University of Illinois Press, 1963). For an insider's report on how censorship worked in Poland see the article by Leopold Unger, "Censorship: Polish Defector Describes How It Works," *International Herald Tribune,*

June 5, 1978. One of the words censored was "censorship" itself: "It is forbidden by a special directive of the office of censorship, which states that "the use of the term censorship is not justified by the laws currently in effect." But those laws were changing, as reported in "The Soviet Censor: Keeping an Eye on the Era of Openness," *International Herald Tribune*, July 19, 1989. "In his three years as chairman of Glavlit—the Administration for the Protection of State Secrets in the Press—Mr. Boldyrev boasts that he has cut the list by half, lifting the ban on such diverse secrets as the works of Alexander I. Solzhenitsyn, the bunnies of Playboy magazine and the crime rate."

14. For a useful example of "Ten Stories the Mainstream Press Ignored" see "The Ten Most Censored Stories of 1986," *MetroTimes*, July 29-August 4, 1987, by Craig McLaughlin. Of course, those stories (among them are "Federal Agencies Conducted Radiation Tests on Humans for 30 Years," "Irradiated Veterans: Veterans Administration Caught Destroying Claims Evidence," and "The Lethal Shuttle: Plutonium Payload Scheduled for Space Shuttle") nevertheless surfaced, but not in mainstream media (maybe that is what makes them "mainstream").

The "Ten Top Censored News Stories of 1993," according to ProjectCensored at Sonoma State University, California, and selected by a panel of media experts, were: "The U.S. Killing Its Young (Nine Out of Ten Young People Murdered in Industrialized Countries Are Slain in the United States, According to UNICEF)," "Why Are We Really in Somalia (Oil)," "The Sandia Report on Education (Did Not Favor the School Voucher System)," "The Real Welfare Cheats (America's Corporations)," "The Hidden Tragedy of Chernobyl (Money Goes to Major U.S. Corporations)," "U.S. Army Quietly Resumes Biowarfare Testing After Ten-Year Hiatus (in Dugway, Utah)," "The Ecological Disaster That Challenges the Exxon Valdez (Selenium-Contaminated Drainwater)," "America's Deadly Doctors (30,000 to 60,000 of Them Impaired or Incompetent)," "There's a Lot of Money to be Made in Poverty (Fraud, Exploitation and Price-Gouging of the Poor by Well-Known Corporations)," "Haiti: Drugs, Thugs, the CIA and the Deterrence of Democracy (CIA Involvement)."

For Year 2000, the Top Ten Censored Stories according to Project Censored were: "World Bank and Multinational Corporations Seek to Privatize Water," "OSHA Fails to Protect U.S. Workers," "U.S. Army's Psychological Operations Personnel Worked at CNN," "Did the U.S. Deliberately Bomb the Chinese Embassy in Belgrade?", "U.S. Taxpayers Underwrite Global Nuclear Power Plant Sales," "International Report Blames U.S. and Others for Genocide in Rwanda," "Independent Study Points to Dangers of Genetically-Altered Foods," "Drug Companies Influence Doctors and Health Organizations to Push Meds," "EPA Plans to Disburse Toxic/Radioactive Wastes into Denver's Sewage System," and "Silicon Valley Uses Immigrant Engineers to Keep Salaries Low." (Released April 11, 2001 by Peter Phillips, Director of Project Censored, Sonoma State University.)

For a more systematic and extended analysis of censorship see Donna A. Desnac, *Liberty Denied: The Current Rise of Censorship in America* (New York: Pan American Center, 1988); and, of course, the magazine index.

15. For a theory of the freedom of the press in the United States, see Frederick S. Siebert, Theodora Peterson, and Wilbur Schramm, *Four Theories of the Press* (Urbana: University of Illinois Press, 1963).

16. See notes 5-9 in the Introduction. There is no denial that Censorship I is also operating in the United States, nor that Censorship II was also operating in the Soviet Union—yet, there was (and probably still is) a difference in emphasis.

17. However, we are more interested in the subconscious than in the conscious political culture. There is something obvious about the latter, as it fits the actor-oriented meta-discourse to be described in chapter 6. Identifying the deliberate manipulators is important, but their elimination from positions of influence will not solve the much deeper problem of missing themes, being located deeper down in deep culture, meaning the collective subconscious.

18. To see how this works a case is needed where we are in possession both of an "original" and the version that appears in the media. Here is an OpEd letter, with deleted parts in italics:

To the Editor of
The New York Times

A Silent World War

You report (Science Times, Jan. 16) that pyronaridine, a drug developed in 1971 in China, cured all of 40 malaria patients in a test in Cameroon, whereas chloroquine, the most widely used drug. cured only 44 percent. *The report also mentioned that 1.5 to 2.7 million victims die from malaria each year, mostly children.*

If the newer drug had been made available to those who needed it over the last 25 years, about 50 million lives might well have been saved, roughly the death toll of World War II.

It has been unavailable because of cost: a course of treatment with pyronaridine costs about $3, compared with 25 cents to 50 cents for chloroquine.

To treat all the 300 million malaria patients with the more expensive drug would cost about $900 million a year, *or less than half of the $2.1 billion cost of a single stealth bomber.* With mass production and further research, the drug's cost could be lowered.

It is time to shift our priorities from building instruments of war to saving lives.

Dietrich Fischer
Robbinsville, NJ, Jan. 18, 1996

The writer, a Professor of Pace University, is a board member of Economists Allied for Arms Reduction.

As is easily seen, the letter has been changed from a statement comparing the money made available for direct violence (and the losses of lives incurred) with the lack of money made available to reduce structural violence (and the losses of lives incurred). With the deletions the letter becomes a statement in pharmacology, obviously not what was intended. In addition, the legitimizing facts about the author for writing as he does have been omitted. (By courtesy of Dietrich Fischer who adds: "This experience reminds me of the old saying, 'An editor is someone who separates the wheat from the chaff—and then prints the chaff.'")

19. This control by the editor over the reporter does not have to be explicit, but could take the form of a much more subtle control. In the hierarchy of the newsroom, for example, we find that institutional policies are often enacted, as one of the present authors once learned when questioning a graduate student who was also employed by a local daily newspaper with a reputation for avoiding investigative-type stories. In defense of his journalistic skills the young reporter explained that he and his fellow reporters were allowed to pursue investigative-type stories, but on their own time. They were always required to cover the list of assigned stories first. As the reporting staff was understaffed by what appeared to be two positions, the young reporters never did have time to pursue those stories which might have employed their investigative skills. Hence, editorial control was achieved.

20. Retrieved from the enormous amount of garbage from the downtown party in Honolulu.

21. Defined as ignorance about the attitudes and behavior of the plurality, or even the majority, as when everybody believes themselves to be special cases because of failure to communicate with each other. For example, it is our experience from

Switzerland that everybody believes himself to be an atypical Swiss.

22. Thus, the book on Watergate by Woodward and Bernstein was a public service, as was the book by Robert McNamara, *In Retrospect* (New York: Times Book, 1995), identifying major misunderstandings underlying U.S. policy in Vietnam. They all took risks, but the major risk-taker was, of course, the man who changed world history through an act of publication (actually, photo-copying): Daniel Ellsberg, *Papers on the War* (New York: Simon and Schuster, 1972).

23. And yet there are limits, and such "revolts" probably occur according to some kind of quota system; for instance, maximum once per year, or per administration. In a very thoughtful article, "The Intimidated Press" (*The New York Review of Books*, January 19, 1989), Arthur Lewis, the sometimes really critical U.S. syndicated columnist, reflects on the difference between the press at the time of the Pentagon Papers and Watergate and the press in dealing with the *contras* as if the premise were ". . . that legitimacy rests in the executive branch of the U.S. government, not in the legislative. Congress, along with the rest of us, owes respect to the secrecy that the executive, with its special knowledge and expertise, deems necessary in the interest of national security." As he points out, it looks as if investigative reporting becomes *lèse majesté*. But there is also an alternative interpretation: the Vietnam war was lost, the task was to deliver the premises for ending it and then to sacrifice a president. As late as 1988, even 1989, the *contras* were still not a lost case for the U.S. establishment. And real investigative reporting of the type done by a Günter Walraff in Germany, published in his report on the exploitation of Turkish workers in *Ganz Unten* (*At the Very Bottom*), is not found in the United States. One reason may be that "Walraff's journalistic style is an extreme example of European point-of-view journalism as opposed to the American striving for objectivity" (Geraldine Pluenneke, "The Bad Boy of German Journalism," *International Herald Tribune*, October 28, 1986). U.S. journalism seems to end up with neither one nor the other.

24. The media performance during the Gulf War is now the subject of a major comparative study directed from the School of Communication, University of Örebro, Sweden.

25. See Richard C. Vincent, "CNN: Elites Talking to Elites," in *Triumph of the Image: The Media's War in the Persian Gulf. A Global Perspective*, Hamid Mowlana, George Gerbner, and Herbert I. Schiller, eds. (Boulder, CO: Westview, 1992), pp. 181-201.

26. For a superb collection see Steven Lukes, *No Laughing Matter: A Collection of Political Jokes* (London, Routledge & Kegan Paul, 1985).
27. This characteristic, *causa sua*, is normally only attributed to God.
28. The point is not that this does not happen outside the institutionalized framework of elections, where it has to happen, according to the rules of a democratic society. Of course rulers are all the time paying attention to popular expression of dissatisfaction. The point is that the rulers themselves want to decide when to oblige and when not. A massive civil disobedience campaign in Alta, Norway, in 1980 to protect a river crucial to the nomadic economy and culture of the *Sami* population from being "developed" in the early 1980s was defined as "extra-parliamentary action" not to be heeded, for instance, whereas the rise of a dark conservative party is heeded by everybody trying to take the wind out of their sails by adapting their policies.
29. In Eastern Europe this used to be known as "switching" and probably still is in the more repressive countries, such as Rumania. There is one discourse for public space and one for private space, and is the same rapid switching of speech, behavior and probably also thought as exercised by Christians/Muslims/Jews when entering or leaving a church/mosque/synagogue.
30. On the other hand, we might also use the A-curve to develop another perspective on the missing jokes in Eastern Europe today. An educated guess might run as follows: (a) because there is no Censorship I operating, hence no effort to express politics in a jocular way, and (b) because there is Censorship II, and probably even a strict one against making jokes about, say, democracy, the free market, and the World Bank.

Discourse of Inadequacy: Twenty Case Studies

The purpose of this chapter can be expressed in one simple formula: to try to show that the way issues have been framed, are being framed, impedes more rational ways of dealing with them. Of course, this can also have been intended, consciously or subconsciously. More likely, however, the discourse, from which speech flows, is rooted in the deeper habits of the individual and collective mind, to be explored in later chapters.

Let us start with two examples from the history of U.S.-Soviet relations (at the time the Soviet Union was far from "ex-").

CHERNOBYL

On May 26, 1986, an accident occurred in a nuclear reactor in Chernobyl, outside Kiev. The radioactivity was picked up in the atmosphere by the Swedes at the Forsmark monitoring station for radioactivity, north of Stockholm, and the news was out. It must have been at some very early stage that the discourse for this important event was set and internalized. The dimension to be explored was: "to what extent did the Soviets try to conceal what happened and disinform the world, including their own citizens," not "to what extent are nuclear reactors dangerous".[1] Or, beyond that: "nuclear war is dangerous"—the Chernobyl accident corresponded in released cesium-137 to a four-megaton fission bomb, a small nuclear war.[2]

That second discourse was almost systematically avoided. One obvious interpretation might be that discussing it would also shed unfavorable light on the nuclear industry in the United States, bringing up (and this was nevertheless done, often) memories of the Three Mile Island accident in Harrisburg, Pennsylvania in 1979.[3]

The first discourse was compatible with the meta-discourse of the Cold War: something had happened for which the blame could unambiguously be placed on the Soviet Union. The claim was that if it had happened in the United States the media would have reported everything immediately. The implicit claim was also that a primary responsibility of the Soviet government was not so much to build fail-safe nuclear reactors as to be accountable to the press and media in general, and U.S. media and press more particularly (and even more particularly, to CBS). To this the Soviet Union retorted that they were accountable to the International Atomic Energy Agency (IAEA) by international agreement, and that the United States had not lived up to its obligation under the same agreement by waiting much too long before reporting Three Mile Island.[4]

Be this as it may. Nobody will deny that the accountability and coming-out-in-the-open issue is important.[5] Giving due attention to the safety of reactors, to the extent to which this could happen elsewhere, to what the accident says about nuclear war and nuclear deterrence, in general should not be a pretext to exclude the important accountability discourse opened by the U.S. media. But that also holds true the other way round. The argument would be in favor of a joint, *both-and* discourse, not in favor of an *either-or* discourse, as some of those who tried, mainly in vain, to open the second discourse sometimes could be interpreted as advancing. But the "only one issue at the time" spirit prevailed. As a consequence minds hardened on both sides by faulting only one issue, and among people by being inattentive to their fears.

IPPNW

Next example: the Nobel Peace Prize was awarded to the International Physicians for the Prevention of Nuclear War (IPPNW) in Fall 1985 (in the United States the word "won" is used as if it were a battle or a sports competition). What this big international organization of physicians from the East, West, and South, at the time co-chaired by a Soviet physician (Dr. Evgenij Chazov, later Soviet Union Minister of Health) and a U.S. physician (Professor Bernard Lown of Harvard University) stands for can easily be summarized. What they document is that the health impact of a nuclear war of credible magnitude would be so disastrous that health services around the world, national and international, not to mention local, would be inadequate to cope with the survivors. Not only would the clinics, hospitals, and homes, all highly vulnerable, be destroyed, but even if they should survive they would be insufficient to cope with the health consequences of a nuclear catastrophe. No curative therapy is available for a pandemic of that magnitude.

IPPNW came up with the alternative: preventive therapy, distinguishing between primary and secondary prophylaxis, depending on whether the focus is on increasing the resistance of the human body against the disease, or on removing the exposure from the outside.[6] Shelters may be a way of increasing resistance beyond skin, clothes, houses, provided the explosion is far away and of low magnitude. But there is no known way of adequately resisting a nuclear war with a yield of several thousand megatons, meaning that secondary prophylaxis has to be relied upon.

The clear implication for IPPNW was nuclear disarmament, and they did not seem to think that nuclear deterrence would guarantee that nuclear weapons will never be used. Nuclear deterrence, in order to be credible, has to include considerable war-fighting capability, is incompatible with a "no use" doctrine, and—according to the U.S./NATO—is also incompatible with "no first use."

This debate was by no means new,[7] having raged in the Western press as long as we have had nuclear arms. But physicians entering the field with their special expertise about health implications and the capacity of health establishments was new. Added to this comes a more important factor than expertise: the moral status of physicians as professionals presumably with no ulterior motive, a status they derive from professional competence and the Hippocratic Oath (which is, however, easily eroded through commercialization and the AMA).

Given the mainstream, pro-government orientation of most of the U.S. press—which is not the same as implying that they are state-controlled[8]—this was not the discourse the press wanted to open in connection with a Nobel Peace Prize. Consequently, another discourse was opened: Chazov's relationship to the person who for a long time was an idol of the U.S. press, Academician Andreij Sakharov. A document signed by Chazov denouncing Sakharov became the major focus of attention. Efforts were made to switch the discourse back to the track on which the Norwegian Nobel Peace Prize committee had launched it, but generally in vain. What was demanded in this discourse was that Chazov should denounce that letter, not that the superpowers should denounce nuclear arms.

In short, a successful operation in discourse switching occurred, not dissimilar to the preceding example. Again the argument is not against the debate along the dimension singled out for attention—human rights in the Soviet Union in general, and the Chazov-Sakharov link in particular. The point is that another even more important dimension was forced to recede into the shadows, made opaque rather than transparent through the discourse switch—the irrationality, let alone the immorality of nuclear arms because so many of the effects are irreparable. As a result Americans once again became the victims of inadequate discourse.

IRANGATE

After these introductory exercises let us now address a much more important example, this time from Fall 1986. A catastrophe occurred in U.S. journalism of such magnitude that it has not yet been openly perceived as such. The most important story of the whole Reagan administration, actually one of the more important stories not only in the United States but for the whole world after the Second World War as an indication of how U.S. foreign policy was carried out, went unreported and essentially undetected by the U.S. press. It had to be brought to public attention by "that rag in Beirut" (Reagan's term), *Ash-Shiraa* (*The Light*), a weekly political magazine,[9] revealing the lack of U.S. professionalism.

The term chosen to identify the issue was already indicative of how the discourse was to be defined. The very term "Irangate" brings up certain parallels to "Watergate." Both were scandals of concealment combined with deliberate disinformation from high quarters, successfully hiding what really happened. The second expression used, "arms for hostages," points to deals between two or more governments, made clandestinely, not in the limelight of the media, possibly not even known to the U.S. Congress. It is difficult to say how much of this story would have been known had it not been for *Ash-Shiraa*. But nothing of any significance was brought to public attention before the "rag in Lebanon" did the job. And today, years later, all we know is that every day we know a little more, that no end is in sight, that efforts at concealment are still massive, and that the story probably will carry in its long wake ever more significant revelations.

Of course, there is some awareness in the U.S. press that this was a journalistic scandal. The *Washington Post National Weekly Edition*[10] discussed the issue in some detail and came up with a set of five reasons why the U.S. press failed to report the story of the decade. The list:

1. *Coziness with sources.* This is certainly not a factor specific to the U.S.; it happens in all countries. The journalist establishes an explicit or implicit deal with the sources, some of them deep inside government: "I *feed* you this, you don't write about *that.*" But what the *Washington Post* is pointing out is somewhat different. The factor is seen partly in terms of Oliver North: "North regarded the media as a tool to be used." He seems to have been very clever with the media, even to the point that he "mesmerized some journalists who dealt with him regularly."

2. *Time pressure.* This was certainly not an easy story to unravel. As we know only too well considerable amounts of energy, including talent in that particular direction, went into covering up the story. One can easily imagine that the energy needed to *uncover* the story would tax the patience beyond any reasonable limit of tolerance. The pressure on the journalist was to deliver the story right away, or else not. It became "not."

3. *False bravado.* The media did not want to be too confrontational, and too easily gave in if their facts were challenged and their motives were questioned by the administration. Of course, there was the appearance of being investigative, of asking the tough questions. But "the news establishment has often been a lot more malleable than it appears."

4. *Changing standards.* The standards were simply different in the 1980s. "Some news managers grew weary of endlessly searching for bad guys and tilting at windmills." Probably the Iran-Contra story belonged to another decade, to the 1970s (where indeed it also belonged factually), making the basic mistake of coming too late.

5. *National-Security jitters.* The administration has had more luck arranging deals with the press, making newspapers

"more willing to hold stories for a day or longer to listen to arguments from the government about whether the story will damage national security or endanger American operatives abroad." In this particular case the problem was, of course, whether "American lives" or, in general, "hostages in Beirut" would be endangered.

However important the points made, this discourse for discussing journalism is in itself highly inadequate. A much more basic point is located in the meta-discourses and meta-scripts (chapters 7 and 8). There was no story to report, if by story is meant something with subject, object, and predicate. There might have been objects and predicates, but where was the subject? *Whodunit?* Where was the subject in singular, the bad guy? As so often is the case, this is the wrong question. In retrospect it seems very clear that the story of Irangate cannot be framed in terms of one single person; this was the work of a well-connected group of considerable size.

But that thought may also lead us astray. To unravel that complex web of relations is no minor task for investigative journalism. To explain and understand the phenomenon, however, the focus has to be more on structural than on personal factors in individuals and in groups. And that is a very weak point in U.S. journalism.

The good question would be: where in the U.S. structure in general, and in the government in particular, would such initiatives emerge? Traditional journalism would smell the rat of "conspiracy" if more than one person is involved; and "conspiracy theories" are often held in low esteem, and consequently avoided. The social analyst would have a different approach, asking such questions as "how will a structure like the U.S. power structure be expected to respond under pressure, with increasing tensions, even cracks, in the *pax americana*; and from which positions in the structure would the defense of the structure be mobilized?"[11]

In this perspective the structure comes first and the actors, the concrete individuals with their names, come second. What matters is not *who* but *where* in the structure; not the names, but the positions of the actors. What then emerges, however, is more like social science analysis, very far from how a journalistic story is usually conceived. Consequently, the problem may not be located in any journalist(s), but in journalism itself, in the structure of journalism rather than in any particular journalists.

Of course, there is always a substitute for the missing villain when there is not only a victim, but even a smoking gun. There is always the president to blame as the personification of the whole power system, and not only in terms of what he did or did not do, but in terms of what he did or did not know. Using this discourse a fully fledged story can be run, complete with subject, predicate, and object. But before that story emerges there has to be some consensus about what there was to know or not to know.

In other words, some story prior to that story had to be broken and that job was done by *Ash-Shiraa*, not by U.S. journalism. Although, as pointed out in the *Washington Post* article, *Newsweek* was already pretty close to picking up pieces of the story about arms sales to Iran in 1985 (which actually was quite late in the game), having "a pile of documents maybe three feet high" but "no first-hand evidence of the arms-for-hostage deal." They resigned themselves to the circumstance "that we had the biggest story of the decade in one of our reporter's notebooks." Good, but very far from good enough. What this means is simply that 1980-vintage U.S. journalism was not up to the job. It may take one generation of journalists to eliminate the aspersion cast on the profession because of this revealing deficit in professional competence.[12]

But the basic point here is the choice of discourse once the issue was made public. Some possibilities have been indicated, such as the president-centered discourse. Did he know? When? How much? But a much more basic problem, still not recognized as part of the official discourse, would be: *who runs U.S. foreign policy?*

Evidently it is not the public, the ruled, nor the media, nor the two together, as they were both kept in the dark—a fact already of some importance in a democracy. But how about the rulers? In Irangate the rulers did not include Congress, as Congressmen were also kept in the dark, with possibly some well-chosen exceptions. Clearly, the center not only of decision making but also of execution of the action-bundle wrapped together as "Irangate" was located in the executive branch of rulers, and in that branch alone.

The next question becomes: *where* in the executive branch? Evidently not in the State Department, since it seemed not to know much about what happened, and apparently wanted nothing to do with it. Evidently not in the Department of Defense either, for similar reasons. Consequently the Secretaries of State (George Shultz) and Defense (Casper Weinberger) during that period seemed to escape unblemished from the hearings, at least so far. But, again, that is relatively uninteresting when the structure is the issue.

That situation limits attention to the part of the executive branch directly under presidential command, and makes a president-oriented discourse more relevant (or, vice versa, with no other bad guy in sight the place to look is the White House). That gives us three possibilities, if we leave the CIA/NSA/OR out of the picture: the president, the National Security Council (NSC), and a de facto shadow government. As a consequence it was not so strange that the media, and later on the hearings, were quick to pick up the first of these perspectives, reactivating the old Watergate question: "how much did the President know?" (or vice versa, because of the Watergate discourse this perspective was picked up).

Nobody will deny that this is an important question. As has been pointed out repeatedly: the issue is not necessarily U.S. foreign policy in general, nor covert action to promote U.S. foreign policy (both of them certainly important issues), but *illegal* covert action to promote, launch, or shape U.S. foreign policies. This is important enough to warrant attention. But as a consequence the press and the media in general, as well as the congressional hearings, and the court case against Oliver North, directed the attention upward, toward the president and toward Oliver North, not downward exploring an even more important issue: if there is a "shadow government," is it still operating? The basic issue may not be whether the president was in command or not, or even in the know, but whether the structure is still operating. "Who is Oliver North's successor?" could have been a more important question than to what extent he followed orders from above or not.

Why was this important discourse, which would map out in great detail the structure, processes, and goals of any "shadow government," not entered into? One possible answer is very simple: that discourse would open for the whole discussion of whether the United States is a democracy or not, not the much more limited question of whether a particular president had some deficiencies.

Of course, in foreign affairs there is a certain discretion given to Congress in the sense that congressional leaders, on a bipartisan basis, may act first, and be accountable to the public later. There is a corresponding discretion given to the president in the sense that he may act first and be accountable to Congress afterwards. And there is a corresponding discretion given to the National Security Council in that it may act first and be accountable to the president only afterwards, provided some rationale for action has been provided by a "finding."[13] But nowhere in democratic theory is there any opening for a "shadow government" acting so independently as it seems to have done, and not only in this particular case but also others, and over a very long period.

At this point our "missing discourse" searchlight might profitably switch from the media to the U.S. political science establishment. A basic threat to U.S. democracy in its very midst, operating out of Washington, well-rooted in the White House, making a mockery of U.S. constitutional institutions (even to the point that the proper spelling might be "demockracy") should not have escaped scholarly attention by U.S. political scientists, provided they are more scientists than just political. But it was a small institute in

Washington D.C., the Christic Institute, staffed by Jesuits and lawyers (categories that do not necessarily exclude each other) that tried to bring this issue to public attention.[14] Not only U.S. media but also U.S. political science can and should be accused of not having passed the acid test.

Why is this so? Why do they only focus on the top of the political iceberg, that which is above water and is covered by a thick layer of constitutional discourse? There are, of course, good reasons. Gross presidential negligence, not to mention acts of commission (not only of omission in the sense of not trying to find out what happens) against laws and amendments passed by Congress could lead to impeachment. But these are all obvious matters, belonging to the surface structure of political phenomena.

But an academic field deserving the name "political *science*" would of course also explore the deep structure of politics, while still remaining very concrete and empirical. The basement of the White House might do as deep structure; in fact, the whole White House architecture is already reminiscent of the proverbial iceberg. It would also be much more easy for political scientists to do this than for the media, isolated as they are from public critique in the ghettos known as university campuses; talking and writing a language that often does not communicate because it is too complicated, as opposed to the media that often do not communicate either because their language is too simplistic.

This brings up another, equally painful memory from recent U.S. history. How was Watergate discovered? Not by the white man, by that piece of *Washington Post* journalism later awarded a Pulitzer Prize by other white men. It was discovered by a black man, a night-watchman who discovered that a doorknob had been tinkered with. He reported this and seems later to have become virtually unemployable—conveniently forgotten, overshadowed by a white U.S. press ready to rise to the occasion once they had been properly alerted. Of course, what we know is still only the tip of the proverbial iceberg; that applies to Watergate as well as to Irangate. The interesting discourse would center on the question: "exactly what were they looking for?" How long do we have to wait? And how long do we have to wait for the truth of Irangate to come out? Not to mention the Mother of Truths, the JFK murder?

Will we be satisfied with the book by Peter Dale Scott, *Deep Politics and the Death of JFK*?[15] The conclusion of this profound work is exactly the same as here—no concrete names, "deep politics did it." If this cannot enter the media discourse, the media, not Scott, should be faulted. The language has to be found, even if it tends to fault the political structure and hence be rejected.[16]

THE HOSTAGE CRISIS

Back to Iran again, but this time to the hostage crisis of 1979-81. The discourse in connection with the 52 "diplomats" in the U.S. "embassy" (quote-unquote because so many of them were engaged in activity so subversive to the host country that other terms might be more applicable), taken hostage for 444 days from November 4, 1979, focused on the consequences of their capture, not on the causes. Like the standard discourse about "terrorism" the press focused on consequences and possible counter-measures, never opting for a rich, cause-oriented discourse. That the activity of the U.S. embassy, and not only in 1979, the year of the triumphant return of the Imam, the late Ayatollah Khomeini, on February 1, could have been objectionable, even obnoxious to the Iranian people was almost never brought up. As an example the captured CIA documents in the former embassy files have not really been made public in the United States, although they were easily available on the streets of Teheran. As with the case of terrorism the ideological reasons for this discourse limitation are only too obvious, and they are still operating. But there are also other and more subtle factors at work, as will be explored in the next case story.

The consequence of a cause-oriented discourse might have been deeper understanding. With a born-again Christian as president, Jimmy Carter, one might even have imagined an apology, and in the wake of that, even early release of the hostages.[17] The discourse used blocked out peaceful transformations of the conflict. The consequences are still with us today, the situation getting even worse.

DISCOURSE AND THE DISSIDENT IMMIGRANT

One such factor has to do with the precise nature of the United States as a country of immigrants. Many of those immigrants are, if not political, at least economic refugees from the countries of birth. They often had very good reasons to leave. But they also have reasons to justify that they left, and this almost immediately leads to two important consequences.

First, they have something to sell in their new host country: their expertise. Soviet dissidents became experts on the Soviet Union, Polish dissidents became experts on Poland, Iranian dissidents under the Khomeini regime became experts on Iran, Nicaraguan dissidents became experts on Nicaragua, and so on. Equally obvious, Iranian dissidents under the Shah regime do not become experts, nor do the Chilean dissidents under the Pinochet regime. Compatibility with basic U.S. foreign policy ideology is the basic criterion. Mainstream U.S.A. selects her experts well.

However, the main point is that the dissident knows that his expertise has a higher market value within mainstream discourse if he can deliver premises for positions already taken. Most people, and power wielders are no exception, prefer confirmation to information. Driven by solid personal reasons to paint in black the regime of the country he left behind, the dissident has no particular difficulty delivering the goods. There is a problem: the detested regime may change, the oppressors are driven out, a new regime enters. Is the expertise transferable? Usually not, as any Soviet expert trying to pontificate on Russia today knows.

But, second, he might also have had another source of motivation. He might have had his own nagging doubts: maybe I should have stayed behind? Maybe that is where I was tested, not in this new country? Maybe I am a traitor, not to a regime I hated and despised, but to the people suffering under that regime? And, as an afterthought, maybe there will be no triumphant return for me; maybe they will all say, "where were you when we needed you?!"

Of course, psychologically it is easily seen how that problem can be handled. All that is needed is to deny that any improvement of the situation is possible, and to issue declarations to the effect that any apparent change to the better is *fake*, a *cover-up* intended to delude public opinion abroad. Or, if this line does not work, if the changes seem to be genuine, then the second set of declarations would be that any change certainly cannot last. The new will be overturned by the old, and old days will come back again, meaning the days when leaving one's own country as a refugee seemed entirely justified—the good/bad old days, in other words.

Thus, there is an unfortunate coincidence between two factors steering foreign policy discourse in the United States. One is the *publicly shared, mainstream ideology* of the power establishment concerned, steering the discourse, consciously or subconsciously, according to the rules of Censorship II. Added to this is the *psychology of the immigrant expert*, delivering expertise about hated foreign countries, the expert being a dissident from that regime. His psychological calculus, well accounted for by the theory of cognitive dissonance, will tend to reinforce mainstream ideology.

Let us use the case of the Soviet dissident working as a sovietologist in the United States during the Cold War as an example. Gorbachev appears on the arena. He, the dissident in the United States, hates the Soviet regime. But he feels uncertain about Gorbachev. There is no way of denying that Gorbachev is a part of the regime, being nothing less than the Secretary General of the

Party, and in addition, the President of the country. In the triangle shaping up between Ego (the dissident-expert), the Soviet regime, and Gorbachev a problem arises: the triangle would not be cognitively balanced if the dissident-expert should develop a liking for Gorbachev. In that case he is in the situation in the triangle at the top of Figure 2.1 where the unbroken line stands for a positive and the broken line for a negative relationship.

There are four ways of solving this dilemma. First, denial of Gorbachev: "Gorbachev is fake, the old approach in new clothes." Second, denial that he will survive: he may not be killed, but will be eliminated by the old regime. Third, a rather dramatic change approach, a carry-over from sympathy for Gorbachev to sympathy for the entire Soviet regime, as became clear in connection with the INF agreement of December 1987. And then there is the *fourth* possibility: decomposition of the triangle, developing positive images of Gorbachev, continuing with the old images of the regime, as if these were disjointed parts of Soviet reality, a little bit ahead of time.

Cognitive consonance, balanced configurations, is obtained in all four cases. The problem was solved, the mind is at rest, but through psychological rather than empirical-logical processes.

The approach finally taken by the media may generally best be predicted by looking at official U.S. ideology, which in turn may be influenced by similar cognitive dissonance resolution mechanisms in the elites. *The leading expert is the expert who agrees with the leaders.* This theme will be developed in more detail later; here it is only given as an example of some of the many factors steering a discourse: dissident, immigrant, the psychology of the expert.

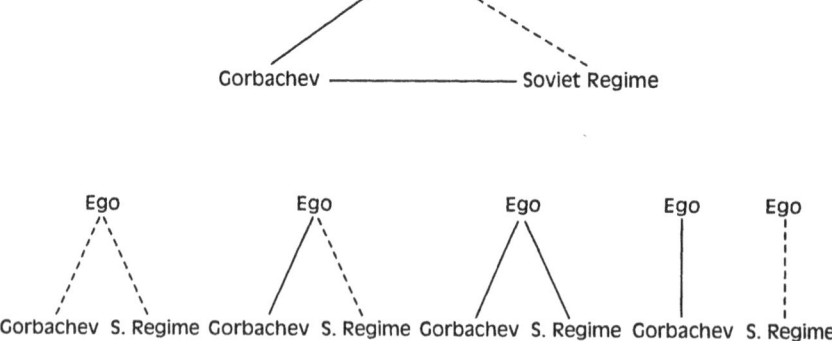

Figure 2.1. U.S. sovietologist: Resolving cognitive dissonance

THE EURO-MISSILES

Let us return to the list of examples after this excursion into theory. The Euro-missile debate played a considerable role, maybe even more so in Western Europe than in the United States, during the years following the "double track decision" of NATO on December 12, 1979 to deploy cruise and Pershing II missiles *and* to pursue arms control/disarmament negotiations with the Soviet Union on the issue of intermediate nuclear forces in Europe. "Double track" also means double discourse, but with important flaws.

Of nuclear powers in Europe there were four: the Soviet Union, the United States, the United Kingdom and France. Of nuclear forces there are many kinds. One simple but useful typology would be "land-based," "sea-based," and "air-based," depending on whether the platform from which the missile is eventually to be launched is on the ground, or in the sea (a submarine, or it could also be a surface ship), or in the air (from a plane, regardless of whether that plane took off from an airport on land or from an aircraft carrier). For a more complete typology, "space-based" will have to be added to accommodate Star Wars-type weapons.[18]

Altogether this would give us what could be referred to as a (4:3)-discourse with 4 x 3 = twelve points. However, from the very beginning it was somehow agreed in the West that instead of a (4:3)-discourse the discussion should be limited to a (2:1)-discourse, focusing only on the Soviet Union and the United States, and only on land-based missiles. The result was a two-point instead of a twelve-point discourse, a reduction of more than 83 percent of the discourse down to a very narrow, and shallow, discourse.

That the reduction is important is seen from Table 2.1, with the type of figures used when the debate culminated in 1983,[19] before the ultimate decision to deploy the missiles was taken, leading to the (unfortunate) Soviet decision to withdraw from the Geneva negotiations. This debate, lasting years, dominated public space. The

Table 2.1. Alternative Discourses For INF In Europe.

	Land-Based	Sea-Based	Air-Based
Soviet Union	455	18	465
United States	0	0	651
United Kingdom	0	64	0
France	18	80	44

numbers involved—464 cruise and 108 Pershing II, adding up to 572—stick in the memory; they are almost indelible. But more important than such numbers is, as usual, the discourse. The 2-point discourse in the inner box portrays the United States and the "West" as totally unarmed relative to the Soviet Union or the "East." The 12-point inclusive discourse gives if not exactly the opposite conclusion at least a strong indication that if balance is the goal, then reduction in number of warheads has to be undertaken by the Western side first.

We were active in that debate. But when one of the present authors gave at least 500 lectures between Fall 1981 and Spring 1985 on this topic, in six languages in twelve countries in Europe, West and East, the other side always refused to enter the expanded discourse. Among those favoring deployment of the missiles a high level of uneasiness could be noticed the moment anybody strayed away from the limited discourse and entered the expanded discourse. They tried to make what to them was politically problematic look as if some kind of intellectual error had been committed, and stuck tenaciously to the limited discourse. The method used, discourse contraction, is the same as what a judge does when he decides what is going to be adjudicated, and, not, for instance, the messages conveyed by activists struggling for desegregation.

Do you not know that U.K. and French missiles were *independent forces*? Yes, it was known that they were referred to as such, but we also know that from the Soviet point of view they were considered hostile, or potentially hostile, as the West would have considered "independent" missiles deployed in, say, East Germany or Bulgaria at the time.

Do you not know that land-based missiles are the only ones that really count because they are much more precise? Yes, we knew that this was said about them, but also knew that land-based missiles are more vulnerable, and it is not obvious that increased precision outweighs what is lost in increased vulnerability. It might very well be that a submarine-based missile, with a lower level of target precision but also a lower level of vulnerability, would look more threatening to the other side.

Does this mean that discourse control is simply and purely a power game? Of course, there is much to that hypothesis. But there are also other factors at work, exemplified by another hypothesis, and a simple one: *simplicity will tend to drive out complexity*. A 2-point discourse is conceptually more easily handled than a 12-point discourse. Just think of the comparisons that have to be carried out with more than one type of weapon system and more than two actors in the military power game. How are we to compare land-based, sea-based, and air-based missiles, given the arguments about precision and vulnerability above? How are we to compare allies with superpowers? Is the United Kingdom 100 percent reliable as an ally, with weapons counting as much as U.S. weapons, or only, say, 90 percent?

In that case, what would be the coefficient for France: 0.9, 0.5, 0.12, 0, -0.5? Five possibilities, including the officially accepted (to the French government the only acceptable) position that the coefficient should be equal to zero. Or, a more sophisticated hypothesis: the French coefficient is highly dynamic, variable in a heisenbergian way, changing the moment one tries to measure it. Moreover, there is certainly a distinction to be made between the coefficient articulated in public space and in private space, secretly, with NATO/U.S. partners.

But what kind of highly variable coefficient would we apply to China over the twenty-year interval 1964 (the first Chinese test) to 1984? Obviously, negative coefficients might also have to be used for some period. But the Chinese could also have been added to Western intermediate-range nuclear forces, being in a position to launch an attack on the Soviet Union from the south, coordinated with a Western attack from west, north, and east—from a Soviet point of view, a not very edifying thought. A fluid situation, indeed. Much better for the peace of mind and cognitive balance to stay with the 2-point discourse. The issues are easy to grasp, no complex knowledge is needed.

Of course, there is another way of arriving at simplicity: to mask the many problems of integration within the Western alliance. The information for the United States, the United Kingdom, and France can be collapsed into one category: "West." That alternative is indicated with the broken line in Table 2.1, pretending more Western unity than in fact there ever was.

In terms of complexity this (2:3)-discourse, with six points, is located in the middle, representing only a 50 percent reduction relative to the broadest discourse (which again could be made much more complicated by subdividing the nuclear forces further). The tone of the argument would then have to change as can be seen from the figures that the reader easily can add up: the West is no longer exactly disarmed. The *Nachrüstung* (catching up) argument is void. Incidentally, it should also be noted that none of the discourses mentioned so far included the Pershing I missiles possessed by the Germans in Western Germany—with U.S. warheads, one more ambiguous case not easily accommodated in equations for balance of power comparisons. Discourse control leads to dishonesty.

LAW OF THE SEA

Returning to the issue of complexity: if a (4:3)-discourse is too complex, what should we say about a (150:150)-discourse? As an observer (in the Norwegian delegation) to the United Nations conference on the Law of the Sea (UNCLoS) in Caracas 1974 Galtung remembers how the delegates were laboring under the complexity of a (150:150)-matrix: 150 participating countries confronted with about 150 issues.[20] It is impossible for the human brain to handle this complexity without introducing some simplifying measures. Countries have to be grouped; issues also have to be grouped. In this case traditional East-West and North-South divides did not work very well. For instance, there was quite a similarity between the United States and the Soviet Union in their views in these matters, not only with regard to the obvious naval rights on which naval powers have always insisted, but also with regard to mining rights and ocean bed exploration and exploitation in general. The North-South divide was not so fruitful either, because poor countries with a long coastline, and particularly very small and poor island states with an Exclusive Economic Zone (EEZ) many times the size of their own territory, suddenly started behaving as big powers. And they were, in this context.

The division of countries that did make sense was in terms of how much ocean the state could lay claim to. On the one end were the land-locked countries that could be found on most continents, with no sea; on the other, the small island states just mentioned, with only sea, nothing but coast; and in between most countries in the world, with some coast. The issues were divided among commissions exploring naval rights, exploitation/exploration of the ocean bed, and more traditional fishing rights. Combining these two dimensions, a simplification down to a (3:3)-discourse, quite adequate, was obtained. When the conference did not succeed it was not because of discourse inadequacy.

We are making this point in order to look at the whole *problématique* of constructing an adequate discourse from another angle. A discourse may obviously be biased, and it may be argued that the only alternative to a biased discourse is a new discourse with a fresh, and hence undetected, bias. A discourse may be too simple and have to be made more complex through discourse expansion to be adequate; that was one way of looking at the Euro-missiles non-debate above.

But the discourse may also be too complex, calling for simplification through discourse contraction. If it is true that the human mind has difficulty handling much more than about seven alternatives and, we would argue, difficulty handling more than three dimensions at a time, then we would end up with (2:3), (2:2:2), and perhaps (3:3) discourses (6-point, 8-point, and 9-point discourses, respectively) as some kind of upper limit. This may or may not be a valid observation, a point to be explored later. But the point made here is that the discourse was reasonably adequate discourse, and not the standard complaint of this book—inadequacy.

ANTI-AMERICAN, ANTI-WASHINGTON, BOTH OR NEITHER?

In connection with debates about U.S. foreign policy, particularly inside the United States, there is one expression that very often arises, opening a most unfortunate discourse: "anti-American." The term is designed to conceive of any critical remark not as an outcome of rational reasoning but as a manifestation of a general, underlying syndrome of "anti-Americanism."[21] If a person is anti-American in general, then to be against U.S. support for the contras, U.S. trade policies, U.S. nuclear deterrence policies, U.S. positions on the seabed, and whatever else, can be seen as nothing but manifestations of that particular mental disorder. Critical remarks are understood as symptoms of a psychological predisposition, not as rational arguments presented in a political discourse. In short, there is no need to listen to the arguments once the labeling of the person behind the arguments has stuck. Better turn to people not suffering from the mental deficit.

It should be noted, in passing, that this dehumanization of the Other may not be very different from social science approaches to people's attitudes in general. A typical sociological approach is to collect information about a number of attitudes from a number of people; compute correlations; use the correlations to arrive at clusters (for instance by factor analysis); and then try to relate the clusters to personality traits, social positions, or both. A social scientist might be more hesitant with the label "anti-American," unless he had good reasons for using it. But the basic inclination is the same; to use attitudes held by population of person P about issue X to say something about P, not about X.[22]

One way out of this effort to kill important debates would be by making a distinction between "anti-American" and "anti-Washington," "Washington" being used the conventional way in foreign policy commentary, newscasts, and so forth, as standing for the foreign policy of a country (without intending any slur on the population of Washington, D.C.). The importance of this distinction lies in the ambiguity of the term "America."[23] The "America" best known abroad would be the face of the U.S. shown abroad—in other words, precisely its foreign policy. The "America" best known from the inside would be the "inner America," as seen by Americans grateful to their country for giving them all the country has to offer, including the famous new beginning for immigrants, even for shorter-term visitors.[24] Different associations come to the minds of the two parties, triggered by the term "America," more precisely, the America they know best.

A critique of "outer America," U.S. foreign policy, may sound so unjust to those inside that the label "anti-Americanism" seems adequate. In the same vein, what is sometimes said about the United States from and by the insiders may sound incredibly naive, even bigoted to the outsider. The disease label used in this case, however, is not "philo-American" but simply "American," assuming that the word already carries a connotation of ignorance and naivete. Another case of dehumanization, and no less serious.

Using both the inner and outer aspects of America we end up with four combinations, as indicated in Figure 2.2. Instead of a 2-point discourse we get a 4-point discourse based on two dimensions, and it is easily seen that we can now make distinctions obscured by the initial oversimplification. Logically, this is satisfactory. The problem is whether psychologically the persons involved are willing to think along both dimensions, and sociologically to speak so, together.

Position A adequately reflects the stand reflected in this book: very much against many aspects of U.S. foreign policy, quite enthusiastic about many aspects of inner U.S. life, such as the truer democracy often found at the local and grassroots level, although often more as a potential rather than as a (to many) scary empirical reality. It should be noted how much that differs from position D, held by many Europeans to the right: a deep contempt for many aspects of the United States as a society, including its grassroots democracy, combined with an admiration for Washington's strong

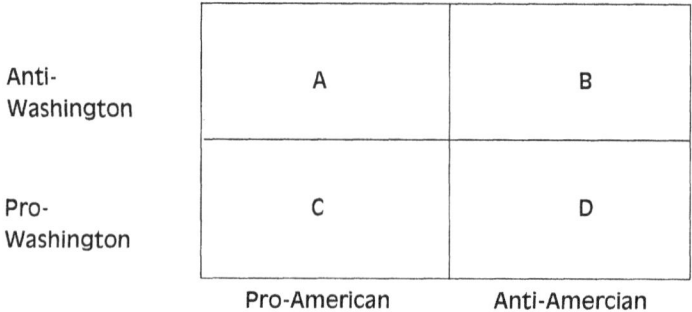

Figure 2.2. Anti-American, anti-Washington, both or neither?

hand, for the effort to be the policeman of the world, providing the type of protection under which they themselves want to be sailing and flying, usually for business, sometimes for other adventures. The Gulf War offered the opportunity.

Position B is the totally anti-American position. This is chronic America-phobia: the person is simply against whatever has a touch of America. The same attitude was held by one of the authors regarding Germany during and after the Second World War for obvious reasons. The behavioral manifestation of that attitude was speak no German, listen to no German (words, music), see no Germans, make no visits[25] (it took 20 years to overcome this.) Anti-American attitudes of that kind may be found among people in the U.S. sphere of influence, for instance in the Caribbean, Central and South America, and in Southeast Asia—true anti-Americanism, in other words, and for good reasons, obvious to any one with a minimum of knowledge of history. No visit, no relation, no America is tolerated. The syndrome often breaks down after some contact.

Position C is the exact opposite of this: chronic America-philia making absolutely no discrimination, just accepting the United States, warts and all, inner and outer. The pattern is frequently found inside the United States. It is often referred to as "patriotism," but the word "jingoism" might be more appropriate; an unquestioning attitude highly incompatible with the type of differentiated positioning expected in a democracy. Led by charismatic demagogues such attitudes could easily become majoritarian.[26]

However, one problem still remains, narrowing the focus to U.S foreign policy conveyed by the term "anti-American." Is an attitude the outcome of a general disposition, regardless of the merits of the particular case, or is it an outcome of a study of one particular case after the other? The allegation could still be made that the person critical of U.S. foreign policy is exactly that, automatically critical, regardless of what might occasionally come out of Washington. In short, the search for differentiated reasoning should still be on, with the diagnosis of a closed mind-set as one possibility. But that closed mind-set can also lead to America-philia, also based on narrow and shallow discourses.

In this search a simple probing question is very useful when encountering the permanently critical: do you see anything positive in the U.S. (foreign) policy? With the obvious parallel question for the permanently uncritical: Is there anything you would disagree with in U.S. (foreign) policy? The method can be used to probe the perimeter of any type of dogmatism. After initial anger the questioning may liberate deep, suppressed reflections.

MARXISM

Let us now try to focus exploration of discourse inadequacy less on media and recent political debates over such issues as nuclear policy, U.S. foreign policy, and the Law of the Sea, turning to general social science and philosophy cases in order to make a slightly different point. Not that these cases are less political, but we may have grown used to ways of thinking and speaking about them because they have been with us, and will stay, for a long time.

What did Marx say? He said a lot, and one point was a revolutionary introduction of a new discourse for social science in general and economics in particular. Imagine a world with two firms or companies, both of them with capitalists and workers, also known as labor buyers and labor sellers, or (less explicitly) as employers and employees. Each pair of terms elucidates one point and obscures other significant aspects of a company, but we leave that point aside. The basic point is that Marx cut this intellectual, conceptual pie in a new way, indicated in Figure 2.3.

In the liberal discourse the primary focus is on the competition between the two companies. The discourse pits one company against the other, and explores the rules of the competitive game. One of these rules limits what a company can lose because of "limited responsibility." The capitalist loser may be driven temporarily out of the market. But he should be preserved in other ways so that he can be recycled and reappear in some other company. The workers are less fortunate. But a basic point in liberal theory is that regulated competition is for the good of everybody, for capitalists, workers, and consumers alike.

Marx enters the discourse struggle also saying that something is pitted against something else. But far more important than company competition is the way the capitalist class, as a whole,

	Company 1	Company 2
Capitalists	C1	C2
Workers	W1	W2

Marxist Discourse

Liberal/Conservative Discourse

Figure 2.3. Liberal versus Marxist economic discourse

bridges the gap between companies, pitted against the workers, as a class, also bridging that gap. However, the working class is considerably less crystallized as a class, being less aware of the interests workers have in common and more fragmented than a capitalist class that easily transcends company and national borders. Moreover, members of the capitalist class obviously have more means at their disposal should they want to become an actor, not only a category. Hence trade unions, working-class parties, and so forth.

One major reason for this "false consciousness" is the liberal discourse. Thus, where a liberal discourse primarily draws a vertical line in Figure 2.3, the marxist discourse primarily draws a horizontal line. The lines cut the same conceptual pie in very different ways, shedding very different light on what happens.

Throughout history we can hear the liberal/capitalist discourse complaining: "you emphasized class solidarity, with strikes and many demands, and as a result we lost the competitive edge on the market, to the irretrievable loss not only for us, the capitalists, but also for you, the workers. The only thing you obtained is that the other company wins!"

And we hear the marxist/worker discourse respond: "you got it wrong, we are not arguing a strike only in your company, we are arguing working-class solidarity so as to raise the wages of all, and not only in our country, but in the whole world! The workers live in misery, dying prematurely in order to keep the capitalists rich, fat, and happy! But you are short-sighted. By treating workers better all of us would gain in the longer run by having a working class with more buying power for your products."

At that point, of course, the difference between socialists (social democrats) and communists shows up. The socialists would make use of both divides to arrive at a more just sharing of the profit cake. The communists would gamble on the second divide first, heading for total abolition of the distinction between capitalists/managers and workers. Some communists would have capitalists and workers cooperate, co-own, and co-work, within the same factory or company, with no distinction between employers and employees. Others would abolish the distinction by abolishing capitalists, making all of them employees of one super-employer, in practice the state. They all differ from liberals and conservatives, who would gamble on dividing expanding cakes.

Socialism in the small versus socialism in the big, in other words. Yugoslavia versus the Soviet Union; in the period of *samo upravljenje* (self-management) in the former, and giant state enterprises in the latter. And then there is Japan, with company unions and manager-worker cooperation, with strong elements of state planning combining the liberal, the micro-socialist, and the macro-socialist approaches, at least at the discourse level.[27]

Who is right, liberals or marxists? The question is misplaced and itself an outcome of the important Western meta-discourse always favoring *two* positions, *two* sides to an issue, *two* points, *two* aspects. We think there can be little doubt that both views are right, and both views are incomplete. There is reality and validity to both discourses. In fact, both of them know this perfectly well in their better moments, only their emphases are different. Unfortunately, even deliberate one-sidedness in our culture passes for some kind of maturity. The carrier of the discourse has "made up," meaning contracted, his discourse.[28]

There is certainly social validity both to market competition as an incentive, and to class struggle as an expression of interests. And there is no reason why only one truth should be predicated of some entity. The only problem is to what extent we are capable of harboring more than one truth in our consciousness, not only individual but also the collectively shared consciousness, particularly when multiple truths have contradictory action implications. This is obviously a major qualitative factor to be added to the more numerical aspect of complexity explored above.

PACIFISM

Let us take another and very similar example: the present state system, explored next to the capitalist system because of their structural similarity (isomorphism). In this case the unit of discourse is not a company but a country, and the country is subdivided into government and people, rulers and ruled, vote buyers and vote sellers. With each pair of terms a new perspective is brought into the picture—but we leave that point aside.

The liberal/conservative discourse sees the world as a place where countries compete, more or less limited by a set of rules. At times they fight, go to war, less constrained by rules. The liberals will emphasize the competitive aspect of the international system, the conservatives the destructive aspect. But both of them would agree that the dividing line that makes a real difference, and should be reflected in a discourse, runs between countries.

Not so, the alternative perspective would respond. The crucial dividing line is horizontal, pitting an international class of governments, rulers, against an international class of people, those ruled over by rulers, demanding them, commanding them, to go to war against each other when the rulers so desire. Governments offer certain services to the people, some of them enshrined in the 1948 Universal Declaration and the 1966 Covenants. But rights imply duties. The people have to give something in return for what they receive. More particularly, people have to show general obedience to the rulers, pay taxes, and be willing to lay down their lives for the national cause when called upon to do so.

Evidently, a contract of that kind was originally written with only the male part of the population in mind. The thick script was the civil and political (later also social and economic) rights, the thin script the taxes that had to be paid, and the script so thin that it was almost illegible, was compulsory military duty.[29] All of this was essentially for males. Females were supposed to offer general obedience to their husbands, be available for reproduction and simple/menial production jobs, and absorb the shocks and burdens of the system, repairing husbands and children.

Who suggested this alternative discourse? If socialists prefer a marxist discourse because they see it as leading to solidarity among workers and a right to strike, then pacifists prefer their alternative discourse because it leads to solidarity among people and peoples, and from there to a global right to refuse military service; in other words, to conscientious objection.

This is, of course, even more unacceptable to governments than a workers' strike to capitalists. What is at stake is not only governmental power and interests, but the governmental self-image as being the very source of law, the *ultima ratio regis*, and for that reason unassailable. Capitalists usually do not claim divine mandate; governments sometimes do. Only if the person called in for military duty can defend adequately the proposition that he also derives his conscientious objection to military service from divine commands might his request be granted. If not, the objection will be referred to as "political" rather than "conscientious,"[30] and be rejected and punished.

The broader military discourse is isomorphic to Figure 2.4.

	Country 1	Country 2	
Governments	G1	G2	Pacifist Discourse
People	P1	P2	

Liberal/Conservative Discourse

Figure 2.3. Liberal/conservative versus pacifist military discourse

The world is seen in a new light the moment the pacifist discourse is considered, which is not the same as accepted. Obviously this discourse has penetrated less than the marxist discourse to which people have somehow become habituated. Marxist discourse is absorbed into general culture, and at an early stage found an expression in labor/socialist/communist political parties. The pacifist discourse is not (yet), although the rapid spread of green parties may be an important articulation.[31]

But again the same point can be made. The problem is not which discourse is right or wrong, but the great improvement in the ability to explore world politics the moment both discourses are used and combined into one overriding discourse, rather than just using one or the other. An adequate science of economics, looking at the preceding example, is impossible without both; so is an adequate science of politics and international relations. Measured by this criterion there is a lot of inadequate economics and political science around. Persistent use of inadequate discourse may be said to subtract from rather than add to the body of knowledge.[32]

HUMAN RIGHTS

Let us then look in more detail at the human rights discourse alluded to above, which is a particular type of legal (not economic, not political) discourse. The very term, "human rights," is positively loaded. Everybody knows that respecting, not infracting, human rights is a positive characteristic of a country. The more a list of what a leading country is rightly proud of coincides with a human rights declaration the higher the status not only of the country, but also of that human rights declaration in particular, and the discourse underlying it in general.

Hence, if we should limit ourselves to seven points, what would be a reasonable list of items in which the United States and the ex-Soviet Union traditionally have taken a certain pride?

Of course, societies do not come in categories so neat that we can say without any reservation that United States has what it is proud of, with the ex-Soviet Union in the same situation for the Soviet list. The rule of law is certainly more valid for some than for others in the United States; the freedom of expression and assembly is less than total if there are FBI agents taking notes and exercising pressure. And the right to take part in government is nice on paper, but in practice somewhat illusory with a two-point party discourse— one of the many reasons why the United States is so low in terms of electoral participation.[33]

Table 2.2 U.S. Achievements and Ex-Soviet Achievements.

U.S. Achievements	Ex-Soviet Achievements
1. Rule of Law	1. Right to work
2. Freedom of movement, internally and externally	2. Sufficient wages for a decent living
3. Right to own property	3. Right to rest, to leisure
4. Freedom of thought	4. Guaranteed basic needs in terms of food, clothing, housing
5. Freedom of expression	5. Guaranteed health care
6. Freedom of assembly	6. Guaranteed education at all levels
7. Right to take part in government	7. Right to take part in culture

And this is correspondingly true for the ex-Soviet Union. The right to work was good, but having something sensible and productive to do at the workplace is also good. Basic needs were guaranteed through heavy subsidies for staple food, real misery practically speaking non-existent. But the level at which the basic needs were satisfied could certainly be criticized. There is one important exception to that last point: higher education, which in the ex-Soviet Union in general was extended to very many, undermining the system by providing a basis for *glasnost/ perestroika* through an educated population.[34]

And finally, taking part in culture is fine but may also be seen as the easy way out for the government: let the minorities dance their own folk dances, talk their own impossible languages, as long as Russians are in control. And they were in control politically (including the police, and economic planning) and militarily, and also of the all-Union Russian super-culture.

However, let us at present leave all such considerations aside. The point we are driving at is the discourse contraction in both countries down to the human rights discourse that guaranteed a high score for oneself and a low score for the officially appointed enemy. In the introduction to this book the second example of this type of debate is mentioned; in fact, it is one of the motivations for writing the entire book. Both were right in a certain twisted, contracted sense, and both were very wrong.

Compare the U.S. list of achievements with these articles from the Universal Declaration of Human Rights (10 December 1948):

1. *Article 12*: No one shall be subjected to arbitrary interference with his privacy, family, home or correspondence, nor to attacks upon his honor and reputation. Everyone has the right to the protection of the law against such interference or attacks.
2. *Article 13*: Everyone has the right to freedom of movement and residence within the borders of each State. Everyone has the right to leave any country, including his own, and to return to his country.
3. *Article 17*: Everyone has the right to own property alone as well as in association with others. No one shall be arbitrarily deprived of his property.
4. *Article 18*: Everyone has the right to freedom of thought, conscience and religion; this right includes freedom to change his religion or belief, and freedom, either alone or in community with others and in public or private, to manifest his religion or belief in teaching, practice, worship and observance.
5. *Article 19*: Everyone has the right to freedom of opinion and expression; this right includes freedom to hold opinions without interferences and to seek, receive and impart information and ideas through any media and regardless of frontiers.
6. *Article 20*: Everyone has the right to freedom of peaceful assembly and association. No one may be compelled to belong to an association.
7. *Article 21*: Everyone has the right to take part in the government of his country, directly or through freely chosen representatives. Everyone has the right of equal access to public service in his country. The will of the people shall be the basis of the authority of government; this will shall be expressed in periodic and genuine elections which shall be by universal and equal suffrage and shall be held by secret vote or by equivalent free voting procedures.

The correspondence point for point is not by chance. The list of seven points of U.S. pride derive from a tradition partly created by the United States: the Declaration of Independence (1776) and the Constitution (1787) with the Bill of Rights.

Let us then do the corresponding exercise for the ex-Soviet Union, quoting from the International Covenant on Economic, Social and Cultural Rights (16 December 1966):

1. *Article 6*: The States Parties to the present Covenant recognize the right to work, which includes the right of everyone to the opportunity to gain his living by work which he freely chooses or accepts, and will take appropriate steps to safeguard this right.
2. *Article 7* a (ii): A decent living for themselves and their families in accordance with the provisions of the present Covenant.
3. *Article 7 d*: Rest, leisure and reasonable limitation of working hours and periodic holidays with pay, as well as remuneration for public holidays.

4. *Article 11*: The States Parties to the present Covenant recognize the right of everyone to an adequate standard of living for himself and his family, including adequate food, clothing and housing, and to the continuous improvement of living conditions.

5. *Article 12*: The States Parties to the present Covenant recognize the right of everyone to the enjoyment of the highest attainable standard of physical and mental health.

6. *Article 13*: The States Parties to the present covenant recognize the right of everyone to education. They agree that education shall be directed to the full development of the human personality and the sense of its dignity, and shall strengthen the respect for human rights and fundamental freedoms. They further agree that education shall enable all persons to participate effectively in a free society, promote understanding, tolerance and friendship among all nations and all racial, ethnic or religious groups, and further the activities of the United Nations for the maintenance of peace.

7. *Article 15 a*: To take part in cultural life.

Again there is correspondence, and not by chance. The socialist countries and Third World countries insisted very much on this Covenant, basically unknown in the United States, and not yet ratified by the U.S. Senate (whereas the second covenant adopted the same day, 16 December 1966, the International Covenant on Civil and Political Rights, was ratified December 1993). The three documents together with the Optional Protocol constitute what is known as the International Bill of Human Rights.

In one sense the situation was almost ideal. Either superpower had its own human rights covenant in terms of which it could declare itself perfect and the other superpower highly imperfect. Seriously drafted United Nations documents provided the setting for the human rights ping-pong match referred to in the second example in the introduction, with either party selecting the discourse that suits them, pointing a finger at the other party, extolling their own virtues—a rather obvious case of the need for joining discourses for a broader and deeper debate. But that only works if both sides are willing to see some good in the other and some bad in the self.

It belongs in the picture, however, that there are some small countries to the north of the United States and in Northern Europe that feel strongly that they have been able to implement all fourteen points at the same time and for that reason are entitled to a "plague on both your houses" stance, combining the two discourses into one relatively holistic human rights discourse. And they feel that the ex-Soviet Union is trying to catch up on the lagging leg (possibly losing the achievements made and the other), but that the United States is not. And it certainly belongs in the picture that there are many countries in a fourth category, short on both sets.

In saying this it should be pointed out that both the Universal Declaration and the Covenants are drafted quite skillfully in the sense that what is in one is also partly in the other, but emphasized less. The reader of the Universal Declaration of 1948 will find in Articles 23-26 much of what is spelled out in more detail in the articles quoted above from the Covenant, and will find in the other Covenant on Civil and Political Rights much of what is listed in the Universal Declaration. And yet they constitute different discourses, and it is quite understandable (but not excusable) that the Universal Declaration, known in the United States and for a long time alone in being ratified by the U.S. Senate, is the one most similar to the U.S. constitutional instruments.

The loser in this discourse contraction game in which Third world countries also participate, playing the Soviet role of focusing on economic rights, is the world population—humankind.

One day, in the not too distant future, an International Bill of Rights will probably become a generally ratified document. In that document there may also be a reflection of what is vaguely called the "third generation of human rights," the collective rights of peoples to independence, development, peace, a clean and balanced environment, and so on. It is also relatively easy to predict when that coalescence of the documents into one will take place—when major world powers are reasonably convinced that they have been able to implement most of it; the ex-Soviet Union (1997: CIS) the civil and political rights and the United States the economic and social rights (the former may actually happen before the latter).[35] This will be a great day for humankind, giving us a unified human rights discourse. And it will be a particularly great day for the Nordic countries who feel at home in both discourses, provided they will still be able, with good conscience, to say: welcome!

SOCIAL SCIENCE AND "SOCIAL LAWS"

Returning to social science and philosophy in general, let us explore the term "law": social regularity. Charles Darwin, in his famous *Voyage of the Beagle* made the point, when encountering the Abakaloufs in South America, that they are so egalitarian that they can never become rich or developed.[36] Only when a society is inegalitarian is it possible to reward the exceptional person, the entrepreneur who is the locomotive of growth and development. But he has a right to expect some kind of return from his labors. That differential return, accumulated, is known as inequality. Absence of inequality carries with it absence of growth: why bother?

Needless to say, this whole idea is heartily embraced by what today passes for economic theory but in reality is the theory of capitalist societies, and probably should be referred to as "capitalistics." In many textbooks in economics "exploitation" is related to mining, and "equity" to bank loans.

To deconstruct the underlying discourse imagine that we introduce two simple dimensions for discussing an economic system, "poor versus rich" and "inegalitarian versus egalitarian." The first dimension can be referred to as "growth," and the second as "distribution" (the former overreported by the media, the latter forgotten or underreported). This gives us a 4-point discourse for discussing economic systems, as indicated in Figure 2.5.

A "social regularity" or "law" in the descriptive rather than normative sense, is indicated in Figure 2.5, both by excluding the (egalitarian, rich) combination, and by tracing a dynamic arrow through the other three combinations.

That arrow may in fact stand for a theory of development according to this type of (liberal, conservative) thinking. We start with a very egalitarian, but also very poor, "primitive" society. Then inegalitarian elements are brought into the picture: accumulation at the top, producing a "traditional" society. In a "modern" society accumulation—savings—is put to profitable use through investment, leading to processes of growth and eventually to a rich society, maintained by, and preserving, inequality.[37] There is no path leading to this corner in Figure 2.5 except the one indicated. And any effort to get into the excluded combination is doomed. Poor, or inegalitarian, or both. *Quartum non datur*—that is the law. Hence, reporting only growth becomes legitimate.

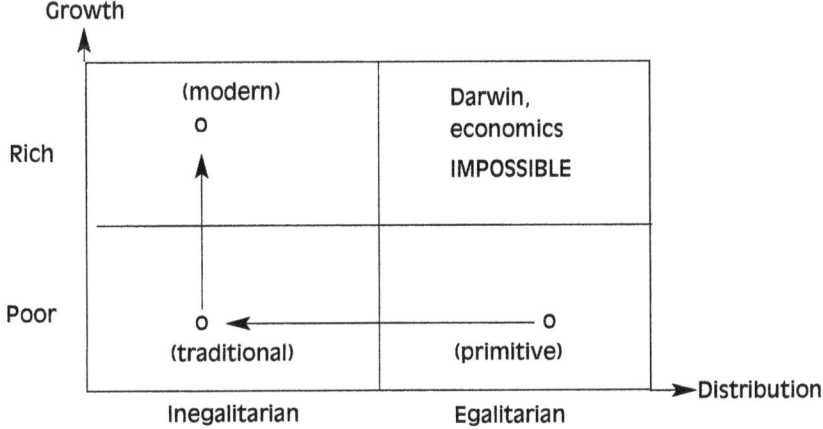

Figure 2.5 A discourse for economic systems

Since rich, egalitarian society is doomed, ruled out as empirically impossible and theoretically unforeseen, however much it may be the preferred order, no discourse is needed to highlight it. We might limit ourselves to two separate discourses, one for growth in terms of poor and rich, and one for distribution in terms of inegalitarian and egalitarian. There is no need to combine these two discourses into a joint discourse as has been done in Figure 2.5. The empirically impossible should rest in the semantic darkness it deserves, not linger on as a potential possibility. The discourses will be separate and unequal, rich-poor being dominant, egalitarian-inegalitarian recessive. There is only one trajectory possible in this image of economic history, toward the rich but inegalitarian modern society—a trajectory also known as modernization. Socialism, rich, and egalitarian is impossible.

This stance has profound consequences. As opposed to the human rights examples in which a normative law impedes entry into forbidden categories (human rights infractions) we are here dealing with a presumably descriptive law standing in the way of that type of excursion. It is bad enough to attempt the illicit-immoral-illegal. To attempt the impossible is not only immoral but something worse according to many—it is stupid. To run your head against a wall will be worse for your head than for the wall, the head receiving the treatment that quality of head deserves anyhow. Again, no need to let the impossible shine in semantic brightness. This way empiricism may stimulate discourse contraction and discourse simplification, letting empirical findings determine the discourse rather than letting the discourse stimulate the search for new reality.

But that means that the descriptive law, the "social invariance" serves the same basic function as normative law: to proscribe, to rule out. Interestingly, the word law is used in both cases.[38] In some Christian epistemology they would come together in the concept of obedience to God's commands. Nature's laws, the laws of nature, were also laws for nature dictated by God the Creator as something Nature had to obey. And God also commanded through Abraham and Moses the laws human beings have to obey, appropriately referred to as "commandments." Only later, through secularization, was this coincidence in meaning lost sight of, making us see scientific "laws" as unbreakable, engraved in a stone called "reality," rather than trying to bend that reality.[39]

CHINA I: ECONOMIC GROWTH AND DISTRIBUTION

Consider a quite different case, also relating to economics, but now taken from a non-Western culture, China, and based on a personal experience. We are again wrestling with the problem of constructing an adequate discourse for economic systems, and enter the field with a 2-point discourse, "capitalism/socialism," and add a rather general discourse for evaluation: "good/bad."

Let us then combine the two into a joint discourse, as is done in Figure 2.6:

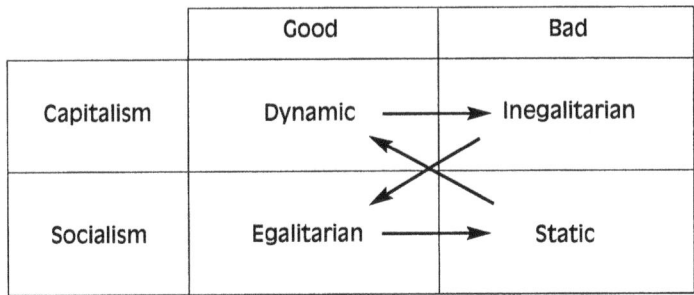

	Good	Bad
Capitalism	Dynamic	Inegalitarian
Socialism	Egalitarian	Static

Figure 2.6. A Chinese discourse for economic systems

Imagine now the following speech given by a common Chinese, having been asked where he stood on capitalism versus socialism (July 1986):

> I like capitalism because it is so dynamic. However, on the other hand, capitalism is also bad because it is so inegalitarian: the poor people become very poor, destitute and prostitute, unemployed, and the rich people accumulate more riches. Hence we have to have socialism which is very good because it is much more egalitarian, lifting up the poor people and setting an upper limit for the rich people. On the other hand, socialism is very bad because it is so static, nothing much is happening. Hence we need capitalism which is very good because it is so dynamic, however, on the other hand, capitalism is also very bad because . . .[40]

The train of thought is indicated by the arrows in the middle of the figure and is in need of no further comment. The basic point is that for the speaker to deliver this speech the 4-point joint discourse was a necessary if not a sufficient condition. It was indispensable for him to be able to use the good/bad distinction for both capitalism and socialism.

Needless to say, in much of Western economic discourse people specialize in either of the two diagonals in the figure, only rarely exploring systematically all four corners. So-called right wing people focus on positive aspects of capitalism and negative aspects of socialism, so-called left wing people on negative aspects of capitalism and positive aspects of socialism, both of them essentially operating within 2-point discourses. But because these two 2-point discourses are not joined anywhere to a 4-point discourse they are prevented from making a speech like this particular, but in no way unrepresentative Chinese.

The Chinese might come to the conclusion that we need a mix, a "both-and," with, for instance, a socialist phase building egalitarianism until the static (read "state"-ic) aspect becomes too overwhelming, then a capitalist phase based on dynamism until the inegalitarian aspect becomes overwhelming, then back to socialism again, and so on and so forth. Western discourse will tend to end up with the conclusion that one is good and the other bad, leading to a battle between the two that may have as a consequence some oscillation between the two systems, but with nobody seeing the oscillation itself as beneficial.

In the Chinese case the oscillation is already built into the discourse, contrary to Western norms of consistency and equilibrium as indicative of maturity and stability. Regrettably, the Chinese do not seem to have a corresponding flexibility in their political discourse, as evidenced by the terrible events in China during the spring and summer of 1989 (to be explored in the next case study).

We shall return to this theme later, as there is a basic distinction here between Western and Chinese discourse theory that should be explored, a warning about the assumption that "Western-Chinese" is not itself a 2-point discourse that cannot be challenged. There is certainly the possibility of both "both-and," "compromise," and "neither-nor," and even these categories are neither mutually exclusive nor exhaustive of all possibilities. We may deplore any mental life passed in slavery under a false dichotomy, and usually detect it more easily in others.

So let us at this early stage end by saying something in favor of dichotomies. More particularly, we will have a look at a very ancient dichotomy, "man/woman." Gays and lesbians, transvestites and hermaphrodites, eunuchs and others draw our attention to the fact that there is more under the sun; there is both-and, neither-nor, in-between and more. And the Chinese *yin-yang* meta-discourse will sensitize us to the man in every woman and woman in every man, and so forth.

Nevertheless, the educated suspicion remains that the dichotomy "man/woman" is not entirely inadequate but actually remains a quite useful, one might even say fruitful, dichotomy. No discourse sophistication should be permitted to kill it.

CHINA II: ECONOMIC AND POLITICAL DEVELOPMENT

The events in China, particularly in Beijing in Spring 1989, from the beginning of the pro-democracy movement demonstrating in Tian'anmen Square and Chang'an Avenue (following the death of Hu Yaobang on April 15 and the editorial in the *People's Daily* on April 26) to the martial law order of May 20, the killing of soldiers June 3 and the massacre of civilians, including students on June 4 along the Chang'an Avenue, stimulated many reflections on economic versus political development. Leaving aside the primitivism of economic development = economic growth, the typical reflection was in terms of the need for having political development = democracy first and then economic development, not vice versa. Gorbachev's Soviet Union was often held out as an example for China to follow, including by the Chinese themselves.

The case is as good as any to point to another missing dimension in a discourse: *sophistication*, in this case with *time* as a variable. A 2-point discourse, "political change first, then economic" and "economic change first, then political" as usual leaves out very important possibilities: "neither-nor" (no change of either kind, needed for completeness, if for no other reason in order to be explicitly rejected), and "both-and." The latter could have two interpretations: "hand-in-hand," and "intermittently", meaning a (short) phase of economic development, then one of political development (or vice versa), then economic development again, and so on. Both of these are actually much more realistic than the simplistic "first one, then the other."[41]

Diagrammatically it can be illustrated like in Figure 2.7:

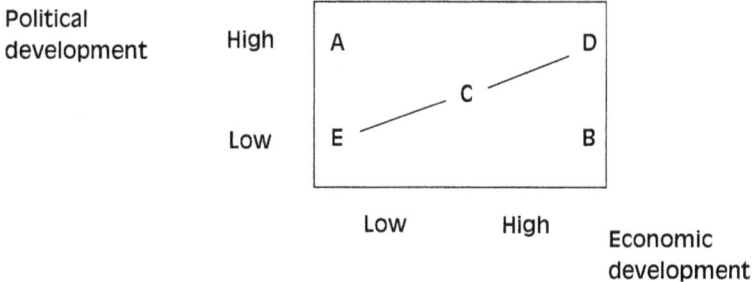

Figure 2.7. Interfaces between economic and political development

A and B are the two roads in the original discourse, supplemented by C for the "diagonal," D for "intermittent," and E for nothing.

The point here is not to argue which of the first four are desirable and/or feasible, but to explore the consequences of the contraction to a 2-point discourse. If these were the only alternatives, then the Western world, so proud of its achievements in these two fields, would have had nothing of which to be proud. What really happened was according to C and D, not A and B, and the amount of time needed from an enlightened absolutism, not that different from that in Mao Zedong China, would have to be measured in centuries, not in decades, and certainly not in years. Political development in the sense of the development of democracy was very modest at the beginning of Western economic development starting with very low levels of growth and distribution. If the ex-Soviet Union/CIS since *glasnost* started in 1985, with no major economic development so far, is insufficient indication that A does not always lead to the bliss of both economic and political development, then India might serve. Of course, the argument may also be that there has been little if any political development, but that is not quite true. To abolish Censorship I, as done by Gorbachev, is no minor achievement.

For the futility of B there are countless contemporary examples—for example, on the Arab peninsula—indicating that economic development may lead to itself and nothing more, just as political development may lead to endless verbal exchanges standing in the way rather than facilitating economic development. *Glasnost* may stand in the way of *perestroika*. After all, the countries in East and Southeast Asia, such as Japan, South Korea (eventually also North Korea), and Thailand, to mention some, follow patterns C or rather D, just as the West did, only much more quickly.

Hence, throwing a 2-point discourse at these countries with the foregone conclusion of A is in a sense to invite them to a road block, leaving them with no alternatives. We may see political development in the sense of democracy with civil and political human rights as an absolute value to be followed up with economic development, and denounce all three alternatives. But in doing so we also denounce our own history, without explaining to others how we would have done otherwise. A richer discourse would invite more explorations. Infantilism does not help anybody.

The usual excuse that the media cannot go into any detail because of brevity of time and shortness of space is not sufficient to explain, not to mention excuse, the frequent use of simplistic 2-point discourses where the mention of two or three more possibilities could contribute tremendously to social, economic, and political imagination. It is tempting to believe that this does not happen because social, economic, and political interests stand in the way. Certainly, but the roots may be in the deep culture.

RACE OR GENDER: A FALSE DICHOTOMY

A white, young, rich woman is gang-raped by black, teen-age, poor boys in Central Park, New York, and beaten into a coma in Spring 1989. The case becomes known all over the world and a debate serves to crystallize a discourse. The general U.S. conflict discourse in terms of individual misfits and individual therapies, rather than any group conflict, prevails. The search for an explanation in the biographies of the boys is on, including why they do not repent but insist it was "kind of fun."

Two collectivist (as opposed to individualist) discourses emerge: the feminist "every rape is a battle in a war between the genders" and the sociologist/criminologist "every crime is a battle in the war between the classes." Obviously, there were two class dimensions involved, given the reality of Manhattan, New York: race and wealth. But only race was clearly visible in a young woman jogging, so let us limit the class discourse to race.

The two dimensions are well taken. The missing dimension in this case is not strictly speaking a dimension, but again the joint discourse, the key to understanding being in the combination of gender and race. Censorship II operates not by ruling out gender or race, but by ruling out the dangerous combination of gender and race. The white male is running the United States; the black female is at the bottom, very often as a lonely, even teen-aged, mother. That structural violence is pandemic, and there is very little the black female can do to a white male to overcome it, at least today. The relation is usually seen as sexually rather than politically explosive.

But there is very much a black male can do to a white female, particularly when her reading of her own society is so unrealistic that she jogs alone in Central Park. They can rape her, and they did. Sexual or political? Both, of course. A battle in the war between the genders or the races? Both, of course, hitting the stronger race at its weaker gender. How can the situation be improved? By making both gender and race less relevant as power dimensions *at the same time*, and accepting the reality of a collectivist element in individual crimes.

From a discourse point of view the problem is how to handle not only two dimensions, but two dimensions together, at the same time. The interaction between them may hold the key, as argued often above (and as will be argued in the next three chapters).

Another race and gender case comes to mind: the televised Senate hearing of the Anita Hill-Clarence Thomas case in October 1991; both Hill and Thomas are black (would a corresponding case between two whites have been displayed so prominently in public space?). Roughly speaking the issue was the following: Anita Hill claimed that Clarence Thomas had harassed her sexually by making propositions backed up by references to the length of his penis, and so forth. Clarence Thomas denied that any such conversations had ever taken place during their work together on equal opportunity cases, handling, among other issues, sexual harassment. The issue became one of credibility, seen as a zero-sum game: either Hill speaks the truth or Thomas. As usual a 2-point discourse, favored by the court structure of a Senate hearing bound to end with a yes/no decision.

As usual, the other two points were missing (except to one senator): they may both be lying or both telling the truth. A scenario for the latter is easily imagined. Hill and Thomas are discussing a sexual harassment case at the end of the day. In the longer run hardly any man can do that without some light, jocular remarks. Thomas, the male, makes such remarks—to him made in a professional context and to be taken lightly. To Hill they are out of order, in bad taste, and harassing. To Thomas they are soon forgotten and then repressed, to Hill they are first repressed and then, long afterwards, remembered. He said/she said. Who speaks the truth?

The discourse changes dramatically if the focus is on Hill versus the Judiciary Committee (male, white) rather than Hill versus Thomas. The issue is sexual harassment. But does that issue have salience to the Judiciary Committee? Is there really a hearing going on at all, or is this a question of a dimension, sexual harassment, surfacing at all, and not a question of who speaks the truth? In other words, are we dealing with a two-step discourse process: first, the dimension has to be recognized as of (at least) equal importance as the other dimensions brought up in a confirmation hearing and second, a decision has to be made. As it would have been far from politically correct to rule sexual harassment out of court in 1991, there was no alternative to giving the issue a hearing. But having done that, the issue could be killed by deciding there was nothing to it, Hill is not credible/least credible/less credible. With this decision, not so much Hill's testimony as sexual harassment as an issue was excluded from the discourse.

THE END OF THE COLD WAR: THE MISSING EXPLANATION?

"Nobody could have predicted this" was the almost unanimous exclamation from the state, executives as well as legislators, and from the media, when the Wall came tumbling down on November 9, 1989. Of course, the event was overwhelming. But unpredictable? As the reader may have guessed by now, a partial explanation for the absence of an explanation that might have brightened the prospects for elite forecasting is found in discourse inadequacy, blurring thought, speech, and action like a *maya* draped over crucial parts of the minds of key persons in state and media. It is probably still there.

More particularly, two important factors were missing from the dominant discourse, and even more particularly, their combination:

1. the political power of people, particularly in the form of associations and organizations, in other words civil society;
2. the power of *nonviolence*, wielded by the people.

The argument is not that this is the whole story behind the inner erosion of the socialist bloc in general and the Soviet Union in particular. There are certainly also such factors as the German *Ostpolitik*, how the Soviets were exhausted economically by the arms race and felt technologically inferior, the Final Act of Helsinki 1975, and so forth. Above all, there was Mikhail Sergeyevich Gorbachev and his new thinking. But who can conceive of the end of the cold war without mentioning the dissident movement, with its clear rejection not only of Stalinism but post-Stalinism and its advocacy of human rights? And the peace movement, with an equally clear rejection of the nuclear arms race, and its advocacy of disarmament?

This is not the place to argue the case for the Gorbachev-dissident movement-peace movement triangle as the *causa efficiens* in the end, given the host of other factors as side causes and side effects. (The economic factor may have been the least important; people were not that badly off, moreover, economic scarcity was nothing new). More interesting in this context are some speculations about the why and how of the missing discourses.

One reason is simple: the Cold War was seen in a context of inter-state relations, and more particularly as inter-alliance. Colossal military, political, and economic power had been mobilized on both sides. The conflict, over the better political system, the better economic system, and over power in Eastern Europe, had clear inter-state articulations even if alliances and countries were not homogeneous. The war, should it come, would almost certainly be an inter-alliance war. Peace, or at least dis-targeting if not disarmament, no longer pointing weapons at each other, should it come, would probably also have inter-state causes, with doves arguing *détente* and hawks arguing armament, deployment, and targeting.

In this image, or discourse, people, even when organized, looked so small and governments looked so large. And yet leaders in democratic countries should at least have been conceptually prepared for the idea that people matter, especially given how much effort they put into concealing major policies from the watchful eyes of their own populations. Of course, the argument would be that in the West they pay attention to people in elections and live up to the mandate from the *demos*, whereas in a dictatorship they never do.

This is where nonviolence enters, a concept almost unknown to the political scientists likely to be among the political advisors of leaders. Politicians in democratic countries were probably thinking approximately as follows: in a dictatorship nonviolence is impossible, as its proponents will be imprisoned or worse; in a democracy it is unnecessary, as the majority will express their political will in a more institutionalized way, in elections. Under some conditions both propositions are probably valid, but not under the conditions in the second half of the 1980s. Both movements had by that time demoralized their respective elites to the point that probably only real hardliners believed in traditional socialism, or in nuclear war under some circumstance, or even in the legitimacy of nuclear deterrence as the road to peace. Both elites were shaky; a little push and the shakiest would yield. The shakiest turned out to be post-Stalinism in the East; it probably might also have been nuclearism in the West, in which case the East would probably have followed suit.

The nonviolent methods used were simple demonstrations, far from Gandhian sophistication. But the group that came out of the *Nikolaikirche*[42] in Leipzig on October 9, 1989, one month before the fall of the Wall, had all reason to believe that the Stasis would arrest, or even shoot them; in fact, they did not, probably because somehow they were touched. And the DDR was the cornerstone of the construction, as important to the Soviet empire as India to the British empire.

The elites were taken by a surprise for which they and their discourses were responsible. With discourses ignoring people and nonviolent power, elite life full of surprises seems guaranteed.

THE GULF WAR: CURTAILING TIME AND SPACE

In the Gulf the war started as a surprise, and ended in a more predictable manner, as one might expect in a war involving 33 countries organized in a U.S.-led coalition with Security Council backing (the famous resolution 678, which included the Clausewitzian "all necessary means"). Of course, wars do not always end the way the mightiest predict, possibly because some power dimension has been omitted from the discourse. But in this particular ending the only surprise was that the coalition did not continue on to Baghdad.

Why was the invasion of Kuwait on August 2, 1990 a surprise? Or was it? Iraq's claim on Kuwait was not unknown to anyone with a minimum knowledge of history (in the Ottoman empire Kuwait was part of the Basra province, one of the three provinces in addition to Mosul and Baghdad constituting Iraq). The regime's strong dissatisfaction with its economic situation after the ten-years war with Khomeini's Iran was known and feared by other Arab countries. Moreover, there is the ambiguity of U.S. action prior to the first Gulf war.

But the discourse that was used brushes all of this aside, curtailing time and space. As by some prior agreement politicians and media started the *time discourse*, the clock for the conflict, on 2 August 1990 as if history did not exist (that clock, by the way, was stopped again when the war was over; reporting was limited to the aftermath of the war, particularly to the degree of compliance with cease-fire conditions). The war is constructed as a self-contained event, with neither antecedents (accumulated frustration) nor consequents (such as the Muslim surge in Maghreb).

The *space discourse* was limited to the Middle East (meaning Iraq and neighboring countries Kuwait, Saudi Arabia, Iran, Israel, and the Kurdish nation), making the Middle East self-sufficient and self-contained as both conflict producer and consumer. There was some concern with possible terrorist fall-out in key coalition countries (United States, United Kingdom, France, Germany). But the idea that causal chains could also, partly, originate far away from the Middle East—for instance, as an urge in Washington D.C. to punish a former client lest others should go the same way (as had been done earlier to Noriega and was to be done later to Aidid)—was ruled out by the discourse control. The space discourse that emerged conformed to the old idea of the Middle East as a powder keg, with fire, fuse, and all located locally, and the two world centers in the West as fire brigade.

What was thought, said, and done within that discourse has certainly been debated, but there has been less debate about the discourse as such. Negotiations between Iraq and the United States were ruled out by the latter not only because Saddam Hussein had to be punished and not be rewarded for aggression, but also because that would portray the U.S. as holding negotiation chips, meaning causal levers, and not only as the disinterested bystander rushing in to punish aggression. Iraq was seen as autistic, not reciprocal.

Another effect is found in the many pilgrimages for peace, made by leading statesmen to peace activists. They acted inside the discourse by traveling to Baghdad and not also to London, Paris, or Washington, D.C. Guilt distribution was assured through discourse curtailment, as opposed to symmetric, shared *karma* perspectives.

THE SOMALIA WAR: THE NATION-STATE FICTION

It looked so simple: starvation because of drought, social collapse after years of war, gang warfare over scarce resources. The answer was humanitarian aid, organized by the military under UN and U.S. auspices. There are several discourse points to be made:

1. *What kind of assistance, and who should deliver it?* If the problem is starvation, "seeds and tools" sounds like a reasonable package, combined with medical assistance. Who should deliver this assistance? Presumably agricultural and medical experts. But a UN expert sent to look into the situation in August 1992 reporting back to the UN headquarters along such lines was told that "this does not fit into our concept." That concept demanded delivery by the military to bolster UN forces, and open to German participation, like the Cambodian was used for and by Japan.

2. *To whom should it be delivered and through which channel?* Presumably to those in need, the starving people, and through those who can reach them. And here a major mistake was made, by buying uncritically into the nation-state concept. Somalia is one of the few states in decolonized Africa satisfying European formulas for nation-states: same language (Somali), same religion (Islam). Hence Somalia must by definition be one, and for further proof the fact that it is treated as one on maps, in the UN, and in inter-state relations should be sufficient. "Nation-building" made sense, by war if necessary. Supplies could be shipped and flown into Mogadishu, the capital, assuming that from there they would flow along the arteries of a homogeneous state to those most in need.

Virtual reality. In reality Somalia can only be understood by seeing the clans as polities, missing in the discourse from the beginning, then introduced, but in a very unfortunate way. The super-clans are *Darood* (clans: *Dulbahante, Majerteen, Ogaden,* and *Marehan*); *Irir* (clans: *Issak, Hawiye, Isa,* and *Godabiirsay*) and *Saab* (*Ahanwayn*). This is a different way of organizing a society, partly territorial, partly by kinship. "Modern" Westerners may decide this is the wrong way and wish it away. But kinship is solid; in addition, who are the Westerners to decide? In practice, this means less solidarity where it should be according to Western cognitive maps, meaning within the nation-state of Somalia as such; and more solidarity where it should not be, along kinship lines and territory under their command. So the society cracks at unexpected places. And the clan leaders, instead of being honored, were fitted into an inadequate discourse as "warlords." The U.S./UN spent enormous resources in terms of time, personnel, and money hunting for some thirteen or fourteen leaders of super-clans, clans, and subclans instead of for more useful work. And in Norway Somali immigrant workers demonstrated outside the Foreign Ministry with posters denouncing the U.S. and the UN as the real warlords—in perfect Norwegian.

The UN should have been skeptical of their own maps and understood the clan organization at least as an additional reality. They should have brought in the supplies by helicopter, bypassing Mogadishu, basing assistance on competent civilian personnel with police for crowd control and order. Instead Somalia became the victim of an inadequate discourse, adding to the violence.

THE WAR IN YUGOSLAVIA: THE APPOINTED ENEMY

That Yugoslavia—a unitary state from 1918 until 1941 when it was conquered by Nazi Germany, a federation from 1945 until 1974 when it became more like a confederation (with each internal unit, the six republics, and the two autonomous regions having a veto)—is fragile and might disintegrate should surprise nobody. Nor is it surprising that their "Kingdom of Serbs, Croats, and Slovenes" (Yugoslavia from 1929) would disintegrate along national lines (adding Slavic Muslims in Bosnia; Albanian Muslims in Kosovo; Hungarians in Vojvodina; Macedonians, and Montenegrins) and not along administrative borders. After all, these were the lines drawn in peoples' minds, solidified through conflicts, and myths of chosenness and past and future glory and trauma; often instrumentalized by cynical politicians within and without.

The state-system, in disregard of facts and filled with contempt for "the Balkans," first resisted disintegration, partly because Yugoslavia was more easily dealt with as a package, and partly for fear (with justification) of what would happen. But the centrifugal forces were too strong, so Slovenia seceded successfully in June 1991. The state-system, or the most powerful forces articulating the state system, meaning the United States, the EU (in the first period, still the EC), and the UN Security Council (including Russia), insisted that Yugoslavia should disintegrate along administrative lines drawn by the Communist leaders at the end of the Second World War, using a territorial rather than national discourse for national relations. Referenda were organized in the name of self-determination.

The result after the round of recognitions was minorities forced by the recognition to live under masters who were their old enemies and in some cases even had committed acts of genocide against them. Not only did these minorities demand self-determination, they were willing to fight to the end. And because the Serbs are the most numerous but also the most dispersed group (30 percent living outside Serbia proper) the Serbs became the most aggressive in the struggle against those borders, for both liberation and possible expansion.

But the Serbs entered that struggle as the perfect candidates for the MFE (Most Favored Enemy) position: the wrong Christianity (Orthodox), the wrong alphabet (Cyrillic), the wrong former empire (Ottoman), the wrong location (to the East), having killed the successor to the Habsburg Empire (which annexed Bosnia-Herzegovina in 1908), having killed many Germans in the Second World War (Germany invaded Yugoslavia in 1941), and housing the capital of a communist country (but leading communists were not Serbs—the Serbian party dates from 1946).

Yugoslavia had some isomorphism with the socialist bloc: small and struggling in the northwest (Slovenia = the Baltic), bigger and Catholic further down (Croatia = Poland), Muslim in the south (Kosovo = Central Asia), and big and Orthodox in the northeast (Serbia = Russia), controlling a federal army (JNA = Red Army). Minds trained for 40 years of adulthood on the Warsaw Pact countries, never having had a real chance to fight the "Big One," cast Serbia in that role. Branded aggressor *a priori*, Serbia did not have a chance of presenting an alternative discourse. The public relations agencies hired by Zagreb and Sarajevo had an easy job.

True, the Serbs in Krajina, the *Grenzer*, the Serbs in Eastern Herzegovina, the *chetniks*, and the Croats in Western Hercegnovi, the *ustashe*, belong among the most violent people in Europe. Also for that reason they are not necessarily on easy terms with Belgrade and

Zagreb, the Serbs preferring (con-)federal arrangements to total integration. But to the West, Serb = Serb; local Serbs struggling not to live under Croat or Muslim rule were not seen as such but as the pawns of Belgrade expansionism. That discourse also harbored some truth, but the argument made here is, as usual, for discourse expansion to accommodate more mature thought, speech, and action.

The agenda setters of the world, imprisoned by their own discourse, could not allow themselves to admit that their map had been wrong from the very beginning, even if the consequence of that conscious or subconscious decision was the inability even to formulate what the wars in Croatia and Bosnia were about. Once recognized as UN members the territories attained a certain sanctity, as dogma, in spite of the clear movements to secede (*"eppure si muove,"* Galilei is reputed to have said, "and yet it moves"). The Serbs in Croatia and Bosnia did not get what the Croats in Croatia and Muslims in Bosnia got. The discourse for Bosnia degenerates into squabbles over the percentage of Bosnian territory, and does not include the constitutional issues underlying the war.

Why did this happen? As in the case of Somalia, because of a high IxA (the product of ignorance and arrogance), the self-interest of major actors (Catholic ascendancy for the Vatican, *Hinterland* for EU-Germany-Austria) and winning the Second and the First World Wars. Discourse inadequacy is cause and effect, and hence well rooted.

Let us now make a jump, after the Dayton Agreement of December 1995, into the streets of Belgrade in December 1996. The conflict is no longer over ex-Yugoslavia but over a key actor, the Serbian president Milosevic, rightly accused of stealing local elections. Students, professors, and many others are in the streets, claiming the elections back, in favor of democratic, and against authoritarian rule. The struggle is nonviolent—dancing, flowers, cakes to the police, drumming out the sound of the official news media at 19:30, reading Aristotle to the police at night, and so forth—highly imaginative.

Leaving aside the amateurishness of the media in reporting nonviolence, what is disturbing is, as usual, a one-dimensional discourse. Some perceptive journalists, however, noticed that working-class people and old people were not in the streets. Why not?

The answer is that because to them this is not only authoritarian versus democratic rule, but also privatization versus public control of the economy. They know who has been hit by privatization in the former socialist countries: workers, state functionaries, and the retired who see guaranteed salaries and pensions dwindle. This does not mean that students and professors are blind to their possible suffering, nor is the implication that the others are anti-democratic. But priorities differ, and are, as usual, close to one's own interests.

Nothing strange in that; this is what politics is about. But, by cutting the issue to only authoritarian versus democratic, the media:

1. Fail to explain all those people who are not in the streets.
2. Fail to explain how and why Milosevic remains in power.
3. Fail to see how solving one issue may depend on the other.
4. Fail to prepare news consumers for complexity in general.

However simplistic newscasting has its benefits: plenty of surprises.

HAWAI'I: SOVEREIGNTY, AUTONOMY, AND INDEPENDENCE

Both authors long lived in Hawai'i, so let us end with a note on the discourses in Hawai'i for thought, speech, and action on the most important problem facing the islands. By historical rights the islands belong to the Hawaiians, and who and how many they are can possibly be decided by blood quantum methods. By majority rights the island belongs to the majority, which in 1959 voted in favor of integration into the United States as the 50th U.S. state, rejecting the two alternatives, independence and free association.

But nothing is final in this world, including the political status of the Hawaiian islands, or East-West relations in Europe, or the borders between Iraq and Kuwait, or the construction of Somalia and of Yugoslavia. Change is normal, and in Hawai'i there has been a jump in consciousness formation about such issues, stimulated by the centenary of the "businessmen coup" in 1993 and the coming centenary of U.S. annexation in 1998. Whereas African Americans came into the limelight of U.S. consciousness through religion, sports, and music, native Hawaiians have come up more through the PhD and JD approach and Hawaiian culture in general. (The hula never caught on the way jazz did.)

The problem is how to construct a discourse that can accommodate a range of future scenarios, and for that to happen there has to be some awareness of the dimensions involved:

1. Which people are we talking about, all and/or Hawaiians?
2. What level of sovereignty, internal and/or external?
3. What territory are we talking about, all and/or a part?

This gives us eight possibilities, Hawaiians have internal control (autonomy) over a part of Hawai'i to all residents have full control over all of Hawai'i (independence). (One of the other combinations, all residents have internal control over the state of Hawai'i, is the present order, aka federalism). The former of the two comes in two versions, territorial as "state-within-a-state," and non-territorial as "nation-within-a-nation." The latter means secession from the U.S., one star off the flag.

Where does the term "sovereignty" fit into this, as in the sentence "X has sovereignty over Y?" X can stand for any people and Y can stand for any territory, the term sovereignty being ambiguous. It can cover any subset in the total set of functions handled by a society; including that total set, and including the zero set in the sense that the people are sovereign "in principle."

There is a need for a catch-all term like that in a very hotly contested field where national emotions are pitted against each other over the very basis for life, territory. For instance, the term can serve to clarify X and Y. But sooner or later the extent of control will also have to be clarified, to translate thought and speech into action, specifying the range of the functions.

In Hawai'i the two positions above, as alternative to *status quo*, are both problematic. Why should the descendants of the owners of the islands have only internal control over only a part? On the other hand, if the whole population takes control over the islands, would the Hawaiians not be subject to settler rule?[43] Were the native Americans better off after 1776? Would Hawaiians be?

We are not going to state any position on these issues here, only point out that a very rich discourse is needed to accommodate the many options, including the status quo. But this also brings up a point that deserves mention toward the end of this long chapter: the need, sometimes, for lack of clarity. We shall not argue in favor of poor discourses; a single dimension with only two points is and remains a very poor way of reflecting social reality. But many dimensions with many points on them and a fuzzy definition of dimensions and points, like a literary, stream-of-consciousness presentation is better than a single precise dichotomy also incapable of capturing a fleeting, flowing, contradictory reality.

But out of this chaos of formulations and positions and non-positions concrete reality may force some clarity. Maybe discourse clarification comes through action just as much as through the work of the wordsmiths. A Hawaiian "occupies" the land of his ancestors nonviolently; the police carry him away. How do the media describe that? Trespassing? Rightfully reclaimed? As there is a parallel between a person owning land and a nation owning its homeland, the connecting link being "property," some care has to be exercised.

One way in which that is done in Hawaiian media is by not spelling out the independence option, but interpreting the generic word "sovereignty" narrowly, as limited autonomy, not independence.[44]

Time will show what comes first, more autonomy/independence politically, or more independence in the discourse in media owned by the mainland. The balance has already shifted markedly to outside control. There is much at stake, as conquering the discourse may be tantamount to conquering at least half the reality.

NOTES

1. There were sensational headlines such as those in some British and U.S. newspapers that claimed 2,000 people had died at Chernobyl. As Hans Blix, Director-General of the I.A.E.A., noted soon after the accident, "the Soviet reporting was late, meager but probably not untrue. The Western reporting was fat, massive and often misleading, notably in casualty figures. Can there not be anything in between?" (Quoted from Philippe Sands, "Burying Chernobyl," *The Nation*, April 30, 1988. Sands is the author of *Chernobyl: Law and Communication*, Grotius Press, 1988).

2. We are grateful to Dr. Michael Jones of the High Energy Physics Group of the University of Hawai'i for the following calculations. The comparison with a 10-kiloton fission bomb is in terms of released radioactivity, the thermic and kinetic energy of Chernobyl being inconsequential. Jones made the comparison for 2 isotopes, iodine-131 and cesium-137, with 8-day and 30-years half-life respectively, meaning that cesium-137 has long-term health consequences. The explosion of a 10-kiloton fission weapon yields 2.1 million curies of radiation from iodine-131 and 2.5 thousand curies from cesium-137 radiation; the Chernobyl explosion yielded 10-15 million curies from iodine-131 and 1-2 million curies from cesium-137.

   In other words, Chernobyl released over 5 times as much iodine-131 and over 400 times as much cesium-137 radiation (data from Samuel Glasstone, ed., *The Effects of Nuclear Weapons*, and an article by Frank von Hippel and Thomas Cochran in *The Bulletin of the Atomic Scientists*, August/September 1986). Depending on what source of radiation we refer to Chernobyl corresponded to a 50-kiloton-4-megaton nuclear war, again only counting the radiation. The scenarios on both sides sometimes mentioned 50 megatons and more.

   Thus, Chernobyl could have led to mature reflections on what nuclear "planners" had in store for humankind. But the issue was not cut that way, for understandable reasons.

3. In a very thoughtful article by the editor of *Harper's* magazine, Lewis H. Lapham, "Soviet Cast as Satan, But Play Misses the Tragedy" in *San Jose Mercury News*, May 15, 1986, a number of other points are made:

- None of the networks remarked on the probable fear and suffering among the people resident within the vicinity of the burning power station.
- It came as something of a shock to discover that the scaffolding of U.S. omnipotence can be wrecked by an anonymous electron or by obscure factory workers 70 miles north of Kiev.
- The American media did not draw the parallel between the Soviet nuclear disaster and the accidents bedeviling the American space program, even though the two stories were being told concurrently, sometimes in adjacent columns in the same newspaper.
- If the Soviets were afraid to speak, so were the Americans. The technical elites in both countries have been obliged to sacrifice much of their judgment and intelligence to the dictates of money and politics.

In short, Chernobyl was one more of those tests the mainstream U.S. press did not pass. The discourse was not wrong, but incomplete.

4. A point repeatedly made by Soviet spokesmen on U.S. television.

5. If not, the communication loop essential to democracy is broken and so is democracy. As far as we know, no theory exists as to the quality and quantity of its activities the executive may conceal from the citizens, beyond general formulas like "security," and "national interest"—as seen by the executive.

6. If health is located in the interface between (pathogenic) exposure and (capacity for) resistance, then the two approaches of preventive medicine are obviously to increase the resistance (by putting everybody in underground shelters?) or to remove the exposure (by eliminating nuclear weapons). The world trend is as IPPNW suggested. The Nobel Peace Prize Committee joined that trend; mainstream U.S. press with its deficient discourse did not.

7. For one of the author's own version of that debate, see Johan Galtung, *Environment, Development and Military Activity* (Oslo: Norwegian Universities Press, 1982).

8. But it is the same as saying that U.S. media are easily manipulated. Just to pick up the issues of one week in Fall 1989:

- All media dutifully reported President Bush saying that the crack cocaine, he held up a plastic bag, had been "seized a few days ago in a park across the street from the White

House." But the "news" had been created ("We had to manipulate him—the teenage pusher—to get him down there," as reported by *International Herald Tribune*, 23-24 September 1989).

- The allegation that during the mid-1980s Mike Hoover, a freelance cameraman working for CBS, filmed various faked events as "news": getting Afghans to make a bomb to look like a toy that he claimed was manufactured and planted by Soviet soldiers to injure Afghan children; presenting a Pakistani air force jet making a practice run as a Soviet bomber; getting Afghan guerrillas to blow up electricity pylons they had already destroyed before he arrived (*Sunday Times*, October 1, 1989). Those who do such things usually defend themselves, saying "it could have been true." Within their own discourse, yes. But what if the discourse is highly deficient?

9. The context for Reagan's remark is interesting: "What is driving me up the wall is that this wasn't a failure until the press got a tip from that rag in Beirut" (*Time*, November 26, 1986). In other words, reality does not matter, only the images of reality, and they have to be managed. The "rag" is actually not that small, but a weekly magazine published in Moslem West Beirut, possibly with a circulation of 25,000 (Stanley Reed, "Beirut Rag," *The Nation*, December 20, 1986).

10. November 30, 1987.

11. John S. Saloma III, in *Ominous Politics: The New Conservative Labyrinth* (New York: Hill & Wang, 1984) tries to do both ("Charting the Conservative Labyrinth" [chapter 1]), both in terms of names and in terms of positions in the structure.

12. Or, the much easier way out: Forget about the whole thing, which is probably what is being done.

13. Because the data underlying the "findings" are not made public the President's judgment has to be believed, also when the President is heavily involved politically. The temptation to produce retroactive "findings" must be considerable.

14. See, for instance, *The Contra-Drug Connection* (Washington: The Christic Institute, 1987). Also important in this connection is the book by Leslie Cockburn, *Out of Control* (New York: Atlantic Monthly Press, 1987). As Jonathan Steele says in his review "All the President's Rogues," *The Guardian*, February 28, 1988: "The fact that they—the findings of the book—have not been branded on to the public consciousness is a tribute to the American press's awesome ability to divert attention and suppress news." But we prefer the expression "inadequate discourse."

15. Berkeley, University of California Press, 1993.

16. Oliver Stone has tried to do exactly that in the two major movies about the JFK Murder and Nixon, and the reaction of the critics in media, also sensing a competing approach, not only a threat to the "system," was predictably negative.

17. Galtung argued this at the time in an OpEd letter to the *International Herald Tribune*, adding that a U.S. president who did so might risk being impeached. Rumors have been heard that Carter at some stage asked for a documentation of whether there was any substance to the anti-U.S. allegations of the Iran revolution. If that documentation was prepared by the Washington foreign policy establishment, the conclusion was probably negative.

18. President Reagan's speech, launching what was dubbed Star Wars, was given in March 1983, meaning at a late stage in Cold War history. See Johan Galtung, "Strategic Offensive: The Real Star Wars Threat," *The Nation*, 28 February 1987, pp. 248-250.

19. These figures were used in Johan Galtung, *There Are Alternatives!* (Nottingham: Spokesman, 1984), pp. 10-11, but with the warning "that all such figures should be taken with more than a pinch of salt." After the Cold War, when they were supposed to disarm in the real sense of destroying missiles and war-heads, it turned out that both sides had "replacement" missiles that had not been counted.

20. See Johan Galtung, "Human Needs, National Interest and World Politics: The Law of the Sea Conference," *Essays in Peace Research, Vol. V* (Copenhagen: Ejlers, 1980), chapter 13, pp. 361-380.

21. During the Vietnam War these sentiments were manifested in the slogan, "America, love it or leave it."

22. See Johan Galtung, "The People were Right," Chapter 3.1 in *Methodology and Development* (Copenhagen: Ejlers, 1988), pp. 93-106, showing how in a major comparative public opinion survey from 1970, people, more than the experts, sensed the predicament the world was moving into.

23. The Latin Americans (in itself a dubious term, naming a continent after the conquering group) refer to the people of the United States (including Canada) as *norteamericanos*; they themselves use often the term "Americans" (not including Canada). What happens, then, to the Mexicans and to the Central Americans when South America is preferred to Latin America?

24. A little like "born-again Christians."

25. See Johan Galtung, "Is There a New Germany Coming?", in Vilho Harle, ed., *European Values in International Relations* (London: Pinter Publishers, 1990), pp. 192-202.

26. See Johan Galtung, *Hitlerisme, stalinisme, reaganisme: Tre variasjoner over et tema av Orwell* (Oslo: Gyldendal, 1984), also in German and Spanish.
27. For a critique of capitalism/socialism and liberalism/marxism see Johan Galtung, *Economics in Another Key*, forthcoming, chapter 4 on "Externalities."
28. There is a saying attributed to the famous mathematician David Hilbert: "People have more or less broad horizons. In some people the horizon actually shrinks to one single point. That point, then, they call their point of view."
29. See Johan Galtung, *Human Rights in Another Key*, p. 10.
30. The problem with that, from the point of view of the authorities, is that where law no longer is of any avail Amnesty International may take over, internationalizing an issue that otherwise might have stayed within the national court system.
31. See writings by Sarah Parkins.
32. On the other hand, most discourses are also easily forgotten, receding into well-deserved oblivion rather than being dismantled.
33. The turnout did jump upwards in 1992, however, when Ross Perot was a third candidate—to 55.23 percent of the voting-age population. See Adam Clymer, "Election Turnout Highest Since '68," *New York Times*, Section B, p. B16.
34. And this, of course, is a theory both for the rise and the decline and fall of Mikhail Sergeyevich Gorbachev. He, and even more so his wife, were intellectuals with important academic degrees, as opposed to their autodidact or semi-intellectually educated predecessors; appealing to the many millions to whom *glasnost* was highly meaningful. His *perestroika*, however, was probably less important to those who work with words, and might even undermine some of their privileges. The working-class support for Gorbachev was probably limited from the beginning.
35. Thus, the Bush administration ratified the Civil and Political Rights Covenant, with the exception of the Optional Protocol, but not the economic/social/cultural rights.
36. "The perfect equality among the individuals comprising the Fuegian tribes, must for a long time retard their civilization. As we see those animals, whose instinct compels them to live in society and obey a chief, are most capable of improvement, so is it with the races of mankind." Charles Darwin, *Journal of Researches into the Natural History and Geology of the Countries Visited During The Voyage Of H.M.A. BEAGLE Round the World* (London: John Murray, 1845), p. 229.
37. Thus, Pareto optimum does not rule out even increasing inequality.

38. Moreover, there is a normative element in the descriptive, and a descriptive element in the normative. See Johan Galtung, "Expectations and Interaction Processes," *Inquiry*, II, 4 (1959), pp. 213-234.

39. See Johan Galtung, "Back to the Origins: On Christian and Buddhist Epistemology," *Methodology and Development* (Copenhagen: Ejlers, 1988), chapter 1.1, pp. 15-26.

40. Written down immediately afterwards, also quoted in *Methodology and Development*, p. 164 (in the section "Contradictory Reality and Mathematics: A Contradiction?").

41. For one effort to analyze the events and the enormous media bias, see "What Happened in Beijing on June 3-4, 1989: What Happens Now?" in J. Galtung and R. Vincent, *Global Glasnost*, pp. 240-244.

42. What happened is described with much detail by Erich Loest in the book with that title, published in Germany (Leipzig: Linden-Verlag, 1995).

43. Thus, typical of Hawai'i is that there is no majority group: the Euro Americans comprise 23.4%, Japanese Americans 23%, Hawaiians 20.6% (pure Hawaiians 0.8% and "mixed part-Hawaiians" 19.8%), Filipino Americans 11.3%, and so on (data from the state Health Department, reported in *The Honolulu Advertiser*, February 23, 1997). Many other distributions would have made the issue much easier, such as a clear majority of Euro Americans or a clear majority of Hawaiians.

44. See Johan Galtung and Poka Laenui, *Imagine An Independent Hawai`i: What Could It Look Like?* (Honolulu: Matsunaga Institute for Peace, University of Hawaii, 1997).

3

Taking Sides:
A Mental/Political Exercise

This chapter is a reflection on the useful book *Taking Sides: Clashing Views on Controversial Issues in World Politics.*[1] The book itself is not a part of the media in the usual sense, but of a larger loop producing and reproducing the general theme of missing themes. The book is a product of the society that produced and consumes it. The table of contents presents twenty foreign policy and world politics issues, very clearly formulated, all of them with two readings, one taking the position "yes" and the other, somewhat predictably, the position "no." The issues and the background papers, generally media texts, are well selected (only that in front of "Soviet" we have to put ex-). Being one more carrier of a very basic problem, the book merits a critique.

The problem is this: do the texts function in a way that prepares the reader for a mature position on "controversial issues in world politics?" Or, could it rather be said that the book is representative in framing the issues in the simplistic way this is usually done in U.S. media? Being based on media material, preparing students for "two-ness" (chapter 7) as a meta-discourse, we shall use it as a second introduction to U.S. political discourse. But this time somebody else, not we, has defined the issues.

Issue #1: Is the United States becoming too friendly with China? Any answer in terms of yes or no presupposes that the United States is already friendly. It is only a question of degree; maybe the United States is too friendly and should be less friendly; maybe the level of friendship is just about right.

An elimination of the word "too" might eliminate some of this bias. Even better would be the typical public opinion poll-style question such as "do you think the United States is on the whole friendly to China, hostile to China, both, or neither one nor the other?" Formulated this way a broader range of positions might emerge.

But the basic point would be that the question does not define what it means to be friendly. For instance, is it "friendly" to use another country as a possible ally against a major enemy? Is it friendly to have a by-and-large paternalistic stance to the country, seeing any relation of influence from the very beginning as one way, "from us to them" and not "from them to us," in the sense that we might also have something to learn? Is it friendly when relationships are judged in terms of punishment and reward, and any act of cooperation is to be paid for with basic change, but only on the other side (like human rights in return for most favored nation status)? Is friendship something that can be delivered, administered, withdrawn? There is an unstated assumption that "friendship" is unproblematic, in need of no further elaboration. But the problem, what constitutes positive world politics, is already embedded in that term.

Tricky economic issues are lurking behind the question. To open for import can be said to be friendly. But if imports are mainly products at a low level of processing, and no orders are placed for more sophisticated products, is that still friendly? Is any economic deal friendly, or can important distinctions be made about quantity and quality of the deal? Too many dimensions to take sides for or against.

Issue #2: NATO: Should Western Europe be left to defend itself? What is assumed here is that Western Europe is in need of defense, the only question being whether Western Europe should defend itself or depend on the United States. In other words, there is an unasked question not even considered worth discussing: was there really any major threat in the days of the Soviet Union to Western European security? The answer is not obvious. But even if the answer should be yes, the word "defend" still covers a major ambiguity. Through retaliatory deterrence, or through defensive deterrence? Through offensive or defensive defense? That second unasked question is important, because if the answer is through defensive deterrence, in other words by means of defensive, non-provocative defense (with short-range weapon systems), then dependence on a big ally with very long-range weapons systems has to be drastically reduced. But none of this is covered by the discourse hidden in this very poorly formulated question.

And even worse: there is a hint in that formulation of the United States somehow being in a position to leave or not leave Western Europe to defend itself. With that kind of discourse, the United States may be in for some surprises as the European Community becomes an ever closer European Union. Decisions may be taken somewhere else.

The objection could be that the question is intended to stimulate precisely that kind of reflection, and others as well. But this not the message in the title of the book. To take sides means avoidance of "both-and," "neither-nor," "in-between" types of answers. And the critique is that the issue is not of that kind.

Issue #3: Is the United States justified in its support of the contras? Again, there are only two possible answers, "support" or "no support." If the answer is yes, the discourse naturally opens for a follow-up question: what kind of support, possibly with an argument in terms of "non-lethal," "lethal," "both." But if the answer is "no," there is no corresponding opening of the discourse because a basic stand has already been taken: Support of the *sandinistas* is excluded from the very beginning.

And yet many would be willing to argue that support of the *sandinistas*, or at least removing obstacles from, for instance, Nicaragua's foreign trade relations, would have given the United States more, not less influence on the Central American situation, if that is what is wanted, and a more, not less stable situation. It would be more possible to stipulate conditions. But the choice between support of the *sandinistas*, yes or no, is very different from a choice between support of the *contras*, yes or no. It seems to be taken for granted that the *sandinistas* should not be "rewarded"; they should rather be punished or at best be disregarded. A basic bias, in other words, that could easily have been remedied by asking both questions, or one question: "Should the U.S. support the *sandinistas*, or the *contras*, or both, or neither?"—not prejudging the issue.

A perfectly reasonable answer wold be "neither," as neither had legitimacy derived from elections. But the problem may not be so much which actor one supports as which type of issues one considers more important, misery or freedom, both or neither.

Issue #4: Should strict sanctions be applied against South Africa? The question puts us in the same unfortunate discourse situation. The way the issue is formulated, the choice seems to be between "strict" versus "not-so-strict" sanctions or "no sanctions at all." If the answer is "yes" to strict sanctions, a second discourse could logically be opened about what kind.

But what if the answer is "no?" The problem from the preceding issue comes up again, in a slightly different way. There is still the argument that more influence can be exercised in a setting of generally positive interaction than in a hostile setting. The present authors would not have argued that position in this case, but we would certainly argue against a discourse formulated in such a way that the position is ruled out from the very beginning. That is the whole point about discourse analysis; not whether or not one supports a position but whether or not one supports that a position can be articulated. And the way this issue is framed the position is ruled out from the very beginning.

Issue #5: Has Israel become an expansionist state? In the way the issue has been formulated there is the unstated assumption that Israel some time ago was not an expansionist state, and then Israel possibly became one. The unstated assumption is that there is such a thing as a non-expansionist Israeli state, a position many Palestinians (and others) will find entirely counterfactual, even meaningless. We may or may not agree with this, but no position should be taken for granted or ruled out in advance. In other words, there is an unasked question to be answered before one approaches the question asked: given Zionism, is a non-expansionist Israeli state at all possible? The follow-up question, in case the answer is "yes," would be: "Is Israel still a non-expansionist state?" As usual, there are more dimensions at work behind the question.

Issue #6: Is the Soviet Union the main threat to world peace? This question is so obviously biased that few, particularly in retrospect, will have any difficulty recognizing the bias. The Soviet Union was essentially a threat to itself and its neighbors; its dissolution may be even more of a threat to world peace. Public opinion polls in Western Europe (probably not in Eastern Europe) tend to point to the United States as a major threat to world peace, meaning by that the United States under the Reagan/Bush/Clinton administrations (public opinion in England and France may be different, though). The issue is simply wrongly formulated, in a very parochial manner. A much better formulation would be: "Is the United States or the Soviet Union the major threat to world peace, or both, or neither?"

Issue #7: Should free trade be replaced by protectionism? Much of the current predicament of the U.S. economic situation is not only hidden in this highly inadequate discourse, but probably even partly caused by the inadequacy of the discourse. Of course, the debate about free trade versus protectionism is an important one. But even more important would be a debate about whether the U.S. has anything worth trading or not, in other words a debate about the quality and price levels of U.S. products in general, and about why U.S. products with high degree of processing (e.g., cars) are in decreasing demand, whereas U.S. products with low degree of processing (scrap iron, waste paper, agricultural products) are in increasing demand. Because the underlying issue is not only trade but the economies of the countries concerned, in general, the unstated question is whether trade is the more adequate response to economic crises rather than, for instance, a reinvigoration of manufacturing and service industries aiming for higher quality at constant or lower prices. None of this emerges from the very limited discourse chosen.

Moreover, there is the usual line drawn between free trade and protectionism. Both are arrangements for inter-state economic transactions. What is lost here is the possibility that people may decide, not necessarily in favor of free trade or protectionism by the state, but in favor of deciding themselves, in front of the shelves and exhibits, whether they buy or not. They might, for instance, organize a boycott, or reward a country by over-buying its goods.

Issue #8: Should the industrialized countries do more to aid the less developed countries? The way the issue is stated, the answers seem to be in terms of doing more versus doing less to aid the less-developed countries. The unstated assumption seems to be that aid in fact is aiding less-developed countries, as opposed to harming them or simply being irrelevant. The question that should have been addressed first would be something like this: "Does aid in general stimulate or impede development in less-developed countries?" Formulated this way the whole question of the real impact of development aid would be open for debate instead of the much more limiting question of whether one should aid more or aid less. Another way of formulating the unstated question could be something like this: "What would be the most important contribution developed countries could provide to developing countries: try to aid, try not to stand in the way, both, or neither?"

Issue #9: Does the International Monetary Fund make unfair demands on borrowing countries? This discourse problem is very similar to the preceding issue. The underlying assumption is that borrowing money, with International Monetary Fund conditionality or not, makes sense in the whole process of development; the question is only whether the demands (the "conditionality") made are unfair or not. The conclusion drawn from the issue formulation is that if the demands are fair, then borrowing makes sense, given the unstated assumption that the whole "development" effort makes sense.

But it might also very well be that "development" itself is some kind of process foisted on other countries and peoples by the industrialized countries, simply because they want access to raw materials and markets and for that reason are interested in the types of social change inside other countries (building infrastructure, "modernizing" attitude and behavior) that facilitate that access. Colonialism was to a large extent carried out for this purpose, "Developmentalism" has followed in its wake under the slogan of "modernization." It differs from colonialism only in emphasizing the capacity of "developing countries" for producing semi-manufacturers so that ever more "sophisticated" jobs can be left to the most developed countries; a reason why "developmentalism" is often referred to as "neo-colonialism."

But nothing of this will emerge from the issue formulation chosen, which successfully hides all these tricky (and sticky) issues. Again we have a clear example of jumping straight to a question that presupposes that specific answers have already been given to a number of unasked questions.

Issue #10: Are multinational corporations capitalist villains? The issue is formulated too negatively, casting them as villains, almost forcing a negative answer or a positive protest answer because the formulation is so extreme. A negative answer to the question would be too ambiguous, however, covering both the possibility that multinational corporations are beneficial and that they are, largely speaking, irrelevant.

But more basic is another problem: is it obvious that multinational corporations are really multinational? Or, could the very term "multinational" conceal a basic asymmetry built into the corporation, making them look universal and global in spite of the highly asymmetric distribution of corporate headquarters; of major decision making over production and distribution; of capital, research, and management resources, and so on. On the other hand, it may also be argued that this is the kind of issue that might come up given the relatively open formulation of the question. But a better formulation would still be something like: "On the whole, are multinational corporations beneficial or detrimental?"

Issue #11: Should the West strictly limit its trade with the Soviet bloc? The unstated assumption is that the quality of trade is unproblematic, the word "limit" preparing the minds only for a quantitative debate. There is no opening for a discourse in terms of quality—what kind of trade. The underlying assumption is that it would not be security-sensitive trade. But that is a very limited discourse, not opening for the whole question of what kind of trade would build peace. That question is not asked; a rather basic shortcoming in the entire economics discourse in the United States, also found in U.S. peace studies. This inadequacy of the discourse probably derives from the idea of trade as something developing "freely," "naturally," not to be tampered with. Except, that is, for the security issue, and drugs, and pornography, and . . . showing that trade is not at all necessarily "free." There are non-economic considerations. A possible alternative formulation: "Should the West have more or less trade with the Soviet Union?" And then the follow-up: "What should be more, what should be less?"

So again the problem is not that questions in this field do not lead to complex issues, but that it is impossible to take sides unless the questions are unpackaged, one dimension at a time.

Issue #12: Would complete nuclear disarmament be desirable? Again a typical misstatement of the problem. Not that nuclear weapons are not terribly important, but there are deeper lying, more inclusive candidates for disarmament, of which nuclear weapons would be a special case. Two such categories are prominent in the Gulf War debate, but certainly not reflected in the formulation of the issue: "weapons of mass destruction" and "offensive weapons." Nuclear weapons are weapons of mass destruction, and in most cases also offensive, as most people would not like to have them explode on their own territory, for instance in the form of nuclear land mines. To state the issue in terms of nuclear disarmament, "complete" versus "not complete," not only limits the discourse but also suggests the idea that problems are really being solved if nuclear weapons are gradually being dismantled (or at least the weapons carriers, like the famous land-based missiles in Europe), even if a new category of highly offensive weapons of mass destruction (Star Wars?) are then ushered in, or highly offensive conventional weapons systems (air/land battle, follow-on-forces attack). As the French say, *un train peut en cacher un autre.*

Formulations in terms of offensive versus defensive weapons might have been more useful. But such questions would go to the very root of military doctrine, the whole purpose of military power in world politics, and so forth. Of course no single question can cover all of that. In the meantime, the single-minded focus on nuclear weapons, certainly also found in the peace movement, is not the way to promote a good dialogue. The answer may be yes, but then what?

Issue #13: Can the Strategic Defense Initiative succeed? Just the very fact that this highly complicated family of weapons systems is only referred to by its establishment name, the Strategic Defense Initiative already reveals the bias. The term "Star Wars" is so much better because it does not prejudge the issue by saying that these capabilities are expressions of a clear defensive motivation. "Star Wars" leaves that issue open, as the term "war" is used, which includes both offensive and defensive activity. But that makes the term "succeed" very ambiguous: does it mean "succeed" in the sense of being an effective umbrella against incoming nuclear missiles, or does it mean "succeed" in the sense of working, functioning at all, within the offensive/defensive ambiguity just mentioned? The whole debate about Star Wars has been successfully stifled and muffled precisely by formulating the issue in such misleading terms. The question prior to the one stated could be something like this: "Is the family of weapons systems popularly known as Star Wars defensive, offensive, both or neither?" And then the follow-up question: "Given your answer, is this technically feasible?"

Issue #14: Do the Soviets cheat on arms control agreements? A more burning question some years ago, but substitute "Russians" or "Ukrainians" and the issue is still there. It is prejudging only to ask whether the Soviets cheat or not, not what the United States might be doing. By stating the issue in those terms the United States is implicitly portrayed as the honest guy who could never even conceive of cheating, whereas the Soviet Union might legitimately be suspected of engaging in that kind of activity.

A formulation that might lead to a better, more mature discourse in U.S. political circles would add a second question: "Does the United States cheat on arms agreements?" and at the end the usual "both" or "neither." A satisfactory formulation is usually not more complicated, but it is certainly more symmetric.

Issue #15: Can military action reduce international terrorism? The formulation of the question somehow makes a distinction between "military action" and "international terrorism," obviously seeing the former as a possible cure or therapy for the latter, which is then seen as a disease. But what if cure and disease are very similar? What happens when or if military action is international terrorism? The U.S. bombing of Tripoli in April 1986 was military action and also international terrorism; and not only "terrorism from above," but also "state terrorism." And "international terrorism" is often a form of military action, only less predictable because there is less continuity in time and less contiguity in space. Terrorism flares up, now here, now there; and nobody knows when.

That is what makes it terrorism, not that there are or may be civilian targets; that is certainly also the case in "regular" wars.

In other words, the basic questions would be under what conditions terrorism emerge, what kinds of terrorism there are, and how what kind of terrorism can be decreased—for instance, by military action, or by identifying and removing some of the possible causes of terrorism? Questions such as these would lead to a more mature, more cause-oriented discourse, not to the somewhat childlike debate the question stated is inviting the readers or listeners to entertain. Thus it will be interesting to see how September 11, 2001 (Pentagon, World Trade Center) and October 7, 2001 (first bombs in Afganistan) hold up after some time has passed.

Issue #16: Should morality and human rights be guiding foreign policy principles? The question is formulated as if there is, in general, a strict dichotomy between "morality and human rights" on the one hand and something else as "guiding foreign policy principles," presumably national interests, on the other. However, adherence to human rights can also be in the national interest, and national interests can be formulated, and often are, in terms of human rights. This kind of false dichotomy is very often conceived of as parallel to another false dichotomy between "idealism" and "realism," as if idealism cannot be realistic and realism cannot be idealistic in the sense of being detached from the real world, rooted in an illusionary world where only naked bribe and naked force are operating, not common interests, morality, and human rights, for instance. A world of that type probably never existed and never will exist. The real world is a kind of mix, as usual.

Moreover, because there are many types of human rights, and the U.S. debate (as mentioned above) is insensitive to the distinction between the (1948) first generation of civil-political human rights and the (1966) second generation of social-economic-cultural human rights, the first question to be asked should probably be how to conceive of human rights and how to conceive of national interests. This would not be an invitation to enroll in a political philosophy course, although it may sound so. Rather, the point is that when such questions are never asked and never debated, the discourse remains sloppy and lazy, unable to accommodate the real issues except as they have been pre-distorted by some discourse producers or even discourse controllers in one particular country, in this case the United States. Thus, the United States tends to see itself as promoting human rights around the world, meaning first generation rights; but is also often seen by others as impeding human rights around the world, meaning second generation rights. With that important ambiguity the question is close to meaningless.

Issue #17: Should Congress limit the President's war powers? Recent experience seems to indicate that this is not the basic problem. The basic problem is whether the country should make use of war at all, possibly stating the conditions under which this could or should be done more clearly. A second basic issue is not only whether Congress *should* limit the President's war powers but whether Congress is *able* to limit them. And a third basic issue is whether the President decides, or (some of) the President's men (or both, or neither). With or without a declaration of war, with or without the War Powers Act being made really operational, with or without a substantial role played by the President, wars happen and Congress seems to prefer not to know too much about it. The major criteria seem to be whether the war is short and successful, and whether victory is almost immediate, with no major opposition building up. The Second Gulf War in 1991 was an ideal example. There are other and more important issues to discuss than the constitutionalist issue stated in the formulation; interesting from the point of view of a course in civics, less so for those concerned with reality.

Issue #18: Should the United States obey the International Court of Justice? We are back to the point of departure in the introduction to this book. And for once we would be inclined to say: we think this issue is adequately formulated! It can be answered in terms of "yes" or "no," and both answers open for a reasonable way of clarifying the basic problems in that connection. Of course, a basic point is whether the issue is open for debate at all or whether the "rule of international law" should not imply automatic obedience. But that issue would come up as one way of justifying a "yes." There are so many problems in connection with international law that the discourse certainly should be kept open at this point. A "no" should not be ruled out by a biased discourse—for example, by asking a question like: "why should the United States obey the International Court of Justice?" Our argument is that most of the preceding questions are of that type.

Issue #19: Is the United Nations a beneficial organization? Again, we would be inclined to say that the formulation is adequate. There is a bias in the sense that the formulation is not symmetric enough. Again there is some advantage to the bland social science public opinion poll question, like: "Would you say that the United Nations is on the whole beneficial, detrimental, or neither one nor the other?" But as it is formulated, the issues will come out in the open. They are not systematically obscured from the very beginning, as they would have been if the question were: "How beneficial is the United Nations as an organization?"

Issue #20: Will world conditions deteriorate seriously in the future? And this type of formulation we positively like precisely because it is obviously so crude and primitive, not pretentious like most of the others. The negative bias in the formulation could easily have been avoided by asking: "Will world conditions deteriorate seriously, not so seriously, not at all, improve, or improve considerably in the future?" But there is also the argument that formulations should not be too bland or too long. They should cut straight to the bone and reflect concerns people have, yet not be so intellectually flawed in the cognitive structure imposed upon people invited to reflect on the issue that thinking is steered away from important concerns and possibilities.

Conclusion: by and large a rather negative report card for the book. Out of twenty questions, seventeen serious misstatements and serious omissions of unstated assumptions that have to be clarified before any effort to take sides can become meaningful at all. In short, we are dealing with a serious tendency in the general direction of creating flawed, biased, immature debates rather than what the world in general, and the United States in particular would need— mature reflection. And, unfortunately, nobody can accuse the authors of not having been faithful to mainstream U.S. media discourse in their efforts to formulate the issues.

One aspect of this problem is the failure to pave the ground, mentally, for third positions, as if the authors have *tertium non datur* engraved on their minds. One way out, used often above, is to add the two categories of "both" and "neither," inviting four possible responses rather than the conventional two. This is not an empty formalism but a rather important expansion of the discourse, opening some exit doors from the prison of not only the dichotomy, but even the false dichotomy. And that is exactly the prison *Taking Sides* invites us to join, as permanent inmates.

NOTES

1. Rourke, John P., *Clashing Views on Controversial Issues in World Politics*, 2nd ed. (Guilford, CO: The Dushkin Publishing Group, 1989) [the latest is the Tenth Edition, now published by McGraw-Hill, 2001]. There is a version for schools, *Current Issues: Critical Issues Confronting the Nation and the World* (Alexandria, VA: Close Up Publishing, 1992). In addition to the book there is also *An Instructor's Manual* for *Taking Sides*, prepared by the editor, with a synopsis of the positions taken, proposals for open-ended questions to ask the students, multiple-choice testing on the issues, with answers. See: John T. Rourke, Instructor's Manual to accompany *Taking Sides:*

Clashing Views on Controversial Issues in World Politics. With the exception of essays in which the students can express themselves more freely, the manual reinforces the dichotomous discourses given by the issue formulations.

A Further Theory of
Discourse Analyses

To proceed further, beyond case studies and their possible political implications, time has now come to introduce some intellectual tools. They are indispensable. Ignorance of such tools shows up clearly in those who try to do without them. On the other hand, they should also be seen merely as tools, like a scaffolding relative to a house. They should not show after construction but be thrown away after the job has been completed and they have outlived their usefulness. Moreover, like all tools they are far from neutral, but shape the object to which they are applied. They should not be a focus of fetishism, but rather used with care.

OGDEN'S TRIANGLE AND ITS USES

We start with Ogden's triangle,[1] a particularly useful tool exploring what discourse theory is about: speech about speech, about the meaning of meaning. Three versions of the triangle are given in Figure 4.1:

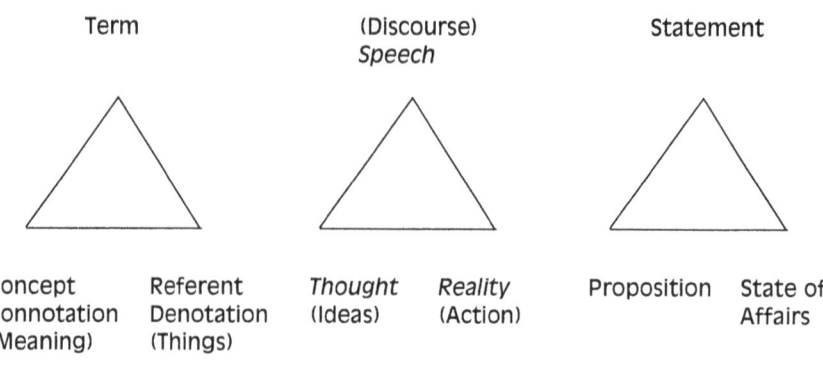

| Term | | (Discourse) *Speech* | | Statement | |

Concept	Referent	*Thought*	*Reality*	Proposition	State of
Connotation	Denotation	(Ideas)	(Action)		Affairs
(Meaning)	(Things)				

Figure 4.1. Ogden's triangle

The triangles are intended to keep the three things at the three corners sufficiently apart and more particularly our speech, our thought, and our action on reality (the triangle in the middle). The three triangles actually convey the same idea, but with slightly different focus.

Starting at the top of the first triangle there is the word *term*. A trivial classroom example: "chalk" (double quotation marks for terms). In the second triangle the terms are seen as components of *speech* or "verbal behavior," oral or written. And in the third triangle terms are chained together in a particular way, adding up to *statements* that have one particular property: they satisfy conditions enabling us to determine whether they are true or false, confirmed-verified or disconfirmed-falsified, valid-invalid or some similar dichotomy on which they may be mapped (in practice such dichotomies have to become trichotomies, including the possibility of "undecided").

Then, at the bottom left hand corner of the triangle is the corresponding *concept*, 'chalk' (single quotation marks for concepts). This is where the *meaning* of the term is located. There is no particular language associated with it; 'chalk' can be expressed not only by "chalk," but also by "tiza" (Spanish) or "kritt" (Norwegian), and so on.

We associate concepts and meanings with our *thoughts* and *ideas*. Whether we accept the notion that thought is subvocal speech or we imagine ourselves, human beings, as totally capable of accommodating speech-free propositions in our mind, we might agree that *propositions* can be expressed in statements belonging to a number of languages, if not all. There are such things as untranslatable statements and inexpressible propositions.

In the bottom right hand corner of the first triangle is what the term refers to, the *referent*, sometimes a "thing." In the classroom example this would be a concrete piece of chalk, in other words something that cannot be put on the printed page. Strictly speaking, the only thing we can put on the printed page is speech, but with the trick of using double and single quotation marks we can at least smuggle in (English versions of) concepts and propositions. The referents belong to *reality*; although one might say that the abstract referents belong to our construction of reality, and the concrete things to the reality that we can perceive with our senses (if we accept this distinction). Reality, in turn, can be seen as a vast assembly of *states of affairs*, against which the statements expressing propositions can be tested for their possible truth, confirmation, validity.

Needless to say, we are now entering territory on which linguists, philosophers, and logicians have considerable claim, and all distinctions and definitions made are controversial. Moreover, we are at best at the entrance gate to that territory, peering into a vast and not too orderly landscape littered with intellectual land mines and such. Nevertheless, the effort to use Ogden's triangle to map that territory in this crude and preliminary way is useful for the purposes of elementary, but nonetheless relatively systematic discourse analysis.

Where, then, does "discourse" enter the picture? Like speech, a discourse accommodates thought and refers to reality, being constructed in such a way as to do precisely that. But discourse is not speech; it is a framework for speech. Speech is here identified with any kind of verbal behavior, whereas discourse is a framework within which speech can be spoken. A discourse is a construct that accommodates thoughts, a house for many thoughts within that discourse. Speech is the verbal raw material out of which a discourse can be *constructed*: the person speaks as if this discourse frames his thoughts. Thus, a discourse is not observed, it is inferred. And vice versa: from a discourse speech can take off in many, but not any, directions.

Having said that it is also obvious that a discourse can be *deconstructed*. A discourse can be torn apart, showing what kind of thoughts it can accommodate, and what kinds of thoughts it subjugates, relegating them to corners of society or the deeper recesses of the mind; what kind of reality it can make transparent and what kind of reality is made opaque. A discourse should be adequate to two tasks: expressing thoughts (including those in the "deeper recesses" of the mind), and reflecting reality (including the more "opaque" aspects, and including potential, not only empirical, reality). An *inadequate* discourse does not do this. Obviously, these are relative terms, to be explored further. But *adequacy* is a central term in discourse analysis, still to be defined in an operational way, guiding us toward adequacy.

The second chapter of this book offered a first, highly non-technical exercise in exploring adequacy/inadequacy, giving twenty examples of how powerful the discourse is in steering our ideas, our speech, and also our actions. Of course, people may proceed straight from ideas to action, bypassing speech. But it would be wrong to assume that in so doing they are not communicating ideas.

Communication, when defined as the transmission of ideas through verbal and nonverbal behavior, can also take place through action, then usually referred to as "non-verbal behavior." An idea does not have to be spoken. Inquisitive Westerners trying to find out what goes on in Japan might often find the Japanese, even when highly competent in English, not very inclined to verbalize what's going on. But non-verbal Japanese behavior is extremely rich and detailed, and very often open to inspection, introspection, and retrospection. "Watch what I do, not what I say."

Correspondingly, it is quite possible to jump directly from speech into action without any conscious thought process. Ogden's triangle can even collapse to any one of the three points only. But action and speech may still *communicate*, evoking ideas in others. There are people who just open their mouths uttering speech, hoping that some thoughts will catch up with their flow of words, sooner or later, if not in Self then at least in Other. Much behavior of that kind can be observed in academic seminars, one reason being intense competition to occupy scarce time slots with words, even sounds. Ideas are not sufficient for time slot occupation purposes if only found in embryonic form inside the brain of the speaker.

An idea alone never laid any claim to time or space; words are needed to hold on to a lectern or a pulpit for time, allotted or not. Oral speech can be rapidly deployed ahead of ideas to lay claim on time; and written speech can be used to occupy space in journals, and so forth. Since both time and space are scarce, speech, oral or written, becomes competitive. Ideas as such are not.

One implication of this is that speech should be used well, and one implication of that again is the effort to clarify what might constitute a *richer* or a *better* underlying discourse. Only the person who knows how to till scarce soil should do so. To bore an audience, or waste paper, are crimes against humanity/nature, and should be understood as such. A necessary, not sufficient condition for not committing that crime is discourse adequacy.

DEFINITIONS AND THE RULES FOR DEFINITIONS

At this point a definition of definition is indispensable. A minimum of precision is needed for communication to ensure that not only ideas, but roughly speaking the same ideas are evoked in the minds of sender and receiver. A definition is a social contract, in a speech community, for what a *term* should stand. Definitions regulate the basic building stones out of which discourses are constructed, lifting the terms out of the speech, inspecting them, laying down rules for their use. The *Oxford English Dictionary* (OED) or *Webster's* or similar compilations in other languages are precisely that: collections of definitions or rules, presumably describing and prescribing usage in that particular speech community.

Those who construct the discourse might then go one step further, adding more precision to the rules (making them more technical), introducing new rules to make the terms serve the purposes intended within specified discourses. The meaning of a term may change with the discourse in which it is embedded ("status" does not mean the same to a sociologist and to an economist), and any such change should be explicitly stated if the purpose is precision. But the purpose may also be vagueness, a range of (surplus) connotations, in which case definitions may be counter-productive. Moreover, denotata vary with the experience of which people may have more or less, and that influences connotata.

Going back to Ogden's triangle, first version to the left: there are obviously two ways of proceeding with the term to be defined, the *definiendum*. The *definiens*, the statement carrying the definition so that it can be substituted for the definiendum, can be arrived at in two ways, corresponding to the other two corners of the triangle. We can anchor the term (definiendum) in a *concept*, or in a *referent*. For the concept we also use the expression "connotation," that which the term connotes, "means"; and for the referent we use the expression "denotation," that which the term denotes, "stands for." These two words also have plurals, "connotata" and "denotata." We can define a term giving the connotata or the denotata, also referred to as "definition in intension" and "definition in extension," respectively. And we can arrive at a definition working from either corner, or from both.

At this point an example is necessary, if not sufficient. Imagine we want to define "terrorism." The denotation would clearly be a listing of acts (giving time and place) seen as "terrorism"; the set of those acts being the denotata. However, an inspection of that list will immediately bring up comments like "but this is not terrorism, this is struggle for liberation"[2] or "this is not terrorism, this is nonviolence"[3] or "this is not terrorism, this is military action in a war"[4] or "I think you have left out the important event that took place . . ." and then follow space and time coordinates. Or, this is not "terrorism," this was "authorized action engaged in by a democratic country."[5]

Obviously, in order to come up with such remarks the speaker has a connotation in mind that may or may not yield the same list of denotata, also dependent on subjective experience. There is a *meaning* lurking underneath, somewhere. That meaning should be uncovered and brought into the limelight, stated as a set of connotata (or criteria, or characteristics) that anything falling under "terrorism" should satisfy. This could then be used to produce a new list of denotata to be compared with the old one. Occasionally different connotata have the same denotata, meaning that the definitions for all practical purposes are the same. Differences may show up later, however.

In our efforts[6] to define "terrorism" we would certainly include "violence" as one criterion, preferring to leave that term undefined in this connection lest we open a set of Chinese boxes of definitions, this time with ever more complicated definiendum.

However, in focus is not just any act of violence; but *violence for a political goal.* We would not include unintended violence or any criminal violence, and leave out acts of violence committed by the clearly cranky and/or criminal individual, not thereby saying that those individuals might not at times be drawn upon by organizers of terrorism, or themselves be organizers, or have political goals. "Cranky/criminal" would not be used as connotata in the definition, thereby leaving it open whether *empirically* all, most, some, or no terrorists in fact are cranks and/or criminals.

On the other hand, if we now simply said that "terrorism is violence for political goals," the definition would be too broad. Wars for liberation of conquest also satisfy that criterion. Should we add "against innocent civilian bystanders?" The problem is that this also happens in a "modern," "totalitarian" or at least "total" war, and in many other wars before that.[7] Moreover, it raises the question of who is innocent, as by implication others would be guilty. In saying that terrorism kills innocent people it sounds as if wars, when not killing innocent civilians would be justified, as they are by implication limited to killing guilty people. It may also sound as if those called innocent are pure objects, not subjects, incapable of promoting or impeding the actions of those presumed to be guilty. Thus, if German civilians had refused to take up arms, rejecting Hitler's policies in general and anti-Semitism in particular, they might have prevented the war. Does that make civilians guilty, at least of acts of omission?

In other words, there are too many assumptions built into that idea. Moreover, no real distinction is made between war and terrorism using that criterion, as military action is often against civilians, and terrorist action often against the military. We need a criterion that can differentiate; if not, we should stop using one of the terms, except for stylistic variation, and simply refer to "terrorism" as "war." Or, as we might prefer, to "war" as "terrorism." But then we would lose the distinction.

The key characteristic that differentiates "terrorism" from "war" is the element of surprise, which we shall conceive of as *non-contiguity in space* and *non-continuity in time*. War is a process, bordering on an institution, moving onwards (backwards when retreating), with contiguity in space (often referred to as a "front") and continuity in time, the armistice marking an interval or a stop. Characteristic of terrorism is just the opposite: it suddenly flares up, here, and then there, at a totally different point; it happens now, and then all of a sudden the day after tomorrow. In other words, whereas contiguity/continuity makes a war much more predictable, lack of contiguity and continuity makes terrorism much less predictable. Terrorism produces an archipelago of violence in the time-space continuum. War is a continent.

Unpredictability instills terror. Am *I* on the hit list? In case, how, where, when? The inability to assign probabilities to such statements is what makes terrorism terrible, not that it kills. Wars also kill, but in a much more predictable manner.

Genocidal wars kill everybody and omnicidal wars[8] kill every thing. Of course, the number of victims of terrorism is microscopic relative to the highly macroscopic numbers exterminated in wars. But the small numbers have to be multiplied by the level of surprise for the terror to emerge. In wars people expect to be killed, in non-wars not.

We end up with two connotata:

C1: violence for political goals
C2: non-contiguity in space, and non-continuity in time.

Equipped with these two connotata we can now inspect the denotata again, weed out some elements on the list, include others, then have a reinspection of the list and the excluded elements and possibly return to the connotata for a revision. The goal of this back-and-forth exercise is total overlap. But that is not the exercise to be engaged in here. The example has served its purpose so far; this is not an essay on terrorism. The important point is the (endless?) comparison of connotata and denotata, between intension and extension.

Another example: "democracy." The connotation could be limited to democracy as the "rule with the consent of the ruled, according to rules that make the rulers accountable to the ruled." We then get a typology according to how consent is obtained: (a) dialogue until consensus (today mainly in small groups?); (b) initiative/referendum for all major issues (today only Switzerland?); and (c) periodic election of rulers by secret ballot on issue-bundles (programs, platforms?), occurring in many countries.

Let us summarize (Table 4.1) and then go one step further: The more connotata the less (at least not more) denotata, because all referents will have to satisfy at least one more criterion. Generally connotation expansion will exclude some elements and shorten the lists of denotata. The definition becomes more narrow, possibly ending up so narrow that nothing or very little falls under the term. The opposite problem would be a connotata number so low that very little is ruled out as falling under the term.

These are the Scylla and Charybdis of definition making. The craftsmanship consists in steering between the two, with neither too many nor too few connotata. With too many connotata most findings become tautologies, because they are already built into the definition; with too few connotata we cannot make findings at all, because nothing is excluded. A "finding" means a "state of affairs," and a state of affairs by definition excludes something.

CLASSIFICATIONS AND THE RULES FOR CLASSIFICATIONS

Having now, through definition-making, arrived at what hopefully is a useful list of referents, the next task is to establish some order, cutting into the set of referents falling under the definition with some

Table 4.1. Defining Definitions.

Definiendum:	The "term," that which is to be defined
Definiens:	*In intension*: Using the meaning (connotation/connotata) *In extension*: Using the set of referents (denotation/denotata)
RULES:	1. Increasing the connotata decreases (or keeps constant) the denotata. 2. With too few connotata the definition becomes too broad; everything fits, no effective regulation of speech is obtained. 3. With too many connotata the definition becomes too narrow, nothing fits, fewer empirical propositions can be found as it is already in the definition.

"variables" or "dimensions." Two other terms used in this connection with the same meaning would be "typologies" or "classifications," and we shall use the latter. Rules for classification are given below in Table 4.2. To make the rules more similar to the rules for definition some awkward terms, "classificandum" for that which is to be classified and "classificans" for the principles for classifying them, have been used in the table. They correspond to two other terms frequently used, "explicandum" for that which is to be explained and "explicans" for that which explains that which is to be explained.

The task of the exercise is to arrive at a classification, in other words classification-making. Like definition-making this is an indispensable tool for the construction of a discourse. Let us again emphasize why. It is only by making the discourse explicit, by making clear what the terms stand for and what kind of subclasses or typologies we have for the things that fall under the terms, that we can hope to understand what the discourse clarifies and what it obscures. The person unwilling to engage in definition-making and classification-making is probably consciously or unconsciously hiding something; among the possibilities are ignorance of the subject matter or unclear thought. The examples given in the preceding chapters are indicative of the crucial nature of what might be hidden. Classification, simply asking the question "what types or classes of X do we have?" very often brings the hidden out into the open.

To clarify let us stick to the example used for definition theory: "acts of terrorism." The always germane question defined above when discussing a problematic term would read "to help me understand what terrorism is, what types of terrorism are there?"

Table 4.2. Classifying Classifications.

Classificandum:	The "referents" to be classified
Clasificans:	*In intension*: Using the meaning (connotation), the *fundamentum divisionis*
	In extension: Using the set of classes (denotation) so that all referents can be classified in one (exhaustive) and only one (mutually exclusive) class
RULES:	1. The more homogeneity within the classes, the better the classification.
	2. The more heterogeneity between the classes, the better the classification.
	3. The more the classification correlates (overlapping denotata) with other classifications with different connotata, the better the classification.

Thus, we might be interested in knowing where the terrorist act originated. One possible dimension would be from below/from above, giving two points implicitly describing a dimension that might be referred to as "position in the social and/or world structure." Another possibility would be non-state/state, which would call attention to the possibility that an act of terrorism might be initiated without or with state approval.

And that gives us already four possibilities: terrorism from below and above; non-state and state generated terrorism. Answers such as these already give a good idea of the underlying definition in intension and/or extension.

For many people it seems to be taken for granted that terrorism comes from below, and if backed by a state then certainly one that is "below" in the world structure, like a "pariah" state, in the U.S. discourse referred to as a "terrorist state." Acts of terrorism from above, ordered by a state high up in the world structure, are seen as inconceivable because of the contradiction involved. Such acts would not be terrorist. They would be police actions inflicting "punishment," or pedagogical action "to teach them a lesson." In either case they are seen as legitimate rather than terrorist acts. They will not show up on a list, regardless of the surprise element, such as in the U.S. action against Libya in March 1986.

This is important, because anyone who would like an adequate discourse about terrorism might like to define terrorism in such a way that both below and above, both non-state and state actors initiating the terrorist act (as defined in the preceding section) are included as possibilities. The alternative is bias.[9]

Let us now look at the relationship between variables-dimensions-typologies-classifications-categorizations on the one hand and values-points-types-classes-categories on the other. The former (e.g., gender) give the meaning of the latter; the latter (male/female) spell out the former. There are two absolute demands that values-points-types-classes-categories should satisfy.

Together they should yield an *exhaustive* and a *mutually exclusive* division of the units that the discourse is about. All economic systems should be classified as one or the other, all acts of terrorism should be classified as one or the other on the dimensions indicated. No units should be left out, no units should be classified in both or more of the values-points-types-classes-categories. These are classical, very useful classification rules.

They can be satisfied by introducing such additional types as "both-and," "neither-nor," "in-between," "unclassifiable." This way gains are made "in extension." Everything can be classified one and only one way, at the expense of losses "in intension" as the meaning of the classification. But the *fundamentum divisionis* becomes fuzzy. If possible such escapes should be avoided.

But sometimes they should not, even if problematic, as seen in this example. Much work in this world has been put into a particular endeavor: to classify all the (soon) six billion human beings into one and only one nationality; for instance, with the lofty goals of giving them one and only one passport; as one brick in that big human construction called "nation-state building." The exercise obviously leads to two well-known problems: the stateless (indicating that the classification is not exhaustive), and those with double or multiple citizenship (indicating that the classes are not mutually exhaustive). Both cases present considerable headaches for bureaucrats in favor of neat classification in this as well as other cases. On the other hand, both problems look like highly attractive solutions to the more anarchically inclined.

Does that mean that there is something essentially bureaucratic about the whole effort to obtain exhaustive and mutually exclusive classifications? Certainly, but this is not necessarily bad. These are simply intellectual tools for certain jobs to be done, making communication less ambiguous. They are highly useful when sender and receiver have a common interest in shared meaning. But great care should be taken in naming the classes. No doubt the residual categories indicated above could also be a sign of intellectual laziness, individual or collective, meaning that more work should be put into the definitions to make the classification better, including recognizing the stateless and the multiple citizenships as bona fide.

But "both-and," "neither-nor," and so forth, could also be openings for flexibility, letting the discourse out of the strait-jacket of a strict typology, the dichotomy (two classes) that may be expanded to a polytomy (more than two classes), demanding of everything that it fits into one and only one value-point-type-class-category. The inadequacy of the polytomy is a signal from a more complex reality.

As already mentioned, a major task of discourse theory is to indicate ways of escaping from false dichotomies; that also holds true for false polytomies, leading our thought-speech-action into blind alleys, insisting that these are the only possibilities. Reality, particularly when we include potential reality, can be endowed with many more facets than we capture in poor discourses. The opposite also holds: going beyond the empirical in our classifications we may bring about the potential as something demanding realization.[10] But there is certainly the requirement that variables-dimensions-typologies-classifications should have what is known as a *fundamentum divisionis*. The classification should have a *meaning*, such as "economic system," "position in the social/world structure," or "private versus public sector." The latter is interesting. No particular single word has crystallized over the years to carry the meaning of this dimension. Obviously "private versus public" is not very different from "non-state versus state," although it may tilt our attention more in the direction of economic power and less toward political power, or more in the direction of the family, the intimate. In other words, sometimes the contradiction above is solved by not naming a meaning, only the classes. In this field, work is always in progress. There is no such thing as a final definition or classification.

Let us then return to Ogden's triangle (Figure 4.1) for a moment. The distinction was made between speech, thought, and reality, the reality also being where action may take place. This distinction is then translated into terms-concepts-referents and statements-propositions-states-of-affairs. How does this correspond to what we have just said in connection with classifications? There are different ways of looking at it. On the one hand, the term at the top of Ogden's triangle may be the name used for a dimension, for instance "nationality." The concept would be the idea of 'nationality' with such connotata as territorial belongingness, usually acquired by birth, certain citizens' rights and duties, usually defined by national law, myths, and traumas, and so forth.

And the denotation would be the concrete list of nations: Albania, United States, Zimbabwe, and so on[11]—in other words, the meaning, or *fundamentum divisionis* of the dimension on the one hand, and the set of types, presumably exhaustive and mutually exclusive (of the units to be characterized) on the other.

But we could also run another Ogden's triangle or subtriangle by putting on top the term not for a dimension-classification but for a point-class, in which case the meaning of the point-class could only be understood by referring to the meaning of the whole dimension-classification. It is very hard to come to grips with "Norwegian" unless "nationality" is part of the picture. The denotata would no longer be a catalogue of nationalities, but four million concrete human beings having Norwegian citizenship.

Incidentally, this also brings up the important problem of whether "U.S.-ian," not "North American," may not be a better term for U.S. citizens than "American," there being many other countries in America. And "Eurunionist" or simply "Eunionist" for the citizen of the fifteen countries[12] in the European Union, not European (and not Western European), there being, say, 53 countries in Europe (and eighteen in Western Europe alone).

Thus, Ogden's triangle can be used in many places and in many ways, but with care, to keep speech, thought, and reality separate, regardless of the subject matter. And also with the warning that they are less separate than Ogden made them: how can action be conceived of without naming it, and how is that possible without some thought crossing the mind of the namer?

CARTESIAN PRODUCTS AND THE RULES FOR CARTESIAN PRODUCTS

Let us then introduce the fourth basic tool: the *cartesian product*. The basic idea, if not the name, is known to everybody with a secondary education. The cartesian system of coordinates, with an X-axis and a Y-axis, is a cartesian product enabling us to think of two classifications and their relation at the same time. The X-axis or X-variable in this case is a classification of numbers in which we might focus on *natural* numbers alone; expanding it to *integers* (including zero and negative numbers); expanding it further to *rational numbers* (including fractions); possibly adding *irrational* numbers so as to arrive at the even more inclusive category of *real* numbers. We could do the same for the Y-axis, with the same level of inclusiveness on both axes so that we are comparing the same type of x's and y's.

What a (cartesian) *coordinate system* then yields is a number of points in 2-dimensional space: a page in a book, a sheet, a blackboard, with the first number standing for the X-value and the second number for the Y-value. The cartesian *product* takes the idea of cartesian *space* one step further, using it for any kind of set, not merely for the highly disciplined set of numbers. To refer to one of the examples in chapter 2: we might make a double classification using nuclear powers along one axis and three types of nuclear forces along the other, as is done in Table 2.1. A cartesian product is nothing but a double (or more generally triple, multiple) classification, as indicated in Figure 4.2, forcing us to explore all combinations.

There is no rule that there should be empirical referents for all combinations, that is, that no combination should be empty. On the contrary, the empty combinations are often the most interesting ones; much like the (daoist) point that clay alone never made a water cup, a tea pot, a vessel: a hole, emptiness, is also needed.

Thus, even if there is no (rich, egalitarian) society in the world the cartesian product (rich-poor by egalitarian-inegalitarian) forces us to think that thought. And the (re)search is on, an important search. The welfare state?[13] Job rotation?[14]

Cartesian products invite us, encourage us, even coerce us, to consider all combinations made available by that discourse. Good speech would explore all combinations implicit in a discourse, hoping for hidden surprises in some corners. Bad speech would pick up only a subset of the combinations, such as those with empirical referents, those proving the speaker's point, those most frequently used in everyday/conventional/mainstream talk. Or only those that are exotic, unexpected, crystallization nuclei for good jokes, and so forth. Better than all this: be systematic, consider all combinations.

Classification A with four classes: a1, a2, a3, a4
    multiplied by
Classification B with three classes: b1, b2, b3
    yields
the double classification/*cartesian product* A x B
with twelve joint classes:

b3	(a1,b3)	(a2,b3)	(a3,b3)	(a4,b3)
b2	(a1,b2)	(a2,b2)	(a3,b2)	(a4,b2)
b1	(a1,b1)	(a2,b1)	(a3,b3)	(a4,b1)
	a1	a2	a3	a4

RULES: 1. The number of joint classes is the product of the numbers of single classes.
        2. Pay attention to all joint classes; leave no combination unexplored!
        3. An empirically empty (no referents) joint class is indicative of
           no empirical reality possible, or
           a potential reality (referents may be found/made).

Figure 4.2. Cartesian products

In conclusion and as an example, an important point can now be made using cartesian products. A discourse can be constructed to accommodate comfortably and compare *data*, *theories*, and values if we define them in extension rather than in intension.[15] In other words, even if the connotata of data, theories, and values are very different, they can nevertheless be compared in terms of denotata. And in that act of comparison major aspects of the (meta-discourse) called "scientific inquiry" can be identified.

Thus, what we refer to as *data* is nothing but a dichotomy in a discourse conceived of as a cartesian product, stating that some combinations have been observed whereas others are unobserved; specifying which combinations, and sometimes to what degree, what frequency. A statistical table, with numbers, is precisely that.

Correspondingly, what a *theory* does is also to divide a cartesian product into two parts, that which is *foreseen* by the theory or, more precisely, by the hypotheses derived from the theory, versus that which is *unforeseen*, specifying which combinations (perhaps with a measure of degree of belief).

And finally, what a *value* does to a discourse is also to divide the cartesian product into two parts, that which is *preferred* according to the value versus that which is *rejected* (or pursued/avoided in more action-prone terms), again specifying which combinations (and the degree of preference/rejection).

The three degrees are known as empirical probability, subjective probability, and utility, respectively—three modes of relating to the world, the same world.

For all three cases the more precise the data-theories-values, the more unambiguous the division into two parts. The cartesian product forces precision on us. For each possible combination we have to decide: Is it observed? Foreseen? Preferred? With less precision we may have to introduce a third category of the "undecided," the cases of doubt; better than premature precision.

In short, *data, theories, and values share the same basic structure.* They are three different ways of projecting some order into a bewildering world of countless combinations. They are all dichotomies that may have to be supplemented with a third category. The terms used for these dichotomies, the underlying concepts, the three meanings, are very different. But they can be compared. And in that comparison scientific inquiry can be located.[16]

More particularly, data can be compared with theories in an exercise known as *empiricism*; data can be compared with values in an exercise known as *criticism*; and theories and values can be compared in an exercise known as *constructivism*. Combining the three we get a tripartite image of what research is about: a never-ending adjustment of data, theories, and values to each other. More particularly, if the foreseen coincides with the observed the hypothesis is *true* (verified, supported); if the observed corresponds to the preferred the state of affairs is *good*; and if the preferred is foreseen by a theory the theory is *adequate*. Bliss is when the preferred is foreseen and in addition observed; hell when it is unobserved and in addition unforeseen by any theory.

At a more mundane level there are also rich consequences. In any debate, intra-personal or inter-personal (and in the latter case private or public, meaning that the debate is publicly accessible), the difference and similarity between the three approaches to a discourse play a considerable role. They are often confused, leading to countless misunderstandings.

> Example:
> Mr. A: I think socialism is on the horizon.
> Ms. B: You mean you have seen it?
> Mr. A: No, I think it will come, real socialism I mean.
> Ms. B: What you mean is that you hope socialism will
> be realized?
> Mr. A: I hope it will come and I think it will come even to
> the point that I feel I know what it is like.

Ms. B: But either you have seen it or you have not seen it!

Mr. A: Do you really have to see it to know it?

Ms. B: Yes.

Mr. A: OK then. I haven't seen it. But I like the word, and the concept. Some basic goods and services are made public and inexpensive, not like in capitalism, which should be called privatism or something like that. Socialism is social; like public education, libraries, transportation, health, and beaches. Subsidized food, subsidized housing.

Ms. B: To many that sounds positive. But I prefer smaller systems that are socially responsible and yet you do not disappear in them. You can be a person at the same time. Do you see what I mean?

Mr. A: No. You mean some kind of "small is beautiful," green society? Green socialism?

Ms. B: Or just green. Do not mix the metaphors so. Socialism sounds too big for me. Like Big State. Not that different from Big Corporation.

Mr. A: You would not like Japan, then: Big State and Big Corporation, the two rolled into one.

Ms. B: Sounds awful. But maybe there would be a little niche there somewhere, nevertheless . . .

Mr. A: But would you be willing to give it a try without knowing in advance that the niche would be available?

Ms. B: At least Japan is available as opposed to your socialism on the horizon.

The reader can easily see how Mr. A and Ms. B are dancing around inside the discourse, combining public/private with big/small, issuing or denying data-, theory- and value-certificates to the points they identify. We also note the usual empirical and logical debating techniques of catching the other in referring to something unobserved; or in a contradiction between theories, between values, or between theory and value. Their efforts may be traced in that cartesian product, and D, T, and V labels stuck to the points, with signatures. Communication works because they operate semantically within the same expanded discourse for economic systems—possibly because they have read this far in the book already. Or possibly because the authors made it up. Either way the conclusion is the same: *a necessary condition for communication is a shared discourse.*

DISCOURSES AND THE EVALUATION OF DISCOURSES

Let us go back to the beginning, starting now with Discourse=paradigm=intellectual framework=cartesian product. There is a difference, however, obscured by the "=". Discourse, the way the term is used, accommodates thoughts, but is intended to generate speech. The terms "paradigms" and "intellectual framework" are perhaps somewhat broader. The cartesian product is a multiple classification for the referents about which the discourse can generate speech. A broader approach to discourse will be pointed out in chapter 6, but we shall build on this approach until it is fully explored and exploited, and then try to go beyond.

In order to construct an intellectual framework we have assumed that three things are needed: *units, variables*, and *values*. Again alternative terms are useful. Instead of "variables" we have talked about dimensions, terms, classifications. Instead of "values," which are subdivisions of variables, we have talked about points as subdivisions of dimensions, types as subdivisions of term, classes as subdivisions of classifications.

To summarize: *variables=dimensions=term=classifications* and *values=points=types=classes*. We have combined dimensions in cartesian products, making multiple classifications, and have identified the outcome with intellectual frameworks or *paradigms*.

What then is a "unit" or "unit of discourse?" The unit is that which the discourse refers to, the referent. It is not unproblematic. Let us take as an example economic growth. One unit of discourse is the nation-state. But economics is not the same as national economics, nor is it the same as business economics, but national and business economics ("VWL" and "BWL" are the acronyms in German)[17] are important fields in and of themselves (to which should be added household economics and world economics). It is also agreed that the economic performance of a nation-state should reflect what the whole population does or has, not only what rich people do or have. One way of arriving at this has been to consider dividing the gross national product by the size of the population so as to get GNP per capita. A homage to democracy; one person, one number in the denominator, as opposed to, or in addition to, one person, one vote in the election.

But it is not so obvious that this unit of discourse is well chosen. Imagine we have calculated GNP per capita for two countries, A and B, which for a long time have been trading with each other, arriving at a high degree of interdependence, one of them being rich and the other poor. Suddenly they undergo a fusion and become the country A+B. GNP per capita for A+B will have to be calculated so as to reflect the total economy of the new country, and will become a weighted average of the two values on the GNP per capita variable for the two constituent units. The case looks unproblematic; a joint GNP per capita value after political fusion, as opposed to two independent economies, with two separate GNP per capita values.

But the world of economic reality consists mainly of intermediate cases, economic systems neither separated nor fused as political systems. Can we really calculate the GNP per capita of any country as if that economy were independent of other countries, only seen as interacting with the rest as "the external sector?" Or, should our measure of economic performance for any pair of countries be located somewhere between total independence for mutual isolation, and total interdependence for fusion, reflecting the *degree* of interdependence? The issue is tricky. The transition from a single nation-state to pairs, triples, and so forth of nation-states as units of discourse would lower considerably the GNP per capita of rich countries, because not only productive, but also counter-productive aspects of the way they interact with poor countries would have to be taken into account. It is similar to calculating the castle and the villages downhill together, not separately.

How this can be done is by no means obvious. What is obvious is only that the way we do it today, with an unquestioning use of political discontinuities rather than economic continuities as units of discourse, is hopelessly biased. How biased can best be seen by the castle/serfs example just given. The GNP does take into consideration the "external sector," but not the impact of economic relations on the trade partners, with the externalities (side-effects), some positive and some negative, inside national economies accruing to any country in economic exchange. Should we analyze Dyadic GNPs, adjusting for "degree of interdependence?"[18]

To summarize: The "unit" is that which the discourse is about. A "variable" is a perspective we want to make use of in developing a discourse about the unit. A "value" is the position of the unit using that perspective. Thus, to stick to economics: The unit could be a country, or a pair, a triple and so forth of countries, or an "economic system" of economic interaction, raising the question of identifying borderlines that may or may not coincide with political borders. The perspective could be "economic ideology" and the dichotomous positions could be "capitalism"-"socialism" or, in other, relatively equivalent terms, "market economy"-"centrally planned economy." Or, the perspective could be "GNP per capita," and the positions would be any number from $0 per capita to $X,000 per capita, again raising the problem of what is the unit of the discourse. Or, both, in a joint discourse. Whatever. What matters at this point is not what we end up with as discourse so much as *discourse consciousness* about units, variables, values.

"Subject" is sometimes used for "unit," and "predicate" for what is here referred to as a "value."[19] Consider the following statement: "socialism tends to kill upwards, in society, using direct violence to remove high-class people standing in the way of socialism; capitalism tends to kill downward in society, using structural and direct violence to eliminate low-class people and particularly their leaders standing in the way of capitalism."

Here something is predicated of two subjects, both of them being economic systems. Two units are chosen, and values are attributed to them on three variables: socialism-capitalism; direct violence-structural violence; killing upwards-killing downwards.

With this discourse we can discuss news coverage. Assuming that news coverage will have a tendency to favor reports about elites higher up rather than people lower down, and about "events" (such as direct violence) rather than "permanents" (such as structural violence), then it goes without saying that political violence arising from the social order will be much more frequently reported from socialist than from capitalist systems. A famous person high up in society actually does not even have to be killed to make news. Imprisonment or exile, even inside the country (like a Sakharov in Gorki) will suffice to bring the person into the headlines. But impoverished masses at the bottom and periphery of a capitalist order, often far away, on other continents, are dying, unreported, and end up as statistics rather than as news. As a consequence, socialism looks much more violent than capitalism. The discourse was not fully used, only the part about socialism.

The basic point about the subject-predicate language is that we are now coming closer to human speech, moving our exploration away from the simple mathematical/logical terms and exercises of the preceding sections, toward speech more as we know it. If we can assign a value on some variable to a unit, or, in grammar speech, predicate something of a subject, then we are able to formulate sentences. We are able to make statements. The discourse defines for us what is a well-formulated sentence and what is not. A sentence must be formulated within the discourse. The discourse must generate speech, otherwise it remains unspoken. The discourse is like a vessel waiting to be filled with a script, and the problem is its adequacy for the subject matter.

Thus, if we have a discourse for economic systems with only two points, capitalist versus socialist, then the sentence "Norway has an economic system which is located somewhere between capitalism and socialism" is not a well-formulated sentence. It is ruled out by the discourse as illegitimate, invalid. A corresponding sentence such as "Japan combines a fully developed market economy with a fully developed planning economy" is not a well-formulated sentence either, because it also goes outside that 2-point discourse. The discourse is a set of rules about what can be spoken and what cannot be spoken. Or, using the terminology just introduced: the discourse defines well-formulated sentences as opposed to badly formulated, not to mention "unformulatable" sentences. Along this line we would also come to Gödel's problem: sentences that are well formulated, but cannot be proven true or false.[20]

This puts us in a position to talk about the discourse not as being poor or rich in absolute terms, but as being more or less narrow, more or less broad, "narrower" and "broader." Evidently these are comparative terms that cannot be used to characterize any single discourse, but to compare one discourse with another as a comparison between two sets. The sets would be the sets of points, values, types, classes, or combinations of them in a cartesian product; in other words, the set of single or composite predicates (defined by the discourse) that can be used as attributes of the subject (the unit of discourse). Obviously these sets can be compared as more or less extensive. And then we have the advantage that sets (of elements, points) can be compared, providing the basis for a definition.

The definition would be: discourse A *is broader than discourse B (= discourse B is narrower than discourse A) if A includes all points in discourse B and at least one more point.*

Obviously, the expansion of the discourse for economic systems from capitalist-socialist to capitalist-socialist-in between-both/and-neither/nor is an expansion from a 2-point to a 5-point discourse, and as the 2-point discourse is included in the 5-point discourse we are able to say that the latter is broader or richer than the former. We might even say broader/richer by the ratio 5:2, or 250 percent, or 2.5. This is the advantage of measurement: at the ordinal scale level interspersing "more" or "less," at the interval (cardinal) scale level how much more and less. Refining the dimension is a rather primitive approach, however.

We would refer to this process of *discourse expansion* as *broadening the discourse*, and to the corresponding reverse process of *discourse contraction* as *narrowing the discourse.* As can be seen from the example one characteristic of the broader (or more "refined") discourse is that it permits more discrimination, finer distinctions; the narrower (or "cruder") discourse forces us to be less discriminatory.

A discourse about distances in meters is broader than a discourse in kilometers, the latter being narrower than the former. Everything that can be said in the kilometer discourse can also be said in the meter discourse, but not vice versa. A discourse may also be unnecessarily broad, not only too narrow; more (discriminatory power) is not especially better. What we are searching for is adequacy, and the golden rule applies: neither too broad nor too narrow.

The cartesian products that define a discourse can be compared not only in extension, but also in intension, and that opens for another aspect of adequacy. *Broadening the discourse*, making more discriminations along the same dimensions, may be a gain, but not necessarily a significant gain. To add more dimensions, *deepening the discourse* by bringing in new perspectives, is almost always a gain. In fact, that was the basic conclusion derived from the 40 case studies in chapters 2 and 3.

The definition would be: *discourse A is deeper than discourse B (= discourse B is shallower than discourse A) if A includes all the dimensions used in B, and at least one more dimension.*

As seen in Chapter 3 this is how underlying assumptions can be brought into the daylight; by asking a pertinent question at the very beginning of the discourse, so to speak before it has unfolded itself and become encrusted, demanding an answer in terms of more alternatives. The presence in our mind of those alternatives is already one more dimension, in *statu nascendi*, about to be born, to be present in our mind and consciously added to the list.

Let us return for a moment to the example about killing in socialist and capitalist societies. Imagine that we modified the sentence to say "socialist societies kill with direct violence; capitalist societies kill with structural violence," leaving out the dimension upward/downward. The sentence still says something, but has become more "flat." We have left out an entire perspective on the whole problem of differential distribution of violence in the two social systems. We are left with a shallower discourse.

To deepen it we have to bring the upward-downward dimension, or some other dimension, back in again. If we do that we get a (2x2x2)-discourse with eight points; all eight combinations of "socialist-capitalist" with "direct violence-structural violence" and "upward-downward." The shallower discourse had only four combinations, contained in the eight combinations of the deeper discourse. In this case the deeper discourse is also the broader discourse.

But that is not necessarily the case. Starting with the 2-point capitalist/socialist we could make a list of all functions carried out in a society (raising children; producing, distributing, and consuming goods and services, including health, education, and leisure, etc.); calculating the percentage of these functions administered by the public/centrally planned sector and by the private sector. This variable, from 0 percent to 100 percent, would fill in the range between purely capitalist and purely socialist, with all kinds of in-between positions. Obviously the discourse is now broader but not deeper, still being based on only one dimension.

We could deepen it, however, by conceiving of both capitalism and socialism as two separate dimensions, not as points on the same dimension. In that case we might even do with three points on each: "no capitalism (socialism)," "medium capitalism (socialism)," "full capitalism (socialism)," yielding a total of nine combinations.

From these nine combinations we might now impoverish ourselves again by scaling it down to five, implicitly referred to very often in the preceding chapters: "fully capitalist," "fully socialist," "in-between," "both-and," and "neither-nor." Whereas the index of what is sometimes called "functional socialism" might have as many as 101 points (from 0 percent to 100 percent socialism), this new discourse has only five points. Obviously it is more narrow, by our definition. But it is also deeper, even 100 percent deeper (from one to two dimensions).

This gives us three ways of expanding a discourse: by making it broader, by making it deeper, and by doing both. It should only be remembered that a dimension has a minimum of two points; one point constitutes no dimension. There has to be some counter-point, at least a 2-point dimension, a dichotomy (a 3-point dimension is known as a *trichotomy*, and an n-point dimension as a *polytomy*).

What we have said above is that a discourse based on three dichotomies, a (2x2x2)-discourse, is *deeper* than one based on two trichotomies, a (3x3)-discourse. And yet it is only an 8-point discourse, whereas the latter is a 9-point discourse. Deeper can be narrower and broader can be shallower, as the example shows.

Finally, what could we possibly mean by a *better* or *worse* discourse, introducing clearly evaluative terms rather than the purely descriptive and well-operationalized properties of discourses discussed so far? As we have seen, we can both broaden and deepen a discourse, both processes being referred to as expansion. But does that necessarily make the discourse better, or only more complex?

Complexity could be operationalized as the number of points in the cartesian product times the number of dimensions minus 1,

$$c = m \times n - 1$$

Thus, a fourfold-table has a complexity of $c = 4 \times 2 - 1 = 7$; for three dichotomies we get $c = 8 \times 3 - 1 = 23$ whereas two trichotomies yield only $c = 9 \times 2 - 1 = 17$. With only one point on one dimension, $m=n=1$, $c = 1 \times 1 - 1 = 0$, zero or no complexity at all. There is no choice of predicate, the case of total repression. The members of this speech community can only predicate one thing of any subject. If complexity is too low the discourse is neither complex enough to reflect a complex reality, nor to accommodate interesting thoughts. But the complexity can also be so unnecessarily high that it is complicated rather than complex (some reader might find this chapter a good illustration).

What we need is a discourse neither too high nor too low in complexity, with c well distributed between m and n (thus, better three dichotomies than two trichotomies). The term for "neither too high, nor too low" is *adequate*. The discourse simply has to be adequate to the task at hand.

Adequacy is a question of balance and trade-off between the broad and the deep, of experienced judgment combined with intuitions of future possibilities, of referents not yet observed, states of affairs not foreseen and/or not pursued, thoughts not yet thought and, indeed, of sentences waiting to be spoken, to be born. The quest for adequacy is a process, always adjusting as the empirical (like the previous examples in chapters 2 and 3) fades into obsolescence and an often richly deserved oblivion, and the potential commands increasing attention, possibly because it may be in the process of becoming empirical, of being born.

In general, adequacy is obtained through expansion rather than contraction of a discourse. Contraction is easy; dropping a point, a dimension, or both. The raw material for expansion is often simple, popular speech like somebody who says, "hey, wait a little, we also have to take into account . . .", prying narrow and shallow discourses open, making the opaque transparent by letting the light of thought and speech into dark corners.

So, let us focus on *discourse expansion*, which is the topic of the next chapter, as the approach to discourse adequacy, always keeping in mind that sometimes *discourse contraction* may be called for, calling a spade a spade, rather than endless complications.

NOTES

1. See C. Ogden and I. Richards, *The Meaning of Meaning* (London: Routledge and Kegan Paul, 1923). For an analysis comparing the approaches made by Ogden and Richards to C. S. Peirce and Ferdinand de Saussure, see John Fiske, *Introduction to Communication Studies* (London and New York: Methuen, 1982), pp. 45ff. Of course, much has happened since the book by Ogden and Richards in 1923, leading to, for instance, the important books by Umberto Eco, *A Theory of Semiotics* (London: Macmillan, 1977) and *Semiotics and the Philosophy of Language*

(London: Macmillan, 1984) via Roland Barthes, *Elements of Semiology* (New York: Hill & Wang, 1968). The general tendency is to detach term and concept (statement and proposition) from the referent (thing) and state of affairs "out there," in the "real world." Obviously, we can communicate about unicorns (the classical example) without being able to point to one. We try to get around this by distinguishing between empirical reality and potential reality, one that can be "conjured upon the wall" (like a unicorn). This will bring us into philosophical difficulties. However, for the purposes of exploring media discourses, presumably used to report about things and state of affairs "out there," Ogden's triangle can still serve us well, identifying the connotation of the term with the concept (meaning) and the denotation of the term with the referent(s).

2. The standard comment in connection with the PLO struggle for a Palestine, assuming that "terrorism" is an etiquette to be avoided. The much more devastating activity that passes under the term "war" seems more acceptable to many, probably because qualifiers like "just" or even "holy" are around the corner. In the same vein "terrorism" could be seen as a technical term, to be defined in the text, and then equipped with any number of qualifiers.

3. A comment frequently heard in connection with the *intifadah*, described by some as "stone-throwing kids." It was and it was not; it could also be seen as highly nonviolent by the standards of the Middle East, the stone-throwing being more symbolical (get away, I shake you off—the latter is the meaning of the word). But one point is probably the frequent confusion of "nonviolence" with "passivity."

4. Wars are surrounded by a set of constraining and thereby legitimizing rules, even "laws of warfare" about war (*ad bello*) and, inside the war, how to conduct it (*in bellum*). Terrorism is not, probably because it does not offer protection for the rulers. In wars they can hide behind the front, in nuclear wars even in bunkers, like that prepared for the U.S. Congress in West Virginia. Note U.S. goverment plans to address such a scenario, however, as a "shadow government" of about 100 senior civilian managers assigned to live and work secretly outside Washington [see: "Shadow government at work," *Washington Post*, March 3, 2002, pg. A3]. The terror of terrorism lies probably in the circumstance that rulers and ruled are more equalized.

5. This is also heard quite often, and probably means that democracies possess a legitimacy that places them above the law, including the laws of war.

6. See Johan Galtung, *World Politics of Peace and War*, chapter 5 on "Terrorism," forthcoming.

7. Thus, from the Gulf war and the "smart bombs" comes the "collateral damage," including death, of "innocent bystanders."

8. See Johan Galtung, *Environment, Development and Military Activity* (Oslo: Norwegian Universities Press, 1982), last chapter, on the omnicidal character of a nuclear war.

9. An adequate discourse would be balanced; there is this case, but then also that case. Of course, to anybody used to an unbalanced, biased, inadequate discourse any balanced discourse, by the very fact that it calls attention to the missing possibility, will shout "Bias!" "Ideology!"

10. An example would be the missing combination in the Darwin/economistic discourse in chapter 2: egalitarian, but rich, presumably unattainable for the egalitarian Fuegans (the inhabitants of Tierra del Fuego).

11. During a debate between the two presidential candidates in 1988, George Bush and Michael Dukakis, Bush pointed to his opponent without looking at him and said, "And he, he thinks that the United States of America is just like any country, somewhere on the UN roll call list between Albania and Zimbabwe."

12. 1996; the number may change upwards.

13. This would be the solution approximated in the belt of countries in the world north, from Canada to the Nordic countries: progressive taxation and a dense web of collective services available to all and in fact used, if not by all, at least by very many.

14. This was a solution attempted in the Chinese People's Communes in 1958-76, rotating horizontally between worker-farmer-student-militia; and vertically between worker-engineer-manager in factories. Horizontal rotation must have been easier than vertical rotation, especially when different levels of skills and knowledge are involved.

15. This is developed in some detail in Johan Galtung, *Methodology and Ideology* (Copenhagen: Ejlers, 1978), chapter 2, "Empiricism, Criticism, Constructivism."

16. Thus, empiricism is rooted in the comparisons between the observed and the foreseen, criticism in the comparisons between the observed and the preferred, and constructivism in the comparisons between the foreseen and the preferred. If the three sets in extension coincide, then we obviously live in the best of all worlds: what we think will happen not only happens but is in addition what we want to happen. Problems arise when there is dissonance, the three sets do not coincide, giving rise to the problem of what is stronger—data, theories, or values.

17. *Volkswirtschaftslehre, Betriebswirtschftslehre*; the teaching of the economies of the "people" and the "firm," respectively.
18. This theme is developed in some detail in Part III, Chapter 3 of *Peace By Peaceful Means* (London, Thousand Oaks, CA, New Delhi: Sage, 1996).
19. This terminology, of course, comes from grammar jargon, a speech system successfully disseminated through the school systems all over the world to teach languages, including the native tongue.
20. See Ernst Nagel and James R. Newman, *Gödel's Proof* (New York: New York University Press, 1958).

5

A Theory of Discourse Expansion

THE TOOLS OF DISCOURSE EXPANSION

Imagine that we start constructing a discourse from scratch, really from point zero. We start in darkness. There is no speech. There may be some concepts, some referents; there may be some propositions, some states of affairs. But we are not only speechless but also unable to reflect thought and/or reality. That is what makes for no discourse at all; an interesting case of which we are usually only aware afterwards—like in deep meditation.[1]

What is the first thing to be done, how do we make the step from a 0-point discourse to a 1-point discourse? The answer is obvious: *Name it! Say the word!* This is even the way of Genesis, according to the New Testament (John): "In the beginning was the Word and the Word was with God, and the Word was God." The person who shouts FIRE! in a crowded theater room introduces a discourse that dramatically changes the situation. Attention is drawn to a possibility, amply filled with drama. It is short-hand for a well-formulated sentence: "This room is now on fire!" Put in different terms: to the unit of discourse, the theater, is attributed a value, "fire," on the dimension "nonfire-fire." The subject has received a predicate. The Word has been spoken.

Shout FREEDOM! under conditions of slavery, in a Gulag or a concentration camp, and the unspeakable has been spoken. Chances are that the guards will rush in and silence and/or punish the person who broke this mental barbed wire barrier erected between a 0-point and a 1-point discourse, in public space.

We may also say that the person broke a taboo. The taboo is a 0-point discourse, a social contract between the members of the discourse (speech) community to the effect that certain things and states of affairs should remain unnamed and unmentioned, preferably even unthought of. Repression is a 1-point discourse, limiting speech to one predicate; taboos do not even permit that.

The importance lies in a basic difference between speech and thought: *speech is in public space, thought in inner space.* In principle anybody can think anything without anybody knowing what is going on. "What are you thinking of right now?" is a very frequent question between lovers—love, and the act of love, also being acts of mutual possession, incorporating one in the other. There is a clear demand for access, including to thoughts, and through access to sharing, or at least to naming. Individual privacy is supposed to yield to the privacy of the couple, the borders of the monad bursting, two monads fusing into a dyad. The same question, incidentally, is also asked in any totalitarian society, demanding deprivatization of thoughts and transformation of even the innermost individual into public property—George Orwell's *1984*, in short. Or for the case of the triad, Margaret Atwood's *The Handmaid's Tale*.[2]

The nature of speech is entirely different. Of course a person may be mumbling to him/herself, but in that case there is probably some suffering from loneliness involved. The speaker creates a community of Self and Other. Speech is by its very nature public. It is shaped in such a way as to be heard.

A speaker generally presupposes a listener. Concretely this means that the person who speaks the unspeakable changes the life of Other by bidding for a change in the social contract. Nobody can deny that this is a dramatic bid. And it will be treated accordingly, from enthusiastic acceptance to violent rejection via well-studied ways of ignoring the breach of a contract of silence. Examples of such taboos: Austrian acceptance of *Anschluss* 1938 and extensive membership in the Nazi party; French collaboration with the Germans during the war; Soviet treaties with Nazi Germany and with militarist Japan. These are all on people's minds, if not on their tongues. Only very recently are these old taboos broken. Much of the same applies to the United States in Việt Nam: better leave it unspoken, as seen by the hostility to Robert McNamara's book.[3]

Dictionaries such as the *Oxford English Dictionary* and *Webster's* contain listings of the first citing of certain words. A date is affixed to them. On that date, then, an escape from the prison of the 0-point discourse took place, introducing a new word or term in the language. Something could be clothed with words that had been veiled in silence or carried a different verbal attire earlier. But then it also goes without saying that by making something mentionable something else might have become unmentionable, if we take for granted that neither individual nor collective memory is unlimited. This is a reason why dictionaries should also list the death, the last citing, not only the birth of words, and have a cemetery of former entries printed as an appendix. They should record discourse contraction, not only expansion.

How do we now proceed from a 1-point to a 2-point discourse? There are two ways: by repeating the act, breaking one more taboo by once more naming the unnameable; or completing the dimension on which the first point was given a name by speaking the word. That word named at most one half of the dimension, in a dichotomy. One way of doing the latter is very simple: introduce the antithesis to the thesis that could be formulated with the first term.

Thus, the negation of "fire" is "not fire"; the antithesis to "There is fire in this room" is "There is not fire in this room." Correspondingly, the term "Freedom!" is probably a short-hand for "We want freedom now!," and the antithesis would be "We want no freedom now!" which is not quite the same as saying "We do not want freedom now!"

An interesting way of studying this early stage in discourse development would be to study infants when they utter their first words. Imagine the first word uttered is "mama." A young child has now become a member of the speech community, the word "mama" probably standing for something like "Mama, please pay attention to me!" The next step might be "dada/papa," in which case a dimension has been constructed. The child can now formulate an antithesis to the sentence just mentioned, something like "Dada/Papa, please pay attention to me!" It should be noted that antithesis is not the same as negation; "dada/papa" does not necessarily mean "please do not pay attention to me!" There are four possibilities: both, either or neither. We might speculate that the child's way of articulating "neither" is through silence.

But the child could also go in another direction, opening for a new possible dimension by saying something like "water/wawa," which in turn may be interpreted as a short-hand for "I am thirsty." If that young member of the speech community could expand from this point to a whole dimension by introducing the negative no! there would already be a discourse space with four points indicating whose attention is demanded and whether the focus of attention should be thirst or possibly something else, at this point only known as absence of thirst; silence on that dimension.

Let us once again move one step and ask the question: how do we get from a 2-point to a 3-point discourse? One possibility would be to build on what was indicated above: introduce a third category that would cover the both-and, neither-nor, and in-between categories. We could also exploit the hegelian formulas that have been made use of implicitly, and refer to all three of them as "synthesis." In that case "both-and" might be referred to as a *positive synthesis*, a third category containing in one way or the other both of the original categories. "Neither-nor" could be referred to as a *negative synthesis*, meaning a category rejecting both the original categories. And "in-between" could be referred to as *compromise*, a category containing something from either of them. The most elegant case of synthesis, a *transcendence*, where the two constituents are no longer present because they have somehow been absorbed in the process of making something of a totally new kind, *sui generis*, might then be seen as a special case of the positive synthesis.

Example: there is a point where the hyphenated sciences (geo-chemistry, social psychology) take on a life of their own, leaving the parents behind, transcending them, or staking out a new course perpendicular to the one they are pursuing. Peace studies grew out of a number of disciplines, then acquired a life of its own; so did women's, black, environmental, and communication studies.

If we now focus for the moment on the negative synthesis, the neither-nor possibility, this could also be referred to as an instance of another hegelian principle, the "negation of the negation." The antithesis is already a negation of the thesis. Thus, socialism is a negation of capitalism. But the negative synthesis known as *anarchism*, neither one nor the other, neither big plan-state nor big market-corporation, negates not only in the sense of negating capitalism or socialism but in the sense of negating the dimension capitalism/socialism as adequate dimension for an economic system discourse. The in-between compromise, the "third alternative," does the same job: *social democracy* may also be seen as a negation of the negation.

And thus it continues, with anarchism being the negation of the negation of the negation and "japanism," the both-and solution, being the negation of the negation of the negation of the negation. Obviously somebody can come up with a fifth negation here, for instance by saying that the basic problem is not that of constructing an economy for material goods and services, but an economy in the sense of a pattern of production, distribution, and consumption for spiritual growth. And so on and so forth.

Going back to what has now become five economic systems rather than two, there are several ways of analyzing this process of discourse expansion.[4]

First, we are evidently dealing with the case mentioned above of expansion from one dimension with two points to two dimensions with three points each, yielding nine combinations, although we only make use of five. Let us refer to this expansion from a 2-point discourse to a 5-point discourse as the construction of a "starfish." In principle it is applicable whenever two points have been named: construct dimensions of the (0, 1/2, 1) or (low, medium, high) types, assign *degrees* for each point, combine them into nine points (3 x 3), select five of them (only one, only the other, in-between, both-and, and neither-nor) and a much richer discourse has been obtained, with c = 5 x 2 - 1 = 9. The "starfish" method can be very generally applied and usually yields non-trivial thought and speech. It is highly recommended in discourse theory, not to mention discourse practice. Key words: in-between, both-and, and neither-nor.

But there is also another way of looking at the process. We accept as a first approach the dimension "capitalism-socialism." But then we open for a second dimension with the pertinent question: does the dimension "capitalism-socialism" exhaust all possibilities? If the answer is "yes" then we are back to the 2-point discourse with capitalism and socialism. If the answer is "no" we might make use of the three alternatives already explored, in-between, both-and, and neither-nor.

The process is as indicated in Figure 5.1.

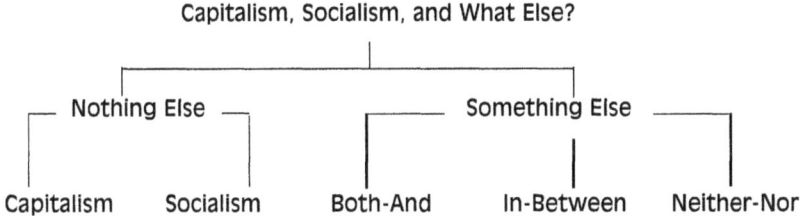

Figure 5.1.

As can be seen from the bottom line we again end up, combining types, with a 5-point discourse. But this time it is written up in such a way that we actually can go one step further and get a 6-point discourse, containing such combinations as (socialism, both-and) by making the cartesian product. Using that discourse the following sentence could be formulated: "on the basis of socialism first, both-and might develop later." Or, "socialism as the leading element, both-and as subordinate to socialism". Or, "neither-nor to start with, capitalism later and forever." Gorbachev, Deng Xiaoping, and Bush respectively?

The important point about the discourses we have just opened, using degree of market articulation as one dimension and degree of planning articulation as the other, is that it empowers us intellectually to search for new combinations that are not seen if market and plan are seen as each other's negation. More particularly, we can now focus on the main diagonal, the *green* (anarchic), the *pink* (social democrat) and the *yellow* or *golden* (Japanese) combinations, instead of only those nineteenth-century products, the *blue* (capitalist) and the *red* (socialist) economic systems. All five fall as ripe fruits into our discourse basket if we use the "starfish" configuration as our underlying framework.

What we have done once we can do once again by opening a discourse within the discourse. Let us focus on the "both-and," the combination of market and plan. As noticed the combination can be at a very high level of articulation of either of them (japanism), at the medium level (social democracy) or at the local level (village economies, green economies). In either case we would definitely like to know more about how two systems, generally considered antithetical to each other, in fact can be combined. To do that an additional discourse is needed, a subdiscourse obtained by expanding a point in the original discourse using the logic of Chinese boxes (or of computers with "windows," like putting the "mouse" on a point in a computer discourse).

Here are five possibilities that might come to the mind of anybody devoting some attention to the fascinating problem of combining market and plan, possibly accommodating thought, speech and action relevant for the "economic crisis" both of an overheated blue economy with recurrent recessions, even depressions, and an undercooled red economy with, among many problems, insufficient financial liquidity put at the disposal of the real economic system. If capitalism is better at growth and socialism at distribution, then discourses should accommodate combinations.

The five dimensions now to be explored are as follows:

Space: the possibility of having two systems co-exist within one country; dividing the country into two spheres, one more socialist and one more capitalist, like free trade areas. In general the condition for doing this would be free mobility of persons, goods, and services (and information) between the two parts of the country. But there is also the possibility of a transition period with only partial mobility. A fascinating long-term possibility would be to have the two parts of a country swap economic roles, like people may do for personal enrichment. Elections in a federal country might bring about exactly that.

Time: as just indicated; there is no law saying that the system has to stick to market/capitalism or plan/socialism for eternity. Human experience is that systems do change. Nothing is forever. Change could be built into the socio-economic formation not unlike what has happened in the People's Republic of China in its pendular or spiraling march through recent history.[5]

Function: have some social functions attended to by market mechanisms and some by plan mechanisms. This is not unknown in the most capitalist society in the world, the United States, where public education is according to socialist logic (with elected boards, publicly appointed officials, planning at all levels, and attendance both compulsory and free), whereas health is run on the basis of capitalist logic (private practice backed up by insurance, including malpractice, free choice for both doctors and patients).

However, much of the higher education in the United States is according to the capitalist logic, whereas some of the most primary health care has elements of socialist logic. In other words, there is nothing particularly unknown or arcane about this from a mainstream U.S. point of view. The point is only to bring the functional dimension to public attention as one among several of the "both-and" possibilities. Not only is there much socialism in the United States (most of the primary and secondary education, national parks, recreation areas, superb public libraries, and museums), but people simply love it, as long as it is never called "socialism."

Level: there are four levels that are of analytical interest: local, national, regional and world levels. Green politics might argue in favor of market economy at the local (municipality) level and more planned economy at the other three. Most of the economy should be local and based on local self-reliance, with production for own consumption, production for barter on a one-to-one basis, and production for sale within economic cycles limited in space.

Blue politics would probably argue in favor of capitalist logic for all four levels, and Red politics in favor of a socialist logic for all four levels. Pink, social democratic politics, would prefer a bland mix at all levels. And the Yellow option, the Japanese solution, would typically be in favor of a strong mix of market and planning at the local and national levels, and probably also at the regional and world levels. Compete inside the country to remain competitive, mean, and lean; cooperate outside with time- or space-sharing of the foreign markets.

All of the above: can these four possibilities be combined? Of course they can, just as the green, pink, and yellow options in general can be combined. Do so and a very adequate way of thinking, speaking, and acting in connection with socio-economic formations emerges, much above the simplistic dichotomy of capitalism versus socialism that was our point of departure.

What has been done here is an exercise in discourse analysis within discourse analysis. It is rather like putting a magnifying glass, even a microscope, on one point in the discourse. We then blow it up, deconstruct it, and then reconstruct, introducing new dimensions, enriching thought, speech, and practice.

Thus we can continue; this process knows no end. New points can be introduced by defining new terms or redefining old ones. The points can then be negated, opening for formulations of antitheses. Between thesis and antithesis a residual category may be introduced, containing the elements of both-and, in-between, and neither-nor. Or, we might negate the negation by denying that this is the relevant new dimension, exploring that negation in terms of both-and (including transcendence), in-between, and neither-nor. In other words, assumptions are brought out into the open; the original rudimentary, poor discourse is deconstructed.

We can also proceed by applying a process of double negation to a 2-point discourse, one negation for each point. If we combine these two dichotomies we get a 4-point discourse. If we then enrich both of the 2-point discourses by making them 3-point discourses we get in principle a 9-point discourse which might then be reduced to the 5-point *discourse starfish*.

Still another way of conceiving what is going on is what we might call the *discourse budding process*, based on the repeated application of the negation of the negation principle. Figure 5.2 illustrates the process, using the example of economic systems drawn upon repeatedly above,

Thus it continues, always negating the negation in the order indicated by the numbers. Or negating the dimension used in the preceding negation, such as saying: "private versus public is not the issue, the issue is pure system versus eclecticism." Or: "you guys all assume the scale of the economy to be national."

Figure 5.3 is an effort to summarize what has been said so far in this chapter. Obviously, all the positions under the main diagonal in Figure 5.3 refer to cases of discourse expansion. And correspondingly, all the cases above are cases of discourse contraction, reducing the number of points. To go back to a 0-point discourse from the 1-point discourse all that is needed is to forget, repress, and suppress *The Word*. From 2-point to 0-point discourse a double use of this mechanism is needed. Of course, from 2-point to 1-point is easier because it is only a question of "forgetting" the negation. A contraction from 3-point to 2-point discourse is tantamount to applying the strait-jacket of a dichotomy, or dropping any exploration of underlying assumptions; in other words, some repression of speech and thought processes.

To/From	0	1	2	3	4	5
0						
1	the Word the Name *thesis*					
2		Negation *antithesis*				
3			Neg. of Neg. *synthesis* both-and, in-between neither-nor			
4			Double Negation 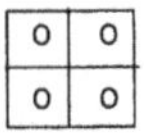 ⊡ (o o / o o)			
5			Starfish 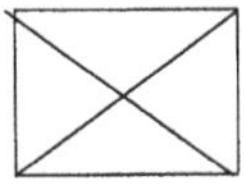 ⊠		Double Compromise Starfish	

Figure 5.3. Discourse expansion and discourse contraction

The outcome is something like the discourse underlying *Taking Sides* in chapter 3, meaning shallower, not only narrower discourses.

As mentioned, the ideal is not an ever-expanding discourse getting broader and broader and deeper and deeper in the sense of having more and more points and more and more dimensions. The ideal is an *adequate* discourse. The discourse is there to make thought, speech, and action reflect and impact on reality. At the same time the discourse is a part of a social contract. An individual's inner space discourse is less important in this connection; what matters is discourse for public communication.

The same applies to the jargon of, say, social scientists, lawyers, and physicians; they are public, but within a very limited speech community. The problem is how to arrive at adequate public discourses for society at large, a social contract between many and diverse senders and receivers facilitating deep communication— discourses worthy of a working democracy: broad, deep, understood.

This can only be obtained through a hermeneutic process combining discourse-construction with discourse-deconstruction, and discourse-expansion somewhere with discourse-contraction somewhere else. Where to start is a chicken-egg problem. Whoever thinks s/he starts with deconstruction obviously is building on somebody else who at some time contributed to the construction of that discourse. Correspondingly, whoever thinks s/he is constructing a discourse might actually be picking up from the ground the debris of an exploded (read: deconstructed) discourse constructed by someone else. Back and forth, from the left to the right and back again, and then back again, that is the nature of the struggle to arrive at a suitable compromise between discourse-expansion and discourse-contraction. And even so, any discourse is temporary, changing when it is entered into and entertained for communication.

Let us now connect what has been said in this chapter with the technical tools of the preceding chapter. There is Ogden's triangle all over the place, emphasizing the separation of term, concept, and referent; also emphasizing that the discourse belongs to the "term" corner of the triangle. But how about definitions, classifications, and cartesian products?

Definitions are used to introduce terms so precise that they can be used to build a discourse with sender and receiver having the same referents in mind, using the principle of a definition as an explicit contract. The introduction of new terms leads to some additional clauses in the general social speech contract, adding clauses in a larger social contract. One way of describing why definitions suddenly emerge might be by using the third hegelian principle; the transition from quantity to quality. Increasing frustration has been felt in the speech community because of an accumulation of misunderstandings, cases of communication not working. Then comes a jump from increased frustration to an aggressive attack on the language, grafting on to it a new definition ("Let us agree to use democracy to mean . . ."). From that point on the language is no longer the same. This is where the basic rules for definitions enter the picture, presumably making the definition an adequate tool not only for speech, but also for thought and action. Lawyers tend to be extremely good at this.

Classifications enter the process the moment a term, or as it is referred to here, a "point," is expanded to a "dimension." The dimension is then seen as a potential classification in need of some rigor where subdivision is concerned. Here the basic rules for establishing classifications in extension and intension enter the picture, making the classification an adequate tool not only for speech, but also for thought and action. What kinds of terrorism are we talking about, what kinds of violence, what kinds of economic systems? The answers will deepen the understanding.

Cartesian products enter the picture the moment we want to combine two or more dimensions or classifications. What we then do is to take two or more disjointed discourses and join them together into deeper, meaning multi-dimensional, joint discourses. Another metaphor: Discourse atoms are joined into discourse molecules.

To bring in examples again: *Star Wars*. If Star Wars is to be discussed as Strategic Defense Initiative (SDI); in other words, if it is taken for granted that Star Wars is defensive, then an adequate discourse could concentrate on whether SDI is effective or not as a defensive technology. "Works/does not work" would be an adequate way of expressing that dimension. But if a rather basic issue is whether Star Wars really is defensive, or could also be used offensively, as a "strategic offensive initiative" (SOI), then we could still use the old discourse "works/does not work," but multiply it with the new discourse so as to arrive at a joint discourse. The result is to the left in Figure 5.4.

In that joint discourse molecule the sentence (C in the left side table) that expresses the evaluation of the situation in this book, "Star Wars does not work defensively, but works offensively" becomes a well-formulated sentence, impossible in either of the separate discourse or discourse atoms. In the U.S. discourse only the SDI discourse is well formulated; SOI seems to be taboo.

To the right in Figure 5.4 is another example, equally "hot" in the political debate of the 1980s-90s in the United States. The economic woes of the country's foreign trade are primarily discussed in terms of trade deficits; in other words, in terms of a negative

	Star Wars	
	Works Defensively	Does Not Work Defensively
Works Offensively	A	B
Does Not Work Offensively	C	D

	Trade Deficit	
	In-Change Positive	In-Change Negative
Exchange Positive Surplus	A	B
Exchange Negative Deficit	C	D

Figure 5.4. Joint discourses: Discourse molecules

outcome (being in the red) of the *exchange* dimension in exchange of goods and services between and among specific nations or sets of nations. The argument here would be that the impact of economic interaction is not only in terms of whether the *ex*-change is positive or negative; in other words, whether there is a trade surplus or a trade deficit, multilaterally or bilaterally relative to any given trade partner (such as Japan, China and the mini-Japans/Chinas).

The impact is also in the change that takes place inside the country, *in casu* the United States, as a result of economic interaction; what we could call the "in-change." This *in*-change, or the inner side-effects, the spin-offs (externalities), can themselves be positive and negative. Generally, the more sophisticated the production process and/or the products (goods, services) the higher the positive externalities of the process: technological spin-offs, science, and education due to the challenge in having to produce sophisticated products, and so forth.

This, however, also applies to such negative externalities as pollution-depletion, a reason why industrialized countries prefer to keep laboratories at home and put the factories in other countries, exporting the negative externalities (pollution) and keeping for themselves the positive externalities (challenges).

Again we have the same situation: in this joint discourse it is possible to formulate, for instance, the present book's view (D in the right hand table): "The problem of the United States is not only that the result of the exchange is negative, but also that the result of the in-change is negative, and the latter is by far the more important." In a disjointed discourse it would have been impossible to state this as a well-formulated sentence.

It should be noted that just as in the preceding case we kept the dimension "positive/negative" and brought into the picture the additional dimension of "exchange/inchange." What was done, however, was not to multiply these two but to expand each point in the exchange/in-change dimension into a 2-point dimension positive/negative, and multiply these two dimensions. Only then were we able to formulate sentence D, escaping from the fool's paradise of talking about monetary trade deficits alone.

In all examples the *problématique* is the same: how can a discourse accommodate that which has to be expressed and reflected? How can it serve as a generous host to our speech and by implication to our thought and action? In short, how can it be adequate? Discourse adequacy remains the general heading over all these exercises, certainly more easily discussed than obtained.

The basic reason for that again comes with a warning from many people who have worked in this or related fields: the best thing we can hope for is to abolish a myth with another myth. We may be good at discovering the inadequacies of a discourse already constructed, and then deconstruct the discourse mercilessly. We may describe the old discourse as designed to steer thought and speech away from reality. But in constructing a new discourse, presumably more adequate to reality, those who deconstruct our construction might point out that we have only exchanged one myth for another, possibly a less evident myth at that, and consequently more dangerous. Just as we did before them. Like the food chain in nature, construction-deconstruction chains may ultimately be self-destructive, self-devouring, like the snake by mistake or design eating its own tail.

We would tend to accept that. In discourse theory and practice we are not testing statements, elevating them to the status of "proposition" if they are confirmed. Statements can be tested against empirical reality. But a discourse should also be capable of reflecting a potential reality that is not there, or not quite there, yet. What *may be* is problematic enough; what ought to be may be even more problematic if we assume that prescriptions give imagination more space than predictions, calling for more complex discourses less tied to the empirical, yet not completely detached. The fruitfulness, another word for adequacy of a discourse, has to be judged both in terms of empirical and potential reality. And that can only be explored by thinking and speaking the discourse.

It will always be fair to say that a discourse excludes something important. One reason is that the discourse itself may establish the conditions under which new aspects of a phenomenon come into the daylight as objects of rudimentary thinking processes, as something observed in the darker corners of "reality," or conceived in the deeper recesses of our minds. The adequate discourse simply undermines itself, like the giant in science providing broad enough shoulders for coming generations to supersede the giant. The substitution of a myth for another is as good an expression as any of what goes on. Reality helps pave the way for a new discourse making the old look as if it is a myth; the new discourse then helps pave the way for a new reality making that discourse also to look just like a myth.

But there is no need for despair. The process still makes very much sense, at least as long as we are not oscillating between two myths only, like in a pendular process, but are spiraling ourselves towards some new myths. The process will go on anyhow, regardless of how we understand what happens, discourse transformation being a part of the human condition.

However, at the risk of stating the obvious, we do not assume that there is always a discourse between us and reality, to the point that the discourse is the closest we come, even to the point that there is no reality "out there." But we humans brush against reality in other ways than through thought and speech. Michel Foucault may well have conceived of the AIDS discourse as merely that, a discourse, but he nevertheless died from it.

Reality "out there" brushes against us and imparts in us pain and/or pleasure, or plain dullness. Reality imparts in the collectivity known as a nation the *kairos* of trauma and glory, or plain *khronos* history. From that point on discourse takes over, the pre-shaped vessel determining how we conceive of this and talk/write about it. But the deep emotions of pain and pleasure are still there. When we have sex we have intercourse, not discourse. But when we start talking about sex, the relevance of everything said above, including what has been said about taboos and poor and rich discourses, is certainly relevant, which brings us to an important point. If we now assume emotions to be real and cognitions that we want to communicate, including to ourselves, to be highly discourse-dependent, then the problem arises: what discourses do we have for emotions?

Tentative answer: this is why we have artists. They translate emotions for us into their languages, which look like ours when coached in poetry and prose and look otherwise when expressed in sounds, shapes, and colors. The discourses are non-verbal even when verbal; a point to be elaborated in Chapter 8.

With this perspective in mind let us now explore further the Chinese example used in Chapter 2. What is new in that example is not that we do not have definitions, classifications, even dichotomies. We even have combinations of dichotomies, as when "good/bad" is multiplied by "capitalism/socialism." What is new is how the relationship between two points on the same dimension are conceived—the ever-present ambiguity also known from art.

It is assumed from the very beginning that the (Western) rules of classification given in Chapter 4 are, in fact, invalid. There is no such thing as the mutually exclusive classification. There will always be an element of the masculine in the feminine and the feminine in the masculine; of capitalism in socialism and socialism in capitalism; of the good in the bad and the bad in the good. In short, the *yin-yang* relationship is not that of a dichotomous classification but of a dialectic relationship, with the *yin* in the *yang* and the *yang* in the *yin*, not to mention the *yang* in the *yin* in the *yang* and the *yin* in the *yang* in the *yin*. They are inseparable.

In this particular case we are dealing with two dialectics at the same time. This implies a limitation on the definition of the unit of discourse. The unit has to be of such a kind that it can accommodate a meaningful dialectic; only in that case has a unit been identified. The next step is to identify the dialectic within the unit. One approach may be in terms of "capitalism/socialism," another in terms of "good/bad," two dimensions of inseparable aspects, one unthinkable without the other.

The *single* use of the *yin-yang* principle makes it possible to build on a particular characteristic of the Chinese language. Many characters in fact consist of two characters joined together, and the meaning of the joint character lies in the dialectic between the meanings of the separate characters. In other words, there is a dialectic already built into the written (and by implication spoken) language. Although this is an empirical hypothesis to be tested, it should also have some impact on thought and action.

Thus, *crisis* = *danger* + *opportunity*, and *contradiction* = *sword* + *shield* (the sword that can pierce the shield; the shield that can withstand the sword; not a bad image of a contradiction).

This also holds for the *double* use of the *yin-yang* principle, or the double dialectic, which leads to a particular form dear to the Chinese mind: the *quartet*. The general form would be A:B = X:Y. Mencius: "Human beings tend toward the good as water flows downward." Four elements are tied together with this syntactic glue, making us consider the four of them together, in all possible ways ("human beings to water as good to downward," and so on). In the example from Chapter 2 the connective : would read "and," not "to." "Capitalism *and* socialism, to good *and* bad"; not "capitalism *to* socialism as good *to* bad." Mainstream U.S. interpretation is as silent on the vices of capitalism as on the virtues of socialism; the discourse covers the road to liberalization/privatization.

What has been done once or twice can now be done more times. There is *yin* in the *yang* in the *yin* and so on, leading to eight combinations. There is contradiction inside contradiction inside contradiction inside; Chinese boxes. An adequate discourse should open the boxes, not close them. Cartesian products are useful, and not only for aristotelian, static classifications but for more galilean, dynamic moves among the various combinations. Objects are not merely classified at rest, they even fall freely.[6] The borderlines between the points in time-space are not watertight but highly porous. Objects move. But *yin/yang* thinking goes further: points or types are inside each other, no longer separable.

Moreover, *yin/yang* thinking carries in its wake, free of charge so to speak, a dynamic hypothesis: there is somewhere a harmony point where *yin* and *yang* are in balance. If there is disharmony, then waning of one and waxing of the other is what happens until the balance point is reached, or there is an overshot. If *yin* is female and *yang* is male, then the harmony point is more toward the *yin* side for women and more toward the *yang* side for men. Moreover, there is a dynamism in the dynamisms, like a switch from tension between classes to tension between age-groups (the 1968 confrontation) to tension between genders to tension between humans and the rest of nature, and so forth.

The image of reality is much more subtle (and, in a sense, also more artistic, rich, suggestive) than the clear-cut, pure cartesian categories. On the other hand, they come with no implicit theory of inner tensions and tensions within tensions attached, leaving us more free to think, say, and do whatever we want with these simplistic building blocs.[7]

Does this lead to a dichotomous discourse about discourse, in terms of Western (aristotelian-cartesian) versus Chinese (daoist), or occidental versus oriental? No, again there is room for "both-and," "neither-nor," "in-between"; we are not forced to make a choice. What matters is to keep the discourse about discourse in general, and about discourse transformation in particular, very open, including to challenges from other cosmologies, epistemologies, intellectual styles. If not, we shall run into some of the problems to be explored in the next chapter.

NOTES

1. A basic point about meditation is to arrive at a state of mind at rest, *tabula rasa*, concentrating, for instance, on your breath, inhaling and exhaling. Cleaning the slate, meeting the world anew, without pre-conceptions, without a pre-set discourse or *mind-set*, could be another way of saying exactly he same thing.

2. Margaret E. Atwood, *The Handmaiden's Tale* (Boston: Houghton Mifflin, 1986).

3. *In Retrospect, The Tragedy and Lessons of Vietnam* (New York: Random House, 1995).

4. For the economic substance, as opposed to the formal aspect, of this see Johan Galtung, *Peace By Peaceful Means*, part III, chapter 4, discussing the interplay of the Blue, Red, Pink, Yellow, and Green schools of economics in building a more pluralistic approach to the economy.

5. For an effort to use this as a perspective on Chinese history from 1949, see Johan Galtung, "Is There a Chinese Strategy of Development? A Contribution to an Everlasting Debate," *Review*, V, 1982, pp. 460-486.

6. This is Ernst Cassirer's distinction between *Substanzbegriff* and *Funktionsbegriff*.

7. See Johan Galtung, *Constructing a Daoist Social Science Epistemology* (Denia: Universidad de Verano, 1993), in *Investigaciones teóricas: Sociedad y Cultura Contemporánea* (Madrid: Tecnos, 1995), pp. 209-221.

Factors Impeding
Discourse Expansion

If we assume that *the ruling discourse is the discourse of the ruling class*, to paraphrase Marx, then we have a suitable, if not very subtle, point of departure for the topic of this section, the antithesis of the preceding section. The ruling classes have their values and interests. In the preceding chapters many examples have been given of very concrete interests that are hiding behind inadequate discourses. In a sense it is unnecessary to belabor the obvious. The basic point would be that when a subjugated discourse is emerging on the surface, new values and new interests are articulated that may not serve the ruling classes, but perhaps serve emerging elites. And the ruling class, for instance the patriarchy, will respond, trying to suppress, subjugating the discourse again, ruling it out of court, suppressing, ridiculing, marginalizing. Killing the word by silence, not repeating it, is to make the word inaudible and invisible; imprisoning it, which may be as effective as imprisoning the speaker, which in turn may be as effective as killing the speaker. In what follows, thirteen mechanisms or ways of killing the word will be explored.

MARGINALIZING THE INTELLECTUALS

One way could be observed not only in the ex-Soviet Union and other socialist countries until recently, but also in the United States; in fact in very many countries. The general formula is the inner exile of those who presumably are the word-masters, or at least artisans of words, the intellectuals, to special ghettos, where life may be quite pleasant, but marginal to society.

In the ex-Soviet Union the name of that ghetto used to be the Academy of Sciences. In the United States the name would be the campus in geographical terms, and the discipline in professional terms.[1] Presumably intellectuals should be among the most innovative when it comes to the creation of new discourses, new intellectual paradigms being indispensable parts of their crafts, to accommodate and develop further new hypotheses and, potentially, new propositions. But instead of serving this impatient, restless function for society as a whole the intellectual is limited to unleashing his/her talents and energies on campus, and/or to becoming famous within his/her discipline, D. But The American D Association or Society is not the same as The American Society; nor is writing an article in the American D Review the equivalent of writing a front-page or major article in a major daily newspaper, as French and German intellectuals do in *Le Monde*, or *Le Figaro*, or *Die Zeit*. And a tiny op-ed piece is no substitute, but often only one more contribution to general shallowness, as the number of perspectives that can be explored in a 300-word piece remains very limited.

A career in D may lead away from society rather than into it. The more the intellectuals are absorbed in campus and discipline activities, the less creativity will be made available for society at large. The rulers may in their lighter and brighter moments know perfectly well that intellectuals are indispensable, yet wish to relegate them to distant corners of society, some seminar room, so that they do not engage in any discourse mischief, stirring up semantic trouble, tinkering with well-established discourses.[2]

The campus/discipline ghettos become like the storage of paintings in the basement of the Louvre, a waiting room until the discourse (even with the name of its creator clipped onto it) can see the light of day, having matured. Which means that the society has matured, has caught up with the discourse, that the discourse has proven useful. But it may also mean not too harmful, for the public, and the rulers at large. By the time the discourse is in it may already be dated, innocuous, and co-opted, incorporated. The sting has been effectively removed by those who control the discourse processes as gate-keepers: not intellectuals and artists, but quasi-intellectuals, or even junk intellectuals, like the journalist/columnist mediators.

Some artists may break out of the ghetto, Gore Vidal being a good example in the United States.[3] But the controllers usually live in real society, not side-tracked into a campus or a discipline. The most knowledgeable are not invited into public space (like Noam Chomsky); those who participate are amateurs.[4] A prime example is the absence of psychiatric scholars in the public discourse on mental health. Both-and would be better.

There is a linkage between populist democracy and the relegation of intellectuals to the corners of society. In the Middle Ages this was definitely not the situation. *The ruling discourse was the discourse of the ruling intellectuals*, the clerics. Europe differed from China, ruled by the *shi'h*, the intellectuals-bureaucrats for at least two and a half millennia.[5] And it differed from the Arab intellectuals, who carried the European intellectual tradition through the clerical Middle Ages.

Social processes changed the composition of the ruling elite, away from intellectuals/clerics to bureaucrats, capitalists, and intellectuals, and in some rare cases to "ordinary people." The intellectuals continued their verbal games, no longer able to impose them on the rest of society. Those who had deposed them not only allowed the games, but even encouraged them as long as the intellectuals did not set the discourse for the whole society. They paid them through private foundations and public budgets, knowing that he who pays the piper also calls the tune. The ghetto was the obvious solution for the intellectuals, as obvious as the Jewish ghetto for Jews, another indispensable irritant. Many American Jews experienced the transfer from a Jewish ghetto in Europe to an intellectual ghetto in the United States, without drawing the parallel. The latter is considerably gentler, paying intellectuals for being on-call as consultants on a "don't call us, we'll call you" basis. With the voice of intellectuals muted, plastic, synthetic intellectuals could take over.[6]

INTELLECTUAL POPULISM

But this means that those who design new discourses will have to pay homage to the non-intellectual rulers in order to get their discourses smuggled into the public arena. In the United States there is a long tradition of intellectuals going populist in order to square this circle, with the predictable result that much discourse richness and adequacy in general are lost in the process. There are no longer publicly available, higher intellectual standards to conform to; they have been flattened, made narrow and shallow.[7]

Such discourses tend to be not only simplistic and moralistic but also dated, mainly relevant to the problems of the past. The ideology, values, and interests of the rulers serve as major steering mechanisms, blocking alternative discourses spelling out deeper values and interests. The typical Western contradiction between intellectuals who dominate debates and politicians who dominate action is gradually solved in favor of politicians having the upper hand in both arenas. The rulers set the agenda, defining not only the themes but also the discourse. Mainstream media follow up, and intellectuals, and not only mainstream, follow suit.

This may be related to presidential as opposed to parliamentary democracy. In Western Europe the Prime Minister is very rarely (Churchill, Adenauer, De Gasperi) also a discourse manager. In the United States the President is both, in deference to the regal aspects and the populist basis of the presidency. The President is not only agenda setter, but also discourse master—but very few with Reagan's grip on society. In Socialist Europe staying within the General Secretary's discourse became a matter of biological survival under stalinism, social survival thereafter.[8]

INTELLECTUAL PROFESSIONALISM

However, there is another strategy an intellectual might choose, but often with even more unfortunate results. Instead of trying to go populist he might try to go professional. S/he might cast his discourse in highly professional, disciplinary terms, meaning s/he not only sticks to an academic discipline, but also disciplines him/herself within that discipline. The gamble is that the professional discourse drives out the non-professional; that a technical discourse drives out the non-technical. In doing this an intellectual might not only push aside or marginalize the moralistic discourse of the population at large, couched in highly non-professional and non-technical terms, but also the more or less successfully concealed dominance discourse engaged in by the rulers. The goal worth the struggle is neither to be marginalized, nor to pay the price of vulgarizing one's own discourse into the unrecognizable, nor to lose campus/discipline respectability—and maybe one day in addition to emerge as a ruler.

In this s/he probably deludes himself; s/he may end up losing it all. The rulers may tactfully, even patiently, listen to the technical-professional jargon, waiting for what they are interested in—the action consequences. They will be willing to accept high loads of professionalism and technicalities, not only verbally, but also support it with private or public funding. But the condition is that the action consequences, the operational part, can be formulated within the discourse the rulers are used to, and be made compatible with the policy implications they have already drawn inside that discourse. The rulers prefer lapdog to topdog intellectuals, who deliver premises for their already formulated conclusions. If this is not the case they will be quick to talk about "excessive professionalism," "ivory tower intellectuals," "people trying to meddle in politics, pretending to be experts in their own disciplines." Seasoned and secure rulers will test the discourse along its edges, in terms of its consequences.

Only inexperienced, naive rulers who have not (yet) learned how this game is played will become repressive. The real rulers flatter the intellectual, support him, but also let him understand not only the rules of the game, but who controls the rule making—the rulers, of course. And the professional intellectual may find himself with one more book on his publication list, possibly having brought about a discourse change in academe. The populist intellectual may not even have that to his credit.

PROFESSIONALISM AND POPULISM

Saying that the strategies of populism and professionalism have their limits is not the same as saying that they never work. A personal experience may be useful. Galtung launched the term "structural violence" in 1969,[9] and it has been interesting to watch the trajectory of this term in geographical and disciplinary space. "Structural violence" stands not only for inequality, inequity, and injustice, but also for repression and exploitation, and for any mechanism built into the structure that impedes basic needs satisfaction and human development, including the violence of too little structure, anarchy.[10] The structure substitutes for the repressive actor, keeping people down with automaticity—no harm intended. The term itself, "structural violence," has a technical tinge to it and can be linked to a general discourse about violence.[11] And it opens also for the horizontal variety, the kind of violence suffered by all human beings by virtue of being members of a social structure, such as having to interact with others, and, as mentioned, for the non-structure.

On the other hand, the term "structural violence" to many no doubt also carries a heavy load of moralism and emotionalism. It is an effort to open for a broader discourse about highly moral and political themes than that carried by the direct, intended violence of concrete social actors who, often designated as "evil," exonerate the structure by focusing all attention on them. As such it is resisted by the backers of status quo as mixing too many things together, as being political values couched in social science terminology. That allegation may be correct, but also applies to other terms such as "freedom" and "justice."

Others, more change oriented, may see the term as a liberating device not only for speech, but also for thought and action. If structures are violent, then maybe they have to be changed, like violent actors. Rather than "evil," a moral category closely linked to intent, structures are "bad" or "inadequate," like slavery and colonialism. Because the term has had a certain success, mainly outside academic circles in its short career so far, it may serve as an example of combining moralist populism and technical professionalism as one approach to discourse expansion.

Take seriously the problems as experienced by common people, making of their concerns the cornerstones of professional philosophical and social science discourses! Thus, most women on earth, repressed/exploited by men, will grasp the essence of structural violence by linking it to patriarchy as an example, and from there contemplate other manifestations. And many men will fear exactly this and mobilize preventive, intellectual resistance.

EMOTIONAL/COGNITIVE INTERFACES

Let us now discuss this issue at a more general level, less in terms of a struggle for power, pitting discourse controllers against discourse rebels, who relish deconstructing old and constructing new discourses. The resistance to discourse expansion can also be discussed using a simple distinction between *emotional resistance* and *cognitive resistance*. The emotional resistance is rooted in emotional unease, discomfort. Taboo areas have been touched, and this is always painful. The carrier of a new discourse may sound "crazy," as out of order as the discourse s/he tries to convey. How could anybody in her or his proper state of mind speak such nonsense as "combining capitalism and socialism?" A gap opens up, a fault-line in one's own favorite intellectual construction. If not clearly perceived, a dull pain is at least felt somewhere at the margin of consciousness. The reaction would, predictably, be emotional, and directed against the source of the pain, the discourse rebel.

Having said this it is clear that the step from emotional to cognitive resistance, and from emotional to cognitive unease, is a short one. The complaint: "I do not understand what you are talking about" most likely is another way of saying "I do not like what you are talking about." The hope would be that the uncomfortable can be written off cognitively, ignored as erratic, wrong, as something to be ruled out and marginalized as only a fad, passing into the oblivion it richly deserves, and so forth. Much intellectual debate is little but the rationalization of unease.

COGNITIVE COMPLEXITY

There are other cognitive problems, however. Resistance to discourse expansion may not be rooted in values and interests and emotions at all, but simply be resistance to a discourse that is too complex and hence too difficult to comprehend. And resistance to a new discourse may arise precisely because it is cognitively too new. In speaking the new Word an act of Genesis (in the sense of the gospel according to John, not in the sense of the first book of the Old Testament) is taking place. The border between much and too much has been passed, coming on top of all the old words that are still there. Curiosity is an unevenly distributed commodity in this world. Deficit in curiosity is abundant; true, generous curiosity is a scarce commodity.

In principle everybody may be in favor of broader and deeper discourses. In practice there is a limit to how much our poor minds can accommodate. In our experience a (2x2x2) discourse is, as mentioned, a very good tool for thought, narrow in having only dichotomies, yet broadened and deep in being based on three dimensions, and not too complex. An 8-point discourse is one most people should be able to handle; it is close to the magical number for maximum cognitive complexity often cited by psychologists: seven.[12]

DISCOURSE SUPERIORITY

Another source of anxiety is the fear of becoming persuaded that the other side in fact has a more adequate discourse that accommodates new and important problems lurking in the individual and collective subconscious. And even worse would be the suspicion that the other discourse, in addition to serving the twin function of reflecting new realities and accommodating new thoughts, also accommodates one's own discourse; being both broader and deeper, providing at least one more important point and one more important dimension. The struggle for discourse control becomes like gladiators fighting with intellectual frameworks as nets, trying to catch each other, like in the wave-particle controversy. "Anything you can speak I can speak better" would be one expression, meaning by "better" precisely what was said above: "anything you can speak I can also speak, but not vice versa." Discourse superiority, in short.

Nobody, and particularly not intellectuals, like to be caught, cornered, capable of articulating nothing that cannot be expressed better in somebody else's discourse. The intellectual would prefer the two alternatives, to catch others in a corner of their own discourse, or a symmetric dialogue between partly overlapping discourses (a condition for communication), with no subsumption of one above the other. This is a major reason why the struggle over terms in seminars and research conferences is never only over terminology, but also over power relations, aiming at discourse superiority.

Such confrontations are bound to become emotional, and the dominant discourse may buy some survival time by pretending to ignore the challenge. Academic standing derives more from ability to frame the problems than to solve them. There is much at stake: will my way of framing the problem, or yours, prevail? This is certainly at the heart of many debates found in academe and equally certainly not limited to this setting.

The more careful intellectual strategist may stake out a less confrontational course, sticking to the official discourse. S/he may not want to be marginalized by launching new dimensions of old problems, or totally new issues. On the contrary, pride may be taken in trying to show that they are wrong on their own terms. The careful one may not succeed in that, as the other side, here assumed to be the rulers, may be better prepared and better at discourse control. There may be success, however, in not being too marginalized as the rulers are less threatened by a disagreement within their discourse than by debates across discourse divides. Discourse agreement is more important than proposition agreement.

The "Star Wars" debate, or non-debate, is a good example here. Seeing Star Wars as S.O.I ("strategic offensive initiative) has two important consequences: marginalization from the official discourse and the substitution of a moral/political discourse for a professional/technical one. Operating within S.D.I discourse marginalization is avoided, but with two grave consequences: helping Star Wars researchers by pointing out flaws in their exercise and missing what the whole exercise may involve.

DISCOURSE SHARING

In the reaction against complexity in the United States there is a democratic, or at least populist, element. The extent to which a technical discourse can serve as a public discourse is limited. In a democracy at least some key discourses have to be broadly shared. In principle *education* should be a discourse-expanding experience. The flip side of that statement, however, would be that the uneducated are less able to expand discourses, less trained in accommodating more than two points and more than one dimension. The good old dichotomy, and only one of them, will do: "Are you for us, or against us?" for instance, or "are you part of the problem or of the solution?" The apparently popular PC (politically correct) movement may be yet another way of stifling debates. The uneducated are numerous, produced and reproduced by such discourse-poor mass media as U.S. television channels and newspapers for third-grade comprehension levels.

This is particularly true in a country ridden by processes that make alphabetization reversible; functional illiteracy coming back in again with increasing distance from schooling, and decreasing functional need for literacy in push-button societies based on oralacy (oral competence) and picturacy (visual competence) rather than literacy (letter competence).

The basic point is not how many people are educated and how many are not, but the level of mutual respect. Populism among the educated has as its consequence a low level of popular respect for the highly educated. "Talk so that common people understand you!" becomes a dominant norm, meaning "stick to the discourse I know!" The educated rather than the uneducated should adjust, as can be seen by studying any U.S. presidential campaign. The presidential debate in France in May 1981 demonstrated the opposite, with Mitterrand and Giscard d'Estaing talking a French shared by very few. Not much populism there; it was a rich discourse when made public on TV. Was this too high a price in terms of the social costs?

PAROCHIALISM

Added to that, in the field of foreign affairs, would come a certain level of parochialism in the United States. A country may be so big that it becomes isolated from the outside, simply not knowing what issues are being debated, and how they are "cut" abroad. Discourses in other countries do not penetrate; the country becomes dangerously self-sufficient in discourse production and consumption. In Europe, where countries are very densely packed together, with many and highly permeable borders, this is less the case. There is discourse seepage, discourse osmosis. Other countries' discourses will be deconstructed and reconstructed with great eagerness. There will even be considerable international reaction, penetration, and participation in the process, particularly if it takes place in such discourse setting countries as England, Germany, or France, because it matters to all neighbors how each frames the problems. One factor in the United States, but only one, is the lack of knowledge of foreign languages, making people less open to other ways of dividing the conceptual pies.

EMPIRICISM

Still another problem generating resistance to discourse expansion is linked to the relative prominence given to *empiricism, criticism,* and *constructivism* as modes of thought, speech, and action.[13] The more empiricist the general mode, the more difficult to change discourses that have served well so far to accommodate existing data, meaning empirical as opposed to potential reality. The only legitimate road to discourse transformation would pass, as already indicated, through new data that cannot be accommodated. The approach has to be empirically guided and inspired; theoretical or ideological approaches alone are insufficient. Any point made has to be documented, demonstrated, with reference to the empirical world. Not so for the critical and constructivist approaches, confronting data with values and values with theories in a potential reality nobody has seen, felt, or touched; rather unconvincing for pragmatic, empirically minded U.S.-ians!

FEAR OF CONTRADICTIONS

Still another source of cognitive unease would be located in the fear of contradictions. There may be contradictions between habits one has grown accustomed to and a new term riding on top of a new discourse wave, such as "sexual harassment." And there may be contradictions at higher levels of complexity with many terms coming together, creating cognitive systems with bewildering, partly shocking instances of cognitive dissonance, such as the economic and military discourses indicated above. The fear that the dissonance may not be resolved causes cognitive resistance and blocks efforts to expand the discourse further. "How can the USA defend its economic interests abroad if we should have only short-range weapons systems" was the reaction of a cadet at the U.S. Air Force Academy in Colorado Springs to a lecture by Galtung on "defensive, non-provocative defense." The answer, "by having only those economic interests abroad you do not have to defend militarily," was far outside his discourse. The contradiction was not resolved; the new discourse was probably successfully rejected.

COGNITIVE OVERLOAD AND DISSONANCE

A true intellectual could counter that both problems are intellectual delights. To the problem of *cognitive overload* he would respond: "here I am, a specialist in classification, making typologies, simplifying by telling you which is the limited number of key classes of elements, of points, you have to pay attention to." To the problem of *cognitive dissonance* the intellectual would respond: "here I am, a specialist in interpretation, pointing out that terms often are ambiguous and that the ambiguity can be removed once you distinguish between this and that meaning of the same term. All of a sudden you will find yourself in a cognitively more friendly environment." To the problem of contradictions that look highly untractable the intellectual may respond: "here I am, I am telling you this is contradictory not because anybody has said anything wise, but simply because an error has been committed somewhere on the way, and I'll identify the error for you." Or: "there is contradiction; why not enjoy it and let it work inside you?" The condition, however, is delight at intellectual craftsmanship, a scarce commodity. Others will not easily submit to them; nor should they. This is hardly a general approach.

ANTI-INTELLECTUALISM

Moreover, isn't it precisely this intellectual inclination to say "you have a problem, let me resolve it for you," that has led to skepticism against intellectuals, and not only in the United States? Intellectuals are seen as people taking others for a verbal ride, being too poor to initiate any real ride themselves. All they have to offer is an intellectual ride during which they will play games with people until people wake up to discover that they have become somebody else's intellectual slave. This might lead to anti-intellectualism in general, and anti-theoretical attitudes in particular. Neither of these syndromes would make the person receptive to discourse expansion. Rather, the order of the day would be to stick to issues as they are conceived of by "regular" (note the double meaning) folks, not by eggheads.

CULTURAL, NOT CLASS DIVERSITY

Added to this comes a particular characteristic of the composition of the U.S. population: diversity in cultural background, from all corners of the world, and right now decreasingly from Europe and increasingly from Asia and Latin America; but less diverse in class background, immigrants usually being of working- and lower-class origins. The multi-cultural background would stimulate a search for a simple, least common denominator discourse that could work across the board; the working- and lower-class origin would be a factor favoring uncomplicated discourses in the name of populism and democracy. Any effort toward discourse expansion might privilege some cultural groups and social classes, and hence drive wedges in the population. Such efforts appeal more to those with a middle- or upper-class educational background. The net result would be in the direction indicated: a tendency to stick to the simplistic, avoiding the complicated, but also the fruitfully complex that might lead to new politics. This, in short, is the lowest common denominator approach.

SELF-REINFORCING DISCOURSES

The self-fulfilling prophecy built into this resistance to discourse expansion is clearly seen from what has been said. A discourse is a social contract not only about present speech practices, but also about those in the future. Built into a discourse contract is the guarantee that nothing new and potentially unpleasant will be spoken because it cannot be spoken, possibly not even be thought. Empiricism adds an intellectual mode that gives loud voice to the past because of the prominence given to data as arbiter of reality. If the discourse accommodates only old practices, and the data are about these practices, then we are obviously in a situation of circular causation. The discourse limits speech to that which already *is*; and that which already is limits the speech. And speech limits both thought and action.

In this setting prediction becomes possible because social invariances become exactly that, invariances. In an invariant, frozen social structure, why change discourse? The system is self-reinforcing because predictions are self-fulfilling and vice versa. There is no way of breaking out of the discourse except by bulldozing it down with new dimensions carried by heavy values, supported by equally heavy social forces—in short, a crisis, which may or may not precede a comprehensive discourse crisis.

Wouldn't this be the case with mainstream economics? Their strategy is interesting: letting externalities (side-effects) like pollution-depletion into the discourse, but only on the condition that they, literally speaking, pay their way; by monetizing the effects and losing their specific quality.[14]

In conclusion, a summary of the thirteen factors indicated above:

Marginalizing the intellectuals	particularly U.S.
Intellectual populism	particularly U.S.
Intellectual professionalism	general
Professionalism and populism	general
Emotional/cognitive interfaces	general
Cognitive complexity	general
Discourse superiority	general
Discourse sharing	particularly U.S.
Parochialism	particularly U.S.
Fear of contradictions	general
Cognitive overload and dissonance	general
Cultural, not class diversity	particularly U.S.
Self-reinforcing discourses	general

Only five of the thirteen factors postulated are seen as particularly prevalent in the United States: populism, nationally shared discourses across cultural and class borders (less across gender and generation, as they are presumably settled in the family, and race that is either seen as irrelevant or insurmountable), and parochialism, all of this at the same time as the potential source of renewal, the intellectuals, are marginalized. The U.S. five might serve to overcome the lethargy brought about by the other eight. Yet with both intellectuals and the external world decoupled from mainstream society, and cultural discourse differences leveled, the sources of new agenda setting would be women, the young and the non-white. For all three this will be an uphill battle.

CONCLUSION

One source of renewal of U.S. discourse is to elect a new president, as pointed out under the heading of intellectual populism above. The only problem is that to be elected he probably has to operate within the old discourse; and to make a difference he has to launch a new discourse. Gorbachev did exactly that, using the expression "New Thinking" for what actually was "new discourse." The question is whether the United States can produce a Gorbachev, a teacher of the nation.[15] Some, certainly not all (see the conclusion), of a U.S. *Glasnost* will have to come from above; not from opposition movements, and not from highly ineffective, alienated intellectuals tucked away in campuses across the country.

If we now see discourse renewal as essential for social renewal, and discourse renewal in the United States as to a large extent dependent on president renewal, we actually have one more argument in favor of single-term presidents, if renewal is wanted.

It is interesting to see President Clinton in this perspective. After the twelve Reagan-Bush years he introduced some discourses reflecting socio-economic differences within the United States, the approach to health being one example. There was a feeling that real problems of the United States were being discussed. However, the reaction to this change of discourse was more negative than positive, the discourse crust being solid, the resistance to discourse expansion easily mobilized. In came the Gingrich Republicans of November 1994, Reaganism without Reagan, and for that reason possibly more genuine, solid. And Clinton moved from the political center to the right, closer to U.S. fundamentalism; away from the dispossessed and underprivileged, into the upper-middle classes.

NOTES

1. The classical text is Russell Jacoby, *The Last Intellectuals, American Culture in the Age of Academe* (New York: Basic Books, 1987).
2. This, incidentally, is a major source of error when intellectuals from abroad try to come to grips with the United States of America. Their encounter is with the intellectual ghetto, C or D version, campus (as visiting scholar) and/or discipline (giving a paper at conference). S/he is well received, even lionized, and listens to brilliant analyses, also of U.S. society, by people from U.S. society. But it is not for U.S. society, only for a very special subsociety with weak linkages to the real thing.
3. See note 3 in the Introduction.
4. Thus, the word "expert" almost invariably stands for a narrowness impermissible and counterproductive in a world at our level of complexity, and above all interconnectedness.
5. This was the rule the brutal Chinese "cultural revolution" tried to end, as indicated by the answers one can get by asking, for each act of brutality, "who were the perpetrators" and "who were the victims."
6. And gradually also dominate academe through the imposition of the TV image as intellectual styles. The remark by President Traina of Clark University in Massachusetts is very perceptive: "Television has also had a profound effect. . . . The students are accustomed to being entertained. They are not accustomed to sustained analysis and attention. They don't read well. They

don't write well." They do, however, have a visual acuity that Traina sometimes envies: "But visual literacy cannot supplant reading and writing. Both remain essential intellectual tools." From "Presidents See Their Roles as Unique and Essential" (*Sunday Telegram*, Worcester, MA, April 2, 1995).

7. And there is no reason to assume that academe is immune to such tendencies.

8. The standard way of submitting was through the quotation introducing a paper, to one of the Big Four (Marx, Engels, Lenin, Stalin) and/or one of the locals (Mao, Ceausescu, Honecker, etc.); like European intellectuals not a long time ago starting with a Bible quote (and U.S. intellectuals a de Tocqueville quote or one from the first generation of presidents and *The Federalist*, not to mention an incredible number of Lewis Carroll quotes) and Muslim intellectuals a general invocation to Alla'h the Compassionate and Merciful.

9. Johan Galtung, "Violence, Peace and Peace Research," *Journal of Peace Research*, VI, 3, 1969, pp. 167-191, in *Essays in Peace Research*, vol I (Copenhagen: Ejlers, 1975), pp. 109-134.

10. Horizontal structural violence is developed in Johan Galtung, *On the Social Costs of Modernization*, Discussion Paper No. 61, Geneva, UNRISD, 1995.

11. Thus, structural violence is obviously both a cause and a frequent consequence of direct violence. Structural violence may lead to direct revolutionary violence to demolish that structure (or, at least, to get out of it); and direct violence may be used to establish structures that are violent.

12. Coming out of the cognitive overload research tradition of J. Milner.

13. See Johan Galtung, *Methodology and Ideology* (Copenhagen: Ejlers, 1977), chapter 2.

14. How to handle the externalities is the basic theme of Johan Galtung, *Economics in Another Key* (Cambridge: Polity Press, 1997); for a shorter version see Chapter I, 3 in *Peace By Peaceful Means* (London, Thousand Oaks, New Delhi: Sage, 1996).

15. The archetype remains Franklin D. Roosevelt and his Hyde Park talks.

7

Discourse and Meta-Discourse

COMPARING META-DISCOURSES

So far we have discussed discourses as if they can be chosen relatively freely. There may be resistance to their introduction in any speech community, whether the intention is political speech or not; and, when introduced, resistance to their expansion—the themes explored in preceding chapters. But the assumption has more or less been that the free individual is able to construct, at least for himself or herself, a broader and deeper discourse, increasingly adequate, even if he is not able to impress, imprint, or engrave it on the minds of others.

The point to be made in this chapter is that *no such free individuals exist*. We are all steered by the discourses behind the discourses behind the discourses and so on, including the steering of how we construct and deconstruct discourses. But acquaintance with these meta-discourses of the first, second, and subsequent orders, and the ability to recognize them (as usual first in others, then perhaps in ourselves), should in principle increase our ability to liberate ourselves. Consciousness of the factors operating upon ourselves is a necessary if not sufficient condition for that liberation; usually insufficient for the simple reason that the factors may be stronger than we are. But efforts to become more free, including more consciousness of those factors, may also make us stronger.

A *meta-discourse* is based on assumptions that are even better hidden, but also more shared. What is shared with many, even most, in the same culture is not easily seen. It becomes natural, normal, located at the level of cosmology[1] rather than ideology.

The ideological nature of assumptions underlying a discourse can often be unmasked using our knowledge of interest groups and valuegroups. But what if these interests and values are deep down in the collectively shared subconscious, even shared by ourselves?

That question, of course, leads to another question: Which collectivity? Humankind? Problematic: who among us would be able to step outside all of humankind, seeing clearly the shared human assumptions? Although we do not claim it is impossible, it is obviously much easier to do so across the usual human divides or fault-lines.

There are essentially six such human divides: gender, generation, race, class, nation, and country, with nations expressed in terms of language, religion, and culture in general. And now the task becomes easier. Men may agree with women that men have a number of assumptions in common, and vice versa. The same agreement may emerge across generation groups, classes, nations, and countries, but across racial groups more easily when gender, age, class, and nation are shared. Race alone is not a very salient dimension, but together with such other divides as gender or class it certainly is. Not only can we communicate across these divides, between Self and Other, but we can also imagine ourselves as Other. In the case of generation, class, and nation we may even move[2] and become Other. But if Self is *homo sapiens*, where is the Other with whom we can communicate, empathize, even cohabit, or switch identities? The most common, and very different, answers—animals and god(s)—are both deeply unsatisfactory. The messages we receive are ambiguous and far from intersubjectively communicable.

So we are led to the study of the meta-discourses shared by gender, generation, class, national, and country groups. Following Gilligan,[3] men's moral reasoning derives, literally speaking, from compatibility with higher, meaning more general, principles (such as Kant's *Maxime deines Willens*, or Kohlberg's highest stage[4]), whereas the moral reasoning of women is based more on immediate human compassion. Two meta-discourses can easily be constructed even on this meager basis. Thus, the shape of the male discourse should be deductive, reasoning from first principles, and female discourse inductive and compassionate. Among males, their meta-discourse would pass as unnoticed as the other meta-discourse among females. Comparative studies of the meta-discourses are important if we want more insight into differences in human communication.

But even more important is what happens when males and females communicate about moral issues, both driven by different meta-discourses. Obvious barriers to communication will arise. Male statements will be seen as cold, devoid of emotion, wrapped up in unnecessary problems of logical coherence; female statements will be seen as emotional, teary, jumping to conclusions, "intuitive" at best.[5] In a situation where discrepant, even incompatible discourses compete, power may enter to define the final outcome according to the principle of the ruling discourse being the discourse of the ruling gender. The ruling gender will enjoy the luxury of continuity between private and public discourse. The subjugated group is condemned to the schizophrenia of the double discourse, one for the public realm, one for private purposes.[6]

Or: the ruling group is condemned to the monotony of the single discourse, whereas the subjugated group becomes bicultural, equipped with at least two tongues, like people in the peripheries of empires or caste/class systems, mastering two idioms, imbued with diversity. In other words, well prepared for world leadership roles in the future, Japanese and Germans would be knowledgeable about U.S. discourse in addition to their own. But the United States would continue being only knowledgeable about themselves.

This leads us to three conclusions for the comparative study of discourses:

1. Discourses can and should be compared by comparing genders, generations, classes, countries, and not only nations (language, religion, culture);
2. But studying relations, not only differences between groups with different discourses, opens for analysis of power relations, including discourse power;
3. And comparisons of relations between different types of groups open for a rich analysis of the web of structures of power relations.

So we get an image of humankind as a nation of nations, each one equipped with its own idiom, separated by differences, and then connected by relations, some of them symmetric (I learn your idiom, you learn mine, and/or we meet in a third idiom), most of them not. Some sets of groups are complementary, together making up humankind with everybody being a member of one group *or* the other, like the genders, the generations, the classes, the nations, the countries. Other sets of groups are supplementary, with people being members of one gender, one generation, one class, one nation, *and* one country. Sociologists refer to that as a status-set.

In both cases discourses can be compared and power relations explored: not only how do women relate to men, but how do they relate to old people, or lower-class people to a specific nation. Such relations, like the two just mentioned, can then be compared.

The field is rich. For the exploration and comparison of meta-discourses let us now focus on nations, as there is a clear agenda involved: language, religion, cosmology in general, and epistemology in particular. In doing so we are also implicitly looking at countries, as they are either uni- or multi-national, the latter being the most frequent.[7]

THE LANGUAGE META-DISCOURSE

Obviously, the *language* of a nation (or of a class, a generation, or a gender group for that matter) is a rather powerful shared set of assumptions; even if some differences are seen as dialects rather than languages. The Indo-European languages have built into them an extremely powerful syntactic framework, referred to above as the *subject, predicate,* and (at times) *object,* or SPO-syndrome.[8] *Somebody* does *something* to *somebody/something.* The focus on a subject that acts, in other words on an actor, will lead to assumptions about the intention and capability of the actor. Subject and predicate are syntactically linked, intention-capability being the nature of the link. What was done may be good or bad in its consequences, but lurking behind or underneath there may also be benign or malign intentions. As the subject demands a predicate, or the predicate a subject for a sentence to be formed, a linkage has to spoken between the two.

A surprising number of consequences flow from this rather simple and general meta-discourse. Let us spell out some of them.

As just mentioned, the SPO-syndrome cries out for completion. A corpse and a smoking gun give us two thirds of the story, PO; a name tag still has to be pinned to a subject. It is not enough that an object to which damage has been done has been identified; nor that a predicate, an act, the way it was done, also has been identified, even to the point of being objectively demonstrated. A story is simply incomplete without subject, predicate, and object. It is not enough to report that damage is being done, in other words object-oriented news. As argued in chapter 2, Irangate was not a "story" for a long time. Clearly something strange was happening, but who did it, and how? Hence no story, not for lack of a smoking gun, but for lack of the subject who pulled the trigger.

This minimum grammar taken out of the grammar of Indo-European languages directs its minimum syntax. A discourse has to respect that powerful meta-discourse; otherwise no story has been told.

Example: U.S. cars have been perceived to be not as good as Japanese cars. But that is only the object side of the story. Where is the subject? Who is responsible, with names and telephone numbers? Thousands of managers more interested in money deals than in engineering, in the finance economy rather than real economy; and tens of thousands of workers gradually transformed by a de-industrializing economy from skilled to junk workers, all "guilty" in the sense of performing a job (car-manufacturing) poorly, does not add up to a story. That constitutes, at most, social science.

The meta-discourse directs the attention to an unlimited number of *persons*, not to a limited number of *categories* of people. Only persons act, not categories, nor does nature, a reason why the environment goes underreported. The object side may deteriorate the way objects do, meaning "objectively." But the meta-discourse does not capture that phenomenon if there is no adequate subjective side to the story. Consequently, the suffering of categories and nature may pass unnoticed, until it is too late. It is easy to fire and replace an inadequate person, but not so easy to replace a whole category. It is easy to convey the suffering of one subject in an SPO-story, even if the verb has to be in the passive mode ("she was killed"). With both sides categories or nature, such as in structural violence by and to people and/or nature, there is no SPO story, and what to do about it certainly goes beyond replacing persons. The imaginative journalist can pick one SPO-triad as a case study, but that is far from the total story.

According to this type of thinking, languages less dominated by the need to complete the SPO-triad should be more able to report without reference to two actors, the subject and the object. This should open for the non-intended, the process with no clear subject, the structural, even for the constant, the non-moving. We find some Japanese newspapers devoting as much space to that kind of material, meaning articles-essays-analyses-background rather than events, as U.S. papers devote to advertising. But this is a field badly in need of empirical research. It should also apply to Chinese media, as it did during maoism, but then as propaganda.

THE RELIGION META-DISCOURSE

This cultural point could then be developed further in several directions. To pick up one point immediately: underlying the cognitive discourse captured in subject-predicate-object terms there is often a moral discourse in terms of good-evil, right-wrong, innocent-guilty. As argued above intention-capability links the predicate-object to the subject brought into focus. The result is a manichean division between good and evil subjects. Imagine then an additional dividing line, introducing another dichotomy in all subjects, the most obvious being once again those big dividers of humanity: gender, generation, race, class, nation, and country. Multiply any one of them with the good-evil distinction and all is set not only for a manichean discourse, but for a polarized view of the world with easily identifiable groups, usually two, spanning the moral universe from good to evil. Armageddon is on the horizon.

    If the speaker/writer belongs to the good group a third step is introduced, a Self versus Other discourse. That particular meta-discourse is always around the corner for anybody in the Occident informed by the three big occidental or Semitic religions, Judaism, Christianity, and Islam, with their strong emphasis on the divides. More particularly, all of these religions have at their core a transcendental (as opposed to immanent) concept of God as above, even residing outside the planet. The fourth stage is very close: Self as chosen gender, generation, race, class, nation (people), and country, chosen by that transcendental God. Other is the unchosen, even rejected group, and we get manicheism as global discourse.

    Combine Self-Other with good-bad and there are in principle four things to be said. But nationalist reporting is eloquently silent on the bad aspects of Self and the good aspects of Other; even more so in mega-national, civilizational discourses. The nationalist meta-discourse, derived from religion, settles that automatically, and so do sexist, ageist, racist, classist, and chauvinist discourses.

THE EPISTEMOLOGY META-DISCOURSE

We could now go still one step further and look at the *general epistemology* of a whole civilization or macro-culture, in other words delve into the deep code of that culture.[9] The ideology of a newspaper or group of newspapers certainly directs the discourses constructed in those media. But ideologies will by definition divide people inside the culture, for instance according to class and nation (cultural group). The epistemology does not divide. It unites, being among the deep assumptions all groups within a macro-culture will have in common; the basic assumptions in a culture underlying what constitutes valid knowledge. In other words, it is even a meta-meta-discourse.

One way of analyzing these assumptions would be in terms of *intellectual style*.[10] Thus, atomistic, deductive reasoning in the Occident would direct the attention towards detailed description of many elements in any "situation" rather than a more holistic effort to catch the situation as a whole. The focus would be on *sets* and *categories*, for instance of people, rather than on *structures*. The West is very good at details, not at patterns.

Even if theory does not generally belong in the meta-discourse for news some short deductive chains might sometimes be in order.[11] And deductive theorizing is in the epistemological meta-discourse just as much as atomism. But a reference to "dialectical struggles of opposites" inside those foci of attention would be out of place. Not being mainstream occidental it would sound "ideological."

On the other hand, one could imagine an oriental discourse focusing on holistic and dialectical approaches. This is perhaps what was attempted in China in its more marxist-oriented period, combining age-old oriental (daoist, buddhist) traditions with one occidental discourse, marxism, which also has some inclinations in that direction.[12] Out of that came "maoist" discourses that sounded strange to Westerners, about contradictions in connection with walking tractors. The word "contradiction," as "dialectics" being associated with marxism in the West vis-à-vis the link to ancient Chinese philosophy was not understood, and this was all perceived as way-out leftist talk. And thus the West cuts itself off.

In general the atomistic-deductive intellectual style, Aristotle-Bacon-Descartes, is so deeply ingrained in Westerners, and through them probably in the vast majority of media consumers, that any departure would meet with enormous resistance. As meta-discourse it would direct attention to fine details in the description of actors and other units of discourse, focusing on similarities and differences, but being relatively blind to the relations among the units. The style will be rich in adjectives for subjects, but poor in adjectives for relations between them. There will be endless reporting on *how* less developed countries are poorer than the more developed, but silence on relations rather than differences among them, rather crucial to understanding why.[13]

THE NEWS META-DISCOURSE

An important consequence of this, indeed a synergistic combination of the language and the epistemology meta-discourses, is the news meta-discourse. From the epistemology comes the atomistic focus on sets rather than structures, and on differences rather than relations. And any language with an SPO-syndrome at its core forces upon us a meta-discourse that is *actor-oriented* as opposed to, for instance, *structure-oriented*. But within that general framework, defining the units of discourse as actors, there is a sub-discourse for news where something more specific is said about the actors chosen for the processing of events into news.

Ideally they should be elite actors rather than ordinary, "elite" being interpreted in two ways; as "elite persons" and as "elite nations." In other words, news will tend to be biased towards elite persons from elite countries/nations, particularly towards top politicians from super-powers or hegemonial powers generally.

It goes without saying that what has happened to the object should be negative, particularly in a culture based on the idea of progress, presumably because the negative then stands out as contrary to the normal, hence worth reporting. In a similar vein the action has to be sudden, discontinuous. The subject has to do something new to the object, beyond the structure grinding out behavior as usual. In other words, it has to be *news*, not *olds*.

We could add more dimensions to this meta-discourse. But the basic point has been made: there is a *news meta-discourse* that directs our attention not only to stories satisfying the general grammar for actor-oriented stories, but introduces the additional requirement that actors should preferably be elites from elite nations, and that negative and sudden actions are preferred to positive and repetitive ones. Only events are news; processes only when discontinuous; permanent conditions never—a heavy meta-discourse.[14]

From this point on a theory of news can be developed based on the two simple principles of *additivity* and *complementarity*. The additivity principle informs us that the better these criteria are satisfied the higher the likelihood that the event will end up as news. And the complementarity principle informs us that if the event is deficient on one or more criteria then it has to compensate by being particularly satisfactory on the others.

The implication is distortion. The additivity principle makes it very difficult for non-elites from non-elite countries or nations to enter the news unless something negative, sudden, or extraordinary has happened. And the complementarity principle adds the consideration that it must be *very* negative and sudden, meaning a heavy emphasis on natural catastrophes, plane or train accidents, *coups d'état*, or political instability in general. Very negative images of how inhuman life is in lower classes and nations and countries, in our heavily vertical social and world orders, are created and reinforced. On the other hand, elite people from elite countries become news with the birth of a baby. This makes them look more human.

In other words, the news meta-discourse is very strong. And the outcome, easily observed, is to be expected: a general, quite uniform news culture around the world, reporting the same events the same way; a news culture steered by a shared meta-discourse.

But if that is the case the meta-discourse should not only operate inside the minds of the news-mediators, the media, and the news-consumers, the readers-listeners-viewers. The meta-discourse should also be a part of the subconscious of the news producers. Just as well as the terrorist would know how to get into the news, the state terrorist would know how to stay outside. The terrorist is guaranteed entry by focusing the violence on elite persons, particularly from elite countries; the state terrorist might prefer killing small people, for example, the organizers of peasants and workers and demonstrations of people fighting exploitation and repression. The terrorist would prefer the sudden attack; the state terrorist the protracted conflict, even with "low intensity" (LIC) that becomes a habit of the mind, with no increment sufficient to catch the attention of the media. This is interactive, not only reactive. The meta-discourse spins a tie, a bond between producer, mediator, and consumer. They are all parts of the same dialectic, and usually unknowingly so, as the meta-discourse is in the collective subconscious rather than in the individual conscious.

News and religion meta-discourses together produce a joint meta-discourse highly present in the U.S. media. Events are seen through the prism of "what does the event mean for us (meaning U.S.)," rather than "what does it mean where it happened."

For or against; anti-American or not. The distant, highly non-elite, depersonalized without individual faces, enduring becomes news, nonetheless, if some kind of relevance to the United States can be imputed to the events; for example, through such badly understood prisms as "fundamentalism" (where are the fundamentalist consumerists? The fundamentalist believers in Mannon, or in Oil? The fundamentalist economists? The reaganites?). Thus, it is interesting to compare U.S. (e.g., CNN) and Japanese (e.g., NHK) newscasts (both available to the authors when in Hawai'i); the latter being much better at reporting events as they matter to the people directly involved (*an sich*), not only to the United States (*für mich*).[15]

Let us now explore this news discourse a little further, bringing in other authors, adding (and subtracting?) to the theory.

Teun A. van Dijk of the University of Amsterdam, a well-known specialist on news discourse, puts it this way:[16]

> An account of news production in terms of the well-known "news value" criteria, first proposed by Galtung & Ruge in 1965[17] may now be complemented with a theory of social cognitions of journalists. These socio-political and cultural representations, shared by journalists as a group, influence the so-called "models" journalists construct of (news) events. An interdisciplinary discourse analysis of news, featuring such a social cognition component, enables us to specify in detail how these models influence the actual production (and understanding) of both source texts and news reports.

In addition to the atomistic focus on lists of news value criteria, a holistic focus on the total representation should be possible, based on studies of journalists and their world images. Among the twelve criteria for newsworthiness two of them were actually more holistic: F4 focused on "meaningfulness" and F5 on "consonance," in other words on contexts for the news item.[18]

Two authors have investigated the security discourse in general, and the nuclear discourse in particular, in this perspective. Glenn Hook[19] states the issue very clearly:

> I have chosen to examine the political role euphemisms and especially metaphors play in shaping the security discourse, for I believe the constitution of the verbal reality of the security discourse is both a product and an expression of political power, whether consciously or unconsciously exercised. To what extent the language of the security discourse highlights, shades or obfuscates aspects of reality is thus a political question.

The examples are many and very well chosen, both of euphemisms and of metaphors. And Carol Cohn makes the same point very forcefully in her now classic article:[20]

> I believe that feminists, and others who seek a more just and peaceful world, have a dual task before us—a deconstructive project and a reconstructive project that are intimately linked. Our deconstructive task requires close attention to, and the dismantling of, technostrategic discourse. The dominant voice of militarized masculinity and decontextualized rationality speaks so loudly in our culture, it will remain difficult for any other voices to be heard until that voice loses some of its power to define what we hear and how we name the world—until that voice is delegitimated. Our reconstructive task is a task of creating compelling alternative

visions of possible futures, a task of recognizing and developing alternative conceptions of rationality, a task of creating rich and imaginative alternative voices-diverse voices whose conversations with each other will invent those futures.

Let us then have a little look at news, discourse, and economy. Youichi Ito, in "The Changing Trade Winds: A Shift From an Information Importer to an Information Exporter"[21] documents in admirable detail the transition from importer to exporter, and then presents the general finding:

At present, however, there are only three countries in the world where the media coverage of Japan is less than the Japanese media coverage of them. They are the United States, the Soviet Union and China. The coverage of Japan in the rest of the world is either about the same as or more than the Japanese media coverage of them.

He has some interesting comments on the type of imports:

The programs featuring American domestic life, human relations and humor disappeared at an early stage. The programs featuring war, crime and violence remain. For this reason some Westerners living in Japan believe that the Japanese public sees the West through a prism of violence and sex. It is felt that inappropriate images are likely to be formed about the West and its people.

Ito makes the point that Japan imports from the West "high quality culture" and "violence and sex"; in-between categories are not successful (like *Readers Digest*, "Dallas").

The problem with Ito's article comes the moment he switches from data to theory. He constructs an image of "the so-called "cultural imperialism," "media imperialism," and "dependency" theories. According to these theories, the world consists of a "center" (economically advanced capitalist exploiting countries) and a "periphery" or "satellite" (the economic and political exploitee). Then there is "the second approach explaining the international flow of information (which) consists of many small theories and hypotheses and there is no comprehensive, systematic theory" (with the last point there is no argument). There is an abundance of trivialities, such as explaining the news flow in terms of geographical proximity and the presence or not of news agencies.

Ito then adds: "there seems to be an assumption that the positions of center and periphery are not interchangeable. They seem to assume that center and periphery will remain static forever." Ito would be hard pressed to find anybody who uses "center" and "periphery" as analytical categories entertaining such a stupid view.

The marxists use theories of uneven development to explain how a country can get an edge over another.

And non-marxists would talk about rank disequilibrium, equilibration of rank profiles, and mobility in the world system, up and down, from periphery to center and vice versa. Japan has moved from marginal (Tokugawa) to regional center (Meiji, Taisho) to world center (Showa, the Pacific War period 1931-45) to latent center in the early occupation period to regional center and then to world center again, this time with economic rather than military aggression. That this makes Japan more newsworthy, to the point of becoming a net information exporter is precisely what we would expect, and not the sensation Ito seems to make of it.

With increasing status more is written abroad, but what is written? Ito has no analysis of the quality of information about Japan. One impression, with no content analysis backing, is that there are two basic types of information about Japan: about Japan's phenomenal rise in economic power, including analysis of why and how; and about the vulnerable aspects of Japan's status, including to what extent markets are closed/open, corruption, the bubble economy.

Whereas the former looks like positive information, the latter is negative, even Japan-bashing; but Ito seems to be concerned only with the "how much," not the "what" of information. The negative information about Japan, often misleading, should be seen in the light of Japan's former status as a non-elite nation, in other words as a lag phenomenon, and in terms of conflicts accompanying rapid upward mobility. The news meta-script translates the elite status of Japan into positive news, and the periphery status (relative to the United States, Russia, and China) into negative news.

But, as Ito rightly points out, to become a net information exporter there is also the strategy of limiting imports. His cultural "competition theory" focuses on Japanese cultural identity:

> It was suggested that the cultural identity problem consisted of three elements, i.e., weakness in the "competitive sector of culture," lack of things to be proud of, and continuity between past and present . . . it was suggested that the cultural imperialism, media imperialism, and dependency theories explained neither Japan's change nor the situation in East Asia.

To the contrary, it shows precisely the strength of these approaches. What Ito shows is how a country can successfully fight against cultural and media imperialism through a strategy of cultural self-reliance, being proud of its own past and by constructing bridges between past, present, and future:

It was shown how this phenomenon, especially the retreat of Western popular cultural products is now occurring throughout East Asia. It was suggested that the major factors which reduced the share of foreign cultural products were: (a) strengthening of the mass media infrastructure including the advertising industry, and (b) the existence of cultural peculiarity that functions as a barrier against foreign cultural products.

Precisely. That is exactly what media and cultural self-reliance are about. Ito has successfully delivered one of the strongest arguments for the theory he thinks he has refuted, possibly because he never took the trouble to understand it. Consequently there is much to learn from Japan in this field when East Asian countries also want to overcome the overabundance of information import from Japan. In that connection it might be worth noting how Japan handles information import: take the best from the West, the high culture, and then take the negative (violence and sex) to preserve a positive Self-Other gradient.

THE "TWO-NESS" META-DISCOURSE

The notion of the dichotomy as a thought form steering our thinking has appeared quite often. Let us refer to this tendency to pick out two items and two sides in any situation as the *"two-ness" meta-discourse*. There have to be two sides, neither less nor more. A statement is "either true or false." *Tertium non datur.*

Of course, the predilection for two-ness is not universal. In very repressive societies we may talk about one-ness: there is only one side to an issue, the prescribed side. Regardless of what is said about two-ness below, it is definitely preferable to one-ness.

In Japan we might equally legitimately talk about a "three-ness," the third category being a combination of maybe, both-and, neither-nor. Subjects and objects may still be present in the discourse, just as in the West. But what is said is more vague, at least to the Western ear used to definitive truth-value certificates.

The underlying occidental idea that something can be predicated, or not, of a subject and with certainty would be less dominant. Maybe it can, but then also maybe it cannot. Maybe it both can and cannot; maybe it neither can nor cannot. Maybe any combination or none of the above. One might even have a feeling that Japanese discourses are operating according to a *maybe* "one-ness" meta-discourse; that no statement may be true, or maybe false for that matter (and that is final!, the saying has it). Maybe.

In the same vein we might talk of a "three-ness" discourse emerging in Europe, West and East, North and South, and in the Third World with the wave of green parties and green politics.

The old dichotomies, market versus plan or capitalism versus socialism with "blue" versus "red" parties yields to a trichotomy with a third, "green" pole rejecting both (national, transnational) markets and plans in favor of local solutions to problems of production-distribution-consumption. Whether that "three-ness" will really emerge remains to be seen, particularly with the regression to "one-ness," capitalism only, after the collapse of the socialist economies in Eastern Europe and the Soviet Union. Moreover, the ecologism has been co-opted by the traditional parties, meaning that a more threatening, deeper discourse has been marginalized.

And this, of course, immediately leads to the suspicion of a possible "four-ness" meta-discourse, building on the "three-ness" discourse just mentioned, including the both-and, favoring both market and plan at the same time typical of the Japanese economy— as argued in the preceding chapter.

Buddhists, with their predilection for multiples of four (as in the Noble Truths and the Eightfold Path), and Chinese with their "quartet" as a major construction, would probably be more inclined to look for four than for two elements. Again, this should be a fascinating field for communication research, and problematic given the contemporary strength of Western meta-discourses as a veil, a maya (in the Hindu sense). The basic point is that "two-ness" is not a general human meta-discourse, but is basically occidental.

To see this issue as a meta-discourse rather than in terms of discourse expansion theory the following graph may be useful (Figure 7.1).

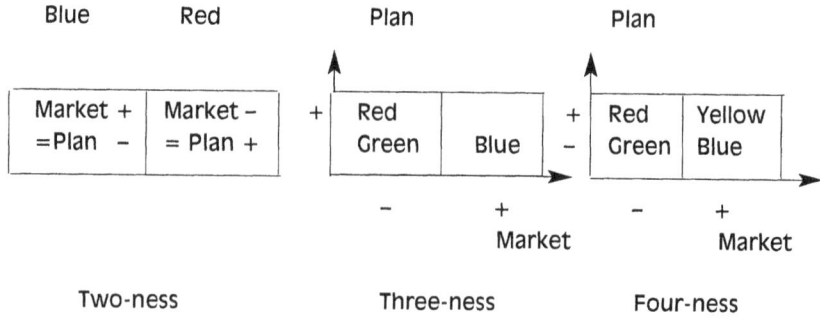

Figure 7.1. Two-ness, three-ness, and four-ness

The point here, transcending the corresponding point made in the preceding chapter, is the point of departure in the meta-discourse. If the meta-discourse is two-ness, then the first solution is adequate to the meta-discourse, and the search for a more adequate discourse stops. A predilection for three-ness would predispose for the second possibility, and a predilection for four-ness for the third.

It should be noted that four-ness is compatible with one-ness, both of them being seen here as essentially Japanese. Given the logic of four-ness a question such as "Is capitalism good?" or "Is socialism good?" can only be answered combining "yes," "no," "both good and bad," and "neither good nor bad." "Maybe" has been seen as a short-hand for these four answers combined. In this light a Japanese saying "maybe" sounds more like a person knowing that his/her meta-discourse is very different from Western two-ness anyhow, and gives up in advance spelling it all out, than like somebody too confused to be able to operate completely inside Western logic, held by Westerners to be universal, civilized, modern; in fact, held to be the only logic worthy of that name.

U.S. TWO-NESS: AN EXPLORATION

We would tend to see two-ness as a particularly important meta-discourse underlying the United States political discourse, and start with an example. A professor of political science at a "university of excellence" declared on one occasion:

> A basic task of a professor is not to confuse his lectern with a pulpit. The professor shall give facts, discursive analyses, not preach values. I myself am proud that my students do not even know whether I am Democrat or Republican.

The naiveté of the statement is hardly lost on anybody. For one thing, there are always values hidden in facts, not to mention facts hidden in values, actually a basic theme of this whole book. Nothing can be pronounced except within a discourse. This goes for "facts" as well as for "values."

But in addition to his rather general facts versus values point, which smacks of naive positivism, there is the even more naive reference to Democrats/Republicans, as if that exhausts the political universe. One reason why students may not be able to guess may be precisely that for them, being younger, that discourse does not exhaust the universe. Those two discourse atoms are only in there together, in some corner of a vast political discourse molecule; like

CocaCola and PepsiCola, often undistinguishable when the etiquettes are invisible. The professor did not pronounce the Word on the label. But then, who cares? The idea of a two-party system is itself an example of two-ness; the reality being closer to one-and-a-half party (even the term "party" may be a misnomer for political action committees), or to one-ness, the U.S. party; the general WASP-dominated party with two, three factions.

Why should the United States be particularly susceptible to two-ness as a meta-discourse? Americans may not be aware of this themselves, because a meta-discourse lies deeper and is more visible to outsiders than to the holders of that discourse themselves. Here, in quick succession, are five non-exclusive efforts to answer the question *why*.

1. *The social factor.* All across the United States one hears: "she or he can see both sides of an issue," or "there must be a winner *and* a loser, like in sports; this is the American way." As mentioned repeatedly in this book, this is considerably better than seeing only one side, in fact 100 percent better. But to see three sides, four sides, five sides is not only better but indispensable, in a complex world where issues have to be cut in complex ways to be understood at all, and particularly to be thought about creatively and even acted upon.[22]

The ability to break out of the prison of the false dichotomy is important, but more difficult: two-ness is a preferred meta-discourse also because of general resistance to discourse expansion (two is the minimum). Low level of really functional education, combined with diversity in cultural but not in class background, would direct attention down to the basics in a search for the lowest common denominator. And basics can best be expressed in terms of binary logic, without unnecessary elaboration. "Two-ness" becomes a meeting ground, internalized into all young U.S. citizens at school in the perennial true-false tests, which is what multiple-choice tests, epitomized in the ubiquitous Standard Achievement Test (SAT) boils down to; mapping each item on a dichotomy.

2. *The legal factor.* Added to this there are many other two-ness roots present in U.S. culture. A nation addicted to litigation[23] will have to buy into the legal paradigm in which the dichotomy of right/wrong in any kind of legal process plays a considerable role. Was O. J. Simpson guilty or not? The judge may pay allegiance to three-ness, beyond the *tertium non datur* of guilty/not guilty, in letting doubts have an impact in assessing punishment, damages, and so forth. But for people in general, guilty/not guilty is the basic dichotomy, as a secular reproduction of the sacred order of the universe.

3. *The party system factor*: The ubiquitous U.S. two-party system is, of course, as mentioned, a major exemplar of U.S. two-ness; partly a consequence of a deeper lying inclination in that direction, partly a factor reinforcing two-ness by training people to think in political dichotomies. The difficulties launching a third party in the United States should not only be seen as due only to the power of an existing and entrenched two-party system, but also to the role of two-ness in general. It is a theological position, not a conjunctural, political expedient. A mind imbued with two-ness surveys the political landscape, sees two parties, and feels confirmed. Anything beyond that is a nuisance. As a result the United States deprives itself of the chance of having third parties articulate in public space new issues that may be taken up by the two parties and be acted upon. A third party does not have to be in power to be politically effective; it may change the nation's agenda simply by being there, like the German Greens.[24]

4. *The theological factor*: Many reasons can be adduced for the two-ness position. Do not propositions come as true and false? Do we not generally use a distinction between good and evil? Do we not talk in terms of right and wrong, sacred and profane, beautiful and ugly? Did the Creator not make us into two genders? Do human bodies not have an undeniable symmetry in right and left? In other words, do we not see the figure 2 written clearly and loudly all over the place?
And if we do, who are we to change the script of the universe, even engraved on reality by the Creator himself? Why should it not also be engraved on our minds as the correct reading of God-created reality? Particularly in the most Christian nation on earth, the United States of America, with God and Satan embodying good and evil, spanning not only the conceptual but the real universe, making sense of up and down, heaven and hell, at the root of it all the only two alternatives.[25]

5. *The historical factor*: Some special reasons can be added to this in the case of the United States. The people who arrived first, the Founding Fathers, were very moralistic in their discourse, with highly explicit and precise opinions as to what is good and what is evil, not hesitant in prescribing the right action in order to promote the good, nor in proscribing the wrong action that would not only promote the evil, but in itself be evil. The simplicity of their black and white world view has been kept alive into our days, given a solid recent reinforcement by the absolutism of the 40th and 43rd, and to some extent also the 41st, presidents of the United States, Reagan, George Bush senior and George W. Bush.[26]

Precisely because those who came first were relatively undifferentiated to start with, White Anglo-Saxon Protestants often of puritan stock, the dichotomy of Self versus Other, "other" meaning "wilderness" (divided into savages, beasts, and wild nature, all to be either tamed or exterminated), laid the basis for today's strong division of the world, with enemies all over. The two-ness prevailed from early on.[27]

Let us then add up these five factors. Take a U.S. child; expose him and her to thousands of tests with myriads of dichotomous choices. Teach him and her about "the two sides to an issue," with the best of intentions, identifying two-ness with objectivity. Let the courtroom enter the living room, vividly portrayed in video and on *Court TV*, leading up to a verdict in highly dichotomous terms, then serving as a model for the general human drama. Choose between two parties only. Celebrate manichean thought in the Judeo-Christian idiom in countless places of worship. And finally, give a stark portrayal of U.S. history as the triumph of good over evil, as a long succession of battles never lost, at least not until very recently (Korea, Viêt Nam, Teheran). What do we get? U.S. two-ness of course, and well internalized.

We get a people who sees the world in terms of capitalism *or* socialism, democracy *or* dictatorship. And when, in that split-second of the eternity of history called 1989, socialism and dictatorship both crumbled in Eastern Europe nothing short of "the end of history" is declared by somebody[28] and even taken seriously, causing debates about a non-issue all over.

With only two alternatives on the economic and political dimensions and only one alternative left, no more change is possible, hence no more history. Two-ness at work, in a sense the only history that could happen in a dichotomous world with *tertium non datur*. It had to happen sooner or later, and the only possibilities were the victory of good over evil, or vice versa. The latter did not happen, so let us celebrate the former. Only a nation brought up on a diet of two-ness could fall so deeply for this message, and also be so surprised when history very quickly proved to have a couple of more things up its sleeve.

On the other hand, the election campaign of Fall 1992 brought in (and out, and then in again) a third candidate, Ross Perot, who managed to get 19 percent of the votes cast. Did Ross Perot teach Americans to count to three? There were elements of triangular debates, not only on television, but also in the population. A basic media concern was, predictably, to whose advantage of the Big Two the Perot factor would work (as Ralph Nader's smaller following also helped George W. Bush in the 2001 elections), and for whom he would recommend votes to be cast, whom he would endorse (when he was out). In other words, highly predictable ways of reducing the discourse down to two again, preserving the two-ness as meta-discourse.

Did many people feel uneasy, not only because he was tinkering with the political game between the Big Two, but because thinking in triangular terms was unfamiliar? The participation in the election was not that much higher, so if there was an uneasiness somewhere it was probably canceled by others who were tired by the old parties and mobilized by a new possibility.

It may take some time before this deep challenge to a sacred numeral is repeated. (Nader did not enjoy the commanding following that Perot did.) Moreover, the party system is a reflection of certain aspects of U.S. political ideology. The parties took shape before a working-class movement, and that movement never managed to get off the ground the way it did in Europe with social democratic, socialist, and communist parties of respectable size. A certain span is reflected in the U.S. system of (zero, one, one-and-a-half, two) parties, but not enough to articulate new images of the good society, as sometimes done by the green parties. Of course there is an upper limit to the number N of parties, but $N = 2$ is too low.

NOTES

1. For definitions and an introduction to cosmology analysis, see Johan Galtung, *Peace by Peaceful Means* (London, Thousand Oaks, New Delhi: Sage, 1996), part IV; "Civilization Theory," particularly chapter 2.
2. The processes are known as aging, social mobility, and migration, respectively.
3. Carol Gilligan, *In a Different Voice, Psychological Theory and Women's Development* (Cambridge, MA: Harvard University Press, 1982).
4. Kohlberg has also fallen for the idea that "universalizability" somehow constitutes a basis for a higher level of ethical orientation. Problem: there is no difficulty in universalizing capital punishment (which Kant favored), defensive warfare and offensive warfare; they all express human inclinations and state logic. Imagine that a Gandhi wants to break out of those vicious circles. In a world with so much institutionalized violence he would have to do so on the basis of some particularism (in his case readings of ancient Hindu texts), maybe hoping that at some later stage in human development norms may have changed so that what was not universalizable could be.
5. Paul Borthwick's famous book *But You Don't Understand What I Am Saying* (Nashville, TN: Oliver Nelson, 1991, rev. ed.) offers a

rich variety of examples that to a large extent are variations on this theme.

6. Thus, the hypothesis would be that women much more than men will engage in switching, the same way this was discussed as a way of coping with censorship in socialist countries in Eastern Europe in chapter 1. But then who would say that the occupation metaphor does not to a large extent apply to the situation of women living in a patriarchy?

7. Approximate numbers: 2,000 nations, 200 countries and 20 nation-states, meaning uni-national countries.

8. See Johan Galtung and Fumiko Nishimura, "Structure, Culture and Languages," *Social Science Information*, XXII, 1983, 6, pp. 895-925.

9. *Peace by Peaceful Means*, part IV, chapter 2.

10. See Johan Galtung, *Methodology and Development* (Copenhagen: Ejlers, 1988), chapter 1.

11. An example would be the classical syllogism *barbara*: "All democracies are peaceful; the United States is a democracy; hence, the United States is peaceful." Premises and conclusions are all debatable, to say the least, but the syllogism as a meta-discourse is impeccable. An interesting example is: "Human beings eat stones; stones are bread; hence, human beings eat bread." The conclusion is O.K., but the premises less than debatable. How much human reasoning, including in the media, is of that type? Even if the truth of the premises do not follow from the truth of the conclusion, many people may believe this to be the case, or, rather, the meta-discourse gives an air of plausibility to the premises.

12. Marx' dialectics supposedly comes from Hegel, and Hegel seems to have learned much from Leibniz' *Denkweise der Chinesen*.

13. Hence, the surface difference between a marxist and a liberal perspective reflects a deep culture difference between two epistemologies: holistic-dialectical and atomistic-deductive. However, a Western marxist is usually not that conscious of the deeper origins of the complex of ideas and may give up the deep structure if the surface ideology suffers a defeat. And a Western liberal may try to co-opt some marxist ideas without understanding the roots, and hence learn very little.

14. For an example of a newspaper that consistently breaks with this meta-script, see the Japanese newspaper *Seikyo Shimbun*, the paper of the Sokka Gakkai. International news are found toward the end of the paper, the front pages have reports with happy endings from common people in their daily struggles, but then also positive dialogues, featuring the president (very much an elite person) with world leaders.

15. Thus, during the Gulf war Japan's NHK seems to have had much more coverage of the damage to civilians wrought by U.S. "smart" weapons than the U.S. media, presumably not because Japan sympathized with Iraq, but because of the "what does it mean where it happened" aspect.

16. In *Discourse Analysis and News Analysis*, paper prepared for the Vrije Universiteit, Amsterdam, workshop 27 April 1988, p. 1. For a detailed exposition of van Dijk's position see his "Discourse Analysis: Its Development and Application to the Structure of News," *Journal of Communication*, 1983, 33, 2, pp. 20-43.

17. Actually 1962, as a working paper, based on work done in 1961. The famous study by the Institute for Communication Research of Stanford University and the Institut Français de Presse of the University of Paris, on the flow of news among thirteen countries was conducted in 1961; Schramm's book about the flow of news is from 1964; see pp. 60-63 for major findings and interpretation.

18. These two hypotheses were tested in an interesting way by Jan Kleinnijenhuis (*Structure of Discourse and Selection of News*, Vrije Universiteit, Amsterdam, 27 April 1988) with the conclusion "that the NET-method for discourse analysis looks useful to investigate news selection hypotheses. The substantial conclusion should be that Johan Galtung's early news selection hypotheses F4 and F5 are supported strongly by empirical evidence. To a large extent the selection of news is dependent upon structural characteristics of the discourse already presented" (p. 6).

19. Glenn D. Hook, *Militarism and Demilitarization in Contemporary Japan* (New York: Routledge, 1996).

20. "Sex and Death in the Rational World of Defense Intellectuals," *Signs: Journal of Women in Culture and Society*, 1987, 12, 4, pp. 687-718. The quote is from pp. 717f.

21. Youichi Ito, The trade wind change; Japan's shift from an information exporter; 1965–1985. In J. A. Anderson (Ed.), *Communication Yearbook* 1990 (pp. 430–465).

22. As mentioned in Chapter 2: try to analyze Bosnia with only two parties!

23. The conflict analysis/mediation/resolution movement is an interesting reaction to litigation, in recent years, no doubt also stimulated by the honoraria commanded by the legal profession.

24. But then other parties will be highly selective, picking the environmental agenda, but not nonviolence, citizen participation, and so forth.

25. It is worth noting that Hinduism works with three deities and three principles (Creator, Destroyer, and Protector); Buddhism with zero, as there is neither God nor Satan.

26. Less so for the 42nd president, the highly malleable William Jefferson Clinton; not necessarily a bad characteristic for a top politician.
27. For one elaboration of this theme, see Johan Galtung, *US Foreign Policy as Manifest Theology* (IGCC, San Diego: University of California Press, 1987).
28. Francis Fukuyama in the book of that title; certainly more Francis (occidental) than Fukuyama (oriental). Francis Fukuyama, (1992). *The End of History and the Last Man*. New York: Free Press.

Script and Meta-Script

The discourse theory developed in the preceding chapters, even with the theory of meta-discourses, at best tells half the story, but a very important half—the vessel shaping the script/story, but not the script/story itself. In other words, it is still a very incomplete discourse about discourse. To make this point clear a comparison must be made with scientific inquiry in general.

To do even the simplest type of research a paradigm is needed, an intellectual framework generating hypotheses within that paradigm, as a discourse generates speech in general. In the preceding four chapters we have explored discourses about discourses, now to be seen as only half the story about discourse.

On the one hand there are the units of analysis through which something is being said or "predicated"; on the other hand the predicates, concepts, variables, dimensions, classifications. The researcher proceeds, knowingly or not (if in the humanities and one half of the social sciences, usually not knowingly; if in the natural sciences and the more mathematically literate half of the social sciences, consciously and conscientiously) constructing cartesian spaces, locating the units, after more or less careful observation, in those spaces. And location = predication.

But then s/he does something more. At some point in classical physics it was decided that time and distance and not color and shape or aesthetic qualities were key variables in connection with moving objects (or non-moving objects when seen as special cases of moving objects). Let us say that cartesian spaces were constructed with time and space coordinates as paradigm pillars, for location.

The physicist, however, did not remain content with saying: "time and distance are important." S/he starts telling a story. What s/he says is simply this: some points in cartesian space of time x distance are included, and others are excluded. The included points together constitute a regularity, an invariance, a natural "law." Galilei even offered a parabolic formula for the law: $s = 1/2gt^2$. In other words, he has a script, a narrative, a story. And the falling object is doomed to enact that script, nobody asking whether the object likes it or not. A human body falling from *la torre pendente* in Pisa might not like the story at all when quickly approaching the ground. So a corresponding story about a human body is usually told in terms of accident, homicide, anguish, suicide. Intent, feelings are not attributed to stones.

Research progresses, as pointed out in chapter 4, by excluding combinations in cartesian spaces, the natural sciences excluding more, the social sciences less, and the humanities sometimes nothing at all, remaining content with rephrasing conceptual spaces as tautologies they are able to recite. This is like saying drama can be divided into tragedies, comedies, and tragic comedies. Useful, but more interesting when related to something else, like epoch, nationality, class, or personality of the author.

In discourse theory the second half of the story would be this: *uncovering the script*, not only the terms out of which the script is constructed, the discourse, and the rules directing the choice of terms, the meta-discourse. This offers us a very fruitful point of departure because it leads to the obvious question: is there a finite number of basic, archetypal scripts driving us so that we merely hook onto one or several of them, interpreting what we see in terms of those scripts, being driven or ridden by them, searching for that which fits, discarding the rest, and thereby reproducing these basic scripts? And, if the answer is yes or maybe, which scripts? Are they something like the Italian Pinocchio theme, the Jewish David and Goliath, the Japanese story of the 47 *ronin*, the Norwegian Espen Askeladd, only deeper?[1]

If we may be permitted a personal remark: The father of one of the present authors tended to be a divine story teller. The guests at his parties were always roaring with laughter. Well deserved; the stories were superb. He knew how first to present that little joke that people already found hilarious, not knowing that this was but the premonition of the real, the greater joke in which the small one was encapsulated, only ten or fifteen seconds away.

Obviously, he was asked how he did it. And he said to his son: "Very simple. There are essentially only twenty good stories around, the rest are variations. All you have to do is to know those twenty stories, and then spice them with detail to get some good variations." Of course the son asked him if he would be kind enough to share with him those twenty stories. He smiled and said yes, one day he might do exactly that. Unfortunately, he passed away before fulfilling his promise (or, maybe that was one of his stories).

So let us try some scripts of our own. Needless to say, they are stories about stories, not stories. They are meta-scripts.

THE OCCIDENTAL STORY

A rather basic story could be called *the occidental story*. It is fairly open-ended, enough to classify as a meta-script rather than a script. It comes out of analysis of civilizations[2] like a ripe fruit, simply taking some basic assumptions in civilization theory in general, and the theory of Western civilization in particular for granted, writing out the general, abstract code as a story.

We then assume that the Western civilization, like the others, is constructed around certain assumptions about nature, self, society, world, time, transpersonal, and knowledge. Very roughly speaking, in the West these assumptions include the West as the center of the world, surrounded by an applauding periphery. But outside that periphery there is evil, personal and transpersonal, lurking in the corners of the self, society and world spaces, waiting for the right, ripe, moment to unleash its wicked designs.

Some very general assumptions about how time unfolds then serve as raw material for the construction of any story. There was once the Golden Age, then came the Fall, the Dark Ages, then the Illumination, the era of Progress, heading for the Crisis with only two possible outcomes, the triumph of good or the triumph of evil, catharsis or apocalypsis.[3] A highly dramatic story, *the cosmic drama*, and the time span may be short and crisis immanent, unlike, say, "the Hindu story."[4] The Bible of Judaism, Christianity, and Islam, in the Christian version encapsulating human history between Genesis and Revelation, is the archetype.[5] And cosmos is the stage.

To understand and fully appreciate this drama/story the basic assumptions about how occidental knowledge operates, in the meta-discourses from the preceding chapter, are indispensable. Thus, the world can best be understood in terms of dichotomies, and more particularly in terms of such highly value-loaded, manichean dichotomies as good versus evil. Good and evil do not mix. They fight, it is either-or, down to the moral atom, the choice between the purely good and purely evil in the single act of will, the decision. The struggle in the world is between them, projected inside each individual human being.

Against this background people are inserted. They are identifiable as individual actors, structurally unconstrained, driven mainly by their intentions, which in turn may be good or evil, and by their capabilities, which may be strong or weak. The actors may also be countries, states, again classified as good and evil, strong and weak.[6] Whatever the nature of the actor they are detachable, operating like atoms in an inert gas and ranked in terms of power and prestige in a highly vertical way. Verticality and individualism are the two basic themes. Nature does not possess individuality, being essentially desouled; and it is at the bottom of the bottom, or below the bottom, non-human. At most it is a context, neither good nor evil where intentions are concerned, but very often treacherous and threatening and hence to be guarded against, although it may also be weak and pleasant, even enjoyable. A She, from a male point of view (die Natur, la nature); Mother Earth. God is a He; Father Sky, God the Father.

At the end comes the transpersonal, the transcendental, in the West concentrated into one point, a male god with his abode outside the planet; the only one, highly jealous of competitors. He is the author of the script, even the choreographer. But it is up to us to perform well or badly, according to that script. Moreover, he is reputed by some to be dying. But there are successor candidates enacting successor scripts that are very similar, only with some changes in the terminology.

Two such successors are enshrined in the doctrines of liberalism/capitalism and marxism/socialism respectively: the market-corporation and the plan-state. The market script is known, and also known to be enacted by an Invisible Hand, for the benefit of all of us, provided we follow the script as revealed (first by Adam Smith). The plan script is also known as a set of detailed goals and regulations. The hand is no longer invisible, now a velvet glove, now an iron fist, but with the definite message that we follow the script as revealed (first by Karl Marx). The state, also the successor to the King, in turn a descendant of God, is sometimes protecting the market, sometimes presiding over the plan.

Science is also a successor to God, disciplining scientists trying to decode nature's hidden script. So is the nation, the Big Self, the ultimate home. And then there are the new priests: the economists for market and plan, the jurists for the state, the scientists for science, the nationalists for the nation; all of them superb story-tellers and meta-script controllers, with tremendous discourse-power. The sum total is called "modernity."

All these key elements in our civilization mesh and combine so as to produce a meta-meta-script. In the beginning is the actor, and because there are many actors we have to focus on some to the exclusion of others. They should be active rather than passive.[7]

Most fascinating are the actors who, in addition, are strong and evil, as they are threatening the status quo, upsetting it, being trouble makers. But good actors should also enter the story, which otherwise would be incomplete. The passive, weak, good actors enter as victims of the active, evil, and strong actors; and the strong, good ones are then activated to stop, even destroy and eliminate the evil ones. Less interesting are the evil and weak actors, although they have to be watched: one day they may become evil and strong. As nature in the shape of a lion cub—pleasant, cuddly, but potentially dangerous, hence threatening.

General Western assumptions about space and time provide the context for the story to unfold. First, the construction of space allocates the *dramatis personae*. The good actors are in the center and in the center of the periphery. The evil actors are in the extreme periphery of the world, social, and self spaces; in the animal self, in the lower classes of the country, and the lower countries of the world; and beyond, lurking and lurching. They creep out of their holes when unobserved to play their evil games, like germs, microorganisms, criminals, terrorists; all archetypal evil actors. Among their victims are also the good and the weak, the "innocent bystanders" of the terrorist script.[8] And they are the animal Id, hidden in the unconscious. Satan is all over.

The story then unfolds in *time*. The evil forces are the causes of the Fall from paradise and the Dark Ages, the Reign of Evil. The crime has been perpetrated. But then the good forces mobilize. They hit back, preparing for the final battle, the real crisis of "either-us-or-them": Armageddon. The story has a happy ending with us/catharsis and them/apocalypse. This is the story structure found in police dramas, movie Westerns, and science fiction. It is also the narrative news-script media use to enhance drama and construct a captivating, audience-involving "story."

If this is the *general* meta-script, how would a *good* meta-script look? Not all stories are equally good. Four criteria for a good story have been defined above by the news meta-discourse.

There should be something negative, evil. The focus should be on persons, not abstractions like structures, peoples, nations, countries. The reference should be to elite persons, not to people in general, reflecting social verticality. Moreover, the reference should be to events involving elite nations/countries, because that is how verticality operates in world space, and how news are produced, script-driven, by the basic meta-script of Western civilization.

However, there is something more to be said. Thus, the story is only a really good story if there is some tension, a certain suspense, like in a good thriller. For that to happen the ending of the story must not be too obvious. In the long run the good forces will triumph. But between now and then much may happen, and for that story to be really exciting the good and the evil forces have to be if not exactly equal, at least on par with each other.

If the evil forces are too weak there is no longer any story; they are just about to be eliminated. And the same applies if the good forces are too weak; all that is needed or called for is a well-written obituary. It is only with balance of power that the good story emerges; possibly another reason why the West is so fascinated with balance of power as the general rule for the power game. Opposite in intention but equal in capability; pitted in a deadly battle, suspense until the very end—the very good story.

Then there is the subscript, not that grandiose, usually referred to as the "smoking gun" script. The point is very simple: The evil actor is caught red-handed, gun in hand, or at least with the gun still smoking, leaving finger prints and DNA codes. Some kind of legal script enters the news stories, demanding proof that can stand up in court. Actually, the gun is not that essential. There may be other types of "evidence" that are much more important in the culture if the problem is whether the actor really is evil: the way he looks, where he comes from, the nature of the deed, the very fact that he plays a role in the meta-script as depicted above and is not on the side of actors readily identified as good. One reason why the United States could reach no clear conclusion in the O.J. Simpson trial was that the nation could not agree that the ex-football hero had turned evil when once a beloved idol.[9]

This is where prejudice has a free play, appointing in advance the good and the evil. Maybe the smoking gun argument only enters in the cases of extreme dissonance, to sort out the evil in our midst; the Other in Self. The person who by all indicators should be good and nevertheless is suspected of evil has to have a smoking gun solidly glued to him to be classified as evil (O. J. Simpson). For the person who by all indicators is permanently evil, no evidence is needed and/or no questions asked (Saddam Hussein, Osama bin Laden).

As an example of this general occidental meta-script take David and Goliath. There is no apparent balance of power; Goliath is by far superior, David is the underdog. He is good and active, but looks weak. However, David has hidden resources, sufficient to overpower an evil that looks strong but is insufficiently active. Active also means cunning, using brain power maximally, identifying power where others find none. Another condition is goodness, or the good cause, otherwise transcendental powers might not provide back-up power. Result: a very good story made even better, now perfect.

But consider the story from the loser's, Goliath's, point of view. Goliath believes in an orderly world where might is right, with Goliath order supported by Goliath strength. But strength might lead to indolence, making people less innovative and cunning. And that becomes Goliath's undoing. His whole world crumbles, like for Per and Pål, the Norwegian Espen Askeladd's elder brothers, entitled to translate primogeniture into privilege. Espen combines acts of goodness with acts of extreme cunning, compensating for the latter with the former in his moral universe, and from a position of weakness conquers "the princess and half of the kingdom." We relish the fall of the high and mighty, Goliath, Per, and Pål. The United States loves those who fight the high and mighty in the absence of any national campaign to muster support for one side or the other.

What happens once can happen twice. Does David end up as the new Goliath, and Espen Askeladd as the new Per and Pål? Is there a new underdog lurking somewhere to unseat them?[10]

A Japanese meta-script in the shape of an adage enters: When you have won, the situation is really dangerous because you may be resting on your laurels. Consider this TV interview some years ago with the somewhat reticent head of Nomura Securities:

> "How did you manage to become No. 1 on the New York Stock Exchange?"
> "Working hard."
> "And now that you are No. 1, what are you going to do?"
> "Work harder."

In one sense the occident *in extremis*. But the occident has its own moral meta-script, as told, to be repeated any number of times, generating any number of stories with happy endings.

THE AMERICAN STORY

Let us then look at a U.S. subscript of this meta-script. Robert B. Reich, in his book *Tales of a New America*,[11] has concentrated American political culture down to "four tales that have shaped our thinking, and which we (and our leaders) continuously retell: The *Mob at the Gates* (about foreigners), *The Triumphant Individual* (about entrepreneurs and routine workers), *The Benevolent Community* (about the poor), and *The Rot at the Top* (about big government and big business)." Let us stop for a moment and use this to describe and explain the tremendous popularity of the very American story told in the Sylvester Stallone movie *Rambo.*

In *Rambo* there certainly was *The Mob at the Gates*: communists, down there in Southeast Asia; the exact location of the country does not matter much, nor the borders. In addition to communism they kept good U.S. prisoners long after the war was over.[12]

There certainly was *The Triumphant Individual,* Rambo himself, making some order out of the whole mess. He was alone; there was no additional *Benevolent Community* to support him. On the other hand, he was fighting a two-front war; not only against *The Mob at the Gates* but also against *The Rot at the Top,* in the shape of big bureaucracy, and at least equally big military.

In terms of Reich's four dimensions *Rambo* covers only three of the four tales. On the other hand, he scores so well on those three that this in itself explains the popularity of the movie. The movie fits the script, but could fit even better if Rambo did not operate alone but was supported by a community of a handful of brave men without power and prestige, winning through some kind of collective action. But wait, how about the movie audience? Are they not the benevolent community?[13] A score of four out of four!

How does this U.S. subscript fit into the meta-script described above? No problem. There is individualism and there is verticality with a steep gradient from top to bottom. And the strength of the strong individual is underlined by the very fact that he emerges from the bottom. The enemy is also located, beyond the periphery, in that evil wilderness beyond the gates. What is original in the U.S. tale is the idea of *The Rot at the Top,* of evil at the very center of society, a common theme in U.S. movies.[14]

This is a more complex topology than center-periphery-evil. The outside is not only out there, but also up here, to be watched, held accountable, changed as often as necessary, and if necessary fought by courageous individuals located lower down on the gradient. *Self* is infected, not only *Other.* Evil is all over.

The film maker must have had some problem obtaining a balance of power between good and evil when there is essentially only one good person and on the bad side hordes of sleazy bureaucrats and subhuman communists, of whom we only see glimpses, and to make it even worse, in Japanese uniforms from the Pacific War. Answer: one truly righteous person suffices against a myriad of evil. This might look like imbalance to many. But parity in numbers to arrive at balance in the customary sense would equate good people with evil. Message: Quality substitutes for quantity; one real person for hordes.

With the theory of the American story we return to the problem of the dialectic relation between (meta-)script and reality. The general idea is that (meta-)discourses and (meta-)scripts are read into reality. They are part of the formula. Pre-programmed for "two-ness," "the American story," and some other scripts, 80-90 percent of the news stories are written in advance.[15] The good author/speaker will know how to draw a standing ovation—by following the meta-script to produce a reassuring *déjà-vu*, yet introducing that little spicy variation that gives a touch of originality. We have the two parts necessary for a "formulaic story": *convention* and *invention*.[16] The readers/listeners feel comfortable: they actually knew (most of) the story in advance. A totally new story would hardly be recognized as one.

But the theory goes beyond that, into the interactive aspect. If reality fails to provide the features not only predicted but prescribed by the meta-script, then reality has to be refurnished. The Soviet Union evaporates as Evil; the search for a substitute (Muslim fundamentalism, Orthodox aggression by Serbs or Russians, Yellow—Japan, China, Korea—Peril) is on. Reality is then reconstructed through the mechanism of self-fulfilling prophecies.

The meta-script becomes a theory creating the conditions for its own confirmation. Embedded in the collective subconscious, the elaborate procedures undertaken to protect the meta-script against irrelevance and subsequent oblivion are hidden even to its authors. Or, to go one step further, could it be that the insane arms races, even with the extinction of the human race as possible consequence, become meaningful only as an enactment of the occidental story?[17] An important example: the military power of Iraq was grossly exaggerated, here interpreted as a necessary maneuver to create the balance that made the Gulf War victory an enactment of the script.[18]

NON-VERBAL COMMUNICATION

Let us once again expand what has been said about discourse and script in a totally different direction, again indicating that we have told less than half the story. Let us try to leave verbal discourse, written or oral, behind and explore a more comprehensive universe of communication. More particularly, do discourse and meta-discourse, script and meta-script still make sense when we cross the border between verbal and non-verbal? Communication is transmission of meaning, whatever the deeper meaning of meaning.

Communication transmits meaning from sender to receiver via a channel. A simple typology is found in the distinction between nonmediated/(direct) or "immediated" communication and mediated/(indirect) communication.[19]

A first approximation to this distinction is between non-verbal and verbal communication. In verbal communication there is a double translation process, an encoding of some intentionality into words, written or spoken, and then a decoding somewhere in the mind of the receiver aimed at recovering that intentionality, which then may or may not coincide with the original intent. The communication is mediated; the verbal symbols are the medium. Words serve like money in economic transactions: like money stores value, words store meaning and can pass it on along the chain.

Compare that with the immediacy of a slap in the face. A chain of people may be mobilized to pass on the slap, but they may also prefer to pass on a heap of verbal abuse for end consumption. As with money the value/meaning may change along the road.

However, there is more to mediated communication than this. The encoding is not only done by those at the beginning of the communication chain, but by somebody else. There are intermediaries or mediators. If two persons, A and B, talk directly with each other we might refer to it as unmediated communication, adding how they also communicate with their clothes, their body language, tone of voice, and what not. It is the moment an author enters telling what is going on in other places, or a journalist does the same, that we have mediated communication.

Mediation is more than words. What an artist does displaying his painting is no different from what an author does displaying his book. Both of them have invited others to be communicated to; both of them are also communicating, from something outside themselves in addition to, from, or via themselves.

Admittedly, these distinctions are not that sharp, nor do they have to be. They may become more meaningful when subcategories are given. Thus, as major forms of non-mediated communication we would take precisely what economists and politicians so often are talking about, with full justification: the free flow of persons and capital, technology, management, goods and services.[20]

Anybody who travels, ordinary or elite persons, communicates by sheer presence, whether that person is staying for some time or is passing by, for instance as a tourist. Any piece of goods communicates, as does any act of service. A SONY cassette player does not stop communicating the moment it is switched off.[21] Just to mention two dimensions in connection with goods/services: the degree of sophistication or processing built into the product, and the level of utility, positive or negative, to the person communicated to. If satisfactory, the name of the company and the country where it is made are usually prominently displayed to tell any receiver who is the sender of that non-verbal message.

Correspondingly, on the mediated side of the divide: elite versus mass media. Elite media serve as channels for theater, books, and the fine arts of exhibitions; the mass media as channels for movies, newspapers/magazines, radio/TV. The distinction between elite and mass media is not sharp, and we object to the term "mass media" with built-in disregard, even contempt for the receivers.[22] However, the term is too frequently used to be eliminated at this stage. Two-way, reciprocal communication is left out; but that is usually also the case for elite communication.

Of course it is much more difficult to do discourse analysis for non-verbal communication. Take a piece of stock-fish lying on the floor of a grocer's shop in Santiago, Chile, September in 1962, with beautiful Danish tins and cans above, and an elegant Swedish Volvo car parked in front of the shop. What is communicated? If you asked one of the authors, at that time a resident Norwegian, what was communicated was degree of sophistication and that his country, the sender of the fish, was communicating a rather low level of that particular commodity. The Danes were doing better, the Swedes, as usual, much better, regardless of how well the needs of common people were served by the stock-fish, *Bacalao de Noruega.*

But others might have a totally different interpretation. The car could be seen as a gasoline guzzler spewing out life-killing exhaust. The tins might be seen as refined but also artificial, heavily bourgeois in an evil sense, a waste of resources. And the stock-fish might be seen as a genuine product of nature, somewhat stinking, but by that very stinking fact bringing us closer to our origins. The "sophistication" dimension turned upside down, into a "close to nature" or "naturity" dimension, like when some tourist pamphlets are talking about "unspoiled nature" and a society is seen as "undamaged by development."

Of course, from the ambiguity of a non-verbal discourse it does not follow that a verbal discourse is self-revealing. If anything has been communicated in the preceding chapters, then it is precisely that this is not the case. To understand the verbal text we also have to read what is not there, the missing dimensions and categories. But to identify them in their not always equally glaring or eloquent absence the missing dimensions somehow have to be present inside us, the person communicated to, the analysts. Our mental grid, and the mental grid attributed to the text, have to be compared; possible surpluses or deficits have to be noted: surpluses to be learned, deficits in order to start reconstructing.

Consequently, there is a lot of interpretation going on and no immediacy in the attempt to unveil the hidden discourse. The tools of discourse analysis that were developed in chapters 4 and 5 are useful in understanding what works when deconstructing and constructing, but will never do the job alone. The analyst is also driven by meta- and meta-meta-discourses and scripts.

And this is precisely what comes out if different persons compare their analysis: the reliability is probably in general relatively low. Two Dutch researchers have come up with the good idea of analyzing movie music in terms of three parallel running discourses: a *verbal discourse*, the written or spoken text; a *visual discourse*, the movie "as such"; and an *acoustic discourse* consisting mainly of music but also of other noises. They all add up to the *total discourse*, and efforts to analyze that one will generally suffer from rather low intersubjectivity (reliability).[23]

But any interpretation is always somebody's subjective interpretation. Why should it be the same as the interpretations put forward by others; why not admit, even encourage subjectivity, individuality? Maybe it could also be interesting to analyze what kinds of people come up with what kinds of interpretation? Maybe the reliability for that study would be higher?

All we know is that communication is a very multi-dimensional phenomenon. Moreover, any set of signs, as the semiotics people tell us, will have a semantic, a syntactical, and a pragmatic dimension. There will be translations from signs to meaning and vice versa—the semantic aspect. Not all combinations of signs into "texts" are permissible in space or time or both; the syntax will permit some and rule out other combinations. And then there is the effect of the communication—the pragmatic dimension.

With that in mind let us return to what was said above about the use of goods and services in international trade as a way of communicating something about the producer country. The astounding variety of products from the capitalist mode of production makes for an equally astounding richness in communication. Socialist countries missed out on that, perhaps believing that products would only be judged in terms of their usefulness, and not also as a means of judging the country of origin. A country like the former Soviet Union failed to realize fully that people draw their conclusions on the basis of the products. Their oil, gas, and so forth may have been very useful but were also seen as crude, being either commodities or industrial products copied from somewhere else (Leica, Fiat). People may conclude that the country is probably equally undifferentiated and unsophisticated, and generally inclined to imitate and not be genuinely creative. But exactly how this works is *terra incognita*, a promising area for future research.

Of course, we project meta-scripts into such communication precisely because it is non-verbal and we have to fill in the gaps. Where did we last see something unsophisticated, non-creative? Maybe from children, including ourselves? What would stop us from seeing the country as coming up, like a child, showing off some little thing, eagerly watching adult eyes for recognition, the adult knowing the value both of giving and withholding praise? Socialist countries and Third World countries were/are treated as children, and praise is withheld. The meta-script answers: "they asked for it"; they have to enact more advanced trade scripts.

The same can be said about persons, for instance about Japanese tourists. Why do they always come in groups? Why do two males so often check in together at the hotel? Because they are gay? No, possibly because Japanese are more "groupy," more tolerant of being together with others, or less tolerant of being alone, depending on how we look at it. Again there are meta-scripts operating, not only classificatory schemes but whole stories lurking in the minds of the receivers. The sender has to know these scripts to have some idea of what is being communicated. And if the sender wants another message to come true, then some theory about what meta-script to trigger off is indispensable, for example, for socialist/Third world countries as trade partners.

With verbal communication there may be more chances to correct the message, not because words are more precise but because verbal dialogues usually permit more messages back and forth more quickly.

One of the authors once (1958-60) conducted an interview in connection with the school conflict associated with desegregation in Charlottesville, Virginia. One segregationist interviewed became rather skeptical listening to the questions, but he answered. His problem was quite clear; it could be read off his eyes, his eyebrows, his body language: who is this person interviewing me, beyond business cards, introduction, and what not? He, totally justifiably, wanted something concrete, in order to get an answer to his question. And out of him came, very explicitly, when the interview was over: "May I accompany you to your car, I would so much like to see what kind of car you have!" The statement was possibly more honest than intended, but he was bursting with curiosity and suspicion. And he found exactly what he expected to find: the ramshackle $100 old car, with a New York license plate, of an underpaid U.S. assistant professor. Nor can we deny that the car conveyed more meaning, and more valid meaning, to him than the little that had already been communicated verbally. For him the interviewer and his car fitted syntactically very well together, the semantics were clear, and the pragmatics equally so: watch out, busybodies from up North, Yankees with foreign accents trying to intervene in our affairs, not even well settled up there. No doubt his findings were communicated, but the curiosity may have overcome the resistance: the interview study was completed.

Correspondingly, people enter each other's houses expecting to be communicated to from the very moment the door opens. There is the syntax of the "living room"; the syntax of the table, dressed up for a buffet or a dinner; the syntax of the whole house. Terms are put together spatially in a script. Most of us are able to read that script, but possibly unable to translate it in any profound way into verbal language. Yet we can read the script of a menu. We know perfectly well that a sentence like fish-dessert-soup-meat is syntactically wrong. It should be soup-fish-meat-dessert, with absolutely no permutation permitted. It takes some time to learn that special dish order, but that is also the case with other languages.

The living room probably offers more flexibility if for no other reason because it is two-, even three-dimensional, whereas the time order of dishes in a bourgeois dinner is one-dimensional, squeezed into time rather than unfolded in space. A Chinese dinner or the Dim Sum luncheon offers more flexibility, as it is also spells out in space, even on a revolving dish to facilitate access.

Non-verbal communication is a big area only recently opened for research, particularly due to that great French interpreter of signs, Roland Barthes. We shall only link up with the missing theme so often eluded to above, the lack of attention given to degree of processing in products traded. The United States communicates with scrap iron and waste paper, hamburgers and fried chicken, cola-drinks and jeans and Disneyland abroad only at its own considerable risk.

Regardless of reduction of trade deficit it is a semiotic disaster. What is communicated is that U.S. civilization is adolescent; that was also the case for the ex-Soviet Union. Whereas the interpretation for the ex-Soviet Union might have been: "So this is the best they are able to do" (with the true believers adding, just wait, in a couple of years it will all be much better), what the United States communicates is adolescence as the final stage, of arrival, not of departure.

The objection to that interpretation is, of course, that this is but one of many possible readings, or one of many possible scripts read into a selected set of messages. Moreover, the United States also produces highly sophisticated goods, even if not for trade. That is, of course, a valid objection.

But imagine now that many have that interpretation. In that case they will start treating the United States as a child, talking slowly when the leaders are around lest they do not catch verbal messages, expecting little and consequently demanding little. Needless to say, that would have a reinforcing impact, locking the big country into the pattern of the prodigy child that did not make it. And not only because of the nonverbal trade messages; equally much because of the missing verbal messages, the political themes that went unheeded for too long because they were not accommodated in the discourse. The problem is that the child metaphor[24] is very wrong for a country with the U.S. level of creativity, but also with as much potential for violence as the United States. So better be careful, no objection, no critique, yes-yes, as the Japanese often do.

We are here at a borderline of insights in discourse and script. No doubt the non-verbal plays a major role, but how? Does it precede, complement, or come after the verbal discourses have been prepared in the mind of sender and receiver? All three? Which one is dominant, capable of driving out the other, the verbal because it is more reflected (if that is the case) or the non-verbal because it is less reflected? Take the Western bourgeois dining room with a clear message of order in space and time; the seating pattern being according to gender, generation, and class; the serving of the dishes according to the order mentioned; the drinks being the undercurrent of percussion as in a music piece. Nothing random here, a strong message of space and time discipline.

Would we not expect people growing up in that context to demand the same from the way their media are framed? Like orderly editing within and between pages, and stories with some appetizer, working up to a climax, then flattening out in a happy ending. The occidental story supported by the non-verbal meta-script, in short.

As we said in the beginning of this chapter, the discourse is like a vessel waiting to be filled with a script (and the meta-discourse with a meta-script). But how adequate is the discourse to the script, and the script to the subject matter? How about the case when the script is highly metaphorical, and the subject matter highly subjective at the borderline between the conscious and the subconscious known as the preconscious? What happens when we really enter abstract, not sensory representational art? Well, this is what art and literary criticism is about, and perhaps the point where social scientists say farewell.

NOTES

1. The Norwegian Espen Askeladd has two elder, highly mainstream, brothers, and whenever there is a problem they can be trusted to be on the conventional road to personal disaster. Espen, on the other hand, is the one who comforts the old

woman (a princess in disguise, of course) on the way, who picks up that rusty nail that comes so handy when the going is tough. In short, with heart and brain he overcomes the odds against him, and in the end always wins the princess and half of the kingdom.

2. Galtung, *Peace by Peaceful Means*, part IV, chapters 2-5.

3. There is the dramatic oscillation between the flow of time (*khronos*; the Golden Age, the Dark Ages, the Progress) and the *Sternstunden* when time stands still (*kairos*; the Fall, the Illumination, the Crisis); all ending with an ever-flowing *khronos* when the universe is sorted out in the perfectly Good (Paradise) and the perfectly Evil (Inferno). And all of this in the life of humankind, and in the life of the individual human being.

4. After one *kalpa* (4,320,000 years, "a day in the life of Brahma") the universe, the gods, and Brahma are all destroyed (with lesser destruction after the shorter cycles), and everything starts all over again after an upward jump.

5. And this archetype, in turn, is encapsulated in the life of the Christ.

6. A giant in U.S. social science, Charles Osgood of "semantic differential" fame saw these two dimensions and active-passive as basic in framing human perceptions.

7. Osgood again; what Osgood did, in our interpretation, was to uncover the Western meta-script.

8. Not to mention in the "collateral damage" of the state terrorist script.

9. O.J. did not fulfill the criteria for the evil actor in the script; among other things he was "rich and famous" (and good-looking; evidently dressed up in court to exude these three characteristics). Countless blacks had been sentenced, even to death, on the basis of being poor, anonymous, and maybe not so good-looking. The verdict of the basically black jury was (also? mainly?) an act of communication to whitey: *This is in return for all those jury decisions of the past; this is what they taste like.* The jury system will hardly come out of the O.J. case unscathed.

10. Albert Camus once turned this into a moral precept, being in favor of the *Knecht* (the underdog) in his struggle against the *Herr* (the topdog) until the *Knecht* became a new *Herr*; then siding with the new *Knecht*.

11. New York: Random House, 1987.

12. This is a major point in Tom Engelhardt's brilliant *The End of Victory Culture, Cold War America and the Disillusioning of a Generation* (New York: Basic Books, 1995). The United States obviously did not win the war in Viêt Nam, and, knowing only two roles, the victor/winner and the victim/loser, transformed

itself into a victim. With the number of people in Viêt Nam killed this was not easy. The MIA (missing in action) formula provided the answer, focusing on that handful relative to the millions killed. The media obliged, given that their role is to mediate elite views downwards, not the views of the real victims upwards.

13. When Galtung saw the movie in New Jersey in 1987, not far from Princeton University, a U.S. banner unfurled in the end, the national anthem was played, and the audience rose to its feet.

14. Particularly in Frank Capra films such as *Meet John Doe, Mr. Smith Goes to Washington*, and *It's a Wonderful Life*.

15. To the extent this is the case it is not strange if media save money by not sending correspondents abroad: some local color can be taken from other media, and the datelines can be faked easily.

16. What makes modern media story telling so effective is its use of genres. Genres employ formulaic devices, comprised of both conventions (good versus bad) and inventions (frontier as dividing line between civilization and wilderness in television and film western) to make for highly popular stories that are easily recognizable yet have some complexity and originality. See John G. Cawelti, *Adventure, Mystery, and Romance* (Chicago: The University of Chicago Press, 1976).

17. Under the name of the "DMA-syndrome," for Dichotomy-Manicheism-Armageddon, this is seen as a pathological deep culture in search of therapies in *Peace by Peaceful Means*, part IV, chapter 5, pp. 253-274.

18. One factor exaggerated beyond any recognition was the "Republican Guard," probably more a unit combining representation, secret police, and military police functions than that of a real fighting force. One day we may also know to what extent the ABC mass destruction capability was real or merely imputed to them. As was to be expected the media obliged, and years after the end of the Gulf War Iraq is still being labeled the largest military threat in the Middle East.

19. An interesting in-between case is body language, like the "typical gesture of the Italians, kings of hand and body language, known as the 'purse'—the fingers form a pocket to express questioning" (from Emmanuelle Ferrieux, "Hidden Messages: A Different Kind of Babel," *World Press Review*, July 1989, p. 39). The same "words" have highly different meanings: thumb and index finger meeting means "OK" to an American, "zero" to Mediterraneans, "money" to a Japanese and "I will kill you" to a Tunisian. Careful with words, careful with "words" (and fingers).

20. The European Union canonizes four of these as "freedoms": the mobility of labor and capital, goods and services, within the

Union (without, labor is not mobile; only three freedoms apply under WTO). What happened to technology and management (assuming that nature can pass under goods and services)? Their non-free flow is essential for the wealth of rich countries, which charge license fees and transaction costs.

21. We are indebted to Fumiko Nishimura for this observation.

22. The term "mass media" is suspect, and may even be said to stand for nothing, as Danilo Dolci says in the very title of one of his recent books, *La Communicazione di massa non esiste* (L'Argonauta, 1987). Either it is communication, and then people are not considered a "mass," or it is precisely with a "mass" but then it is not communication but propaganda, manipulation, advertising, marketing, public relations, or what not.

23. See Harry van den Berg and Kees van der Veer, *On the Structure and Function of Musical Discourse in Television Documentaries*) (Amsterdam: Vrije Universiteit, 1988, 16pp). Television documentary analysis is divided into verbal, visual, and musical discourses, with the verbal discourse carrying a point of view, the film images functioning as support, contrast, or neutral elements in relation to the verbal discourse, and the musical discourse producing "connotations" (p. 9). These connotations are then analyzed using a method similar to Osgood's semantic differential, with 14 pairs of opposites (from activating/ deactivating via soothing/disquieting to mocking/sincere; p. 10). As expected the inter-subjective reliability is not very high; ". . . as the relatively high level of abstraction contained in the anonymous formulations gives rise to a wide range of differences in interpretation, even among well-trained judges" (p. 12). It is not obvious that high reliability is so important given the subjective nature of music appreciation. The approach is nevertheless interesting and could be related to characteristics of the judges.

24. The classic work about metaphors is, of course, George Lakoff and Mark Johnson, *Metaphors We Live By* (Chicago and London: The University of Chicago Press, 1980). Metaphors are based on some imputed isomorphism: the author/writer tries to convince, or at least to communicate, by switching content, pretending to keep the relations, reasoning inside the metaphor, exiting with a conclusion in the field the metaphor is supposed to map. One way of countering a metaphor is, of course, with a counter-metaphor, not by pointing out that the relation is not isomorphic.

Discourse, Script and the New Technologies

There is a revolution underway, whose scope will exceed that brought about by the invention of printing. This revolution will come about because of the advent of cheap and powerful logical devices. . . . The ice age of thought is thawing, and channels for the flow of minds are opening daily like the geometric emergence of the new branches of a tree. Now is the time to tune in to the current. It will soon be all around you.[1]

The computerization of text implies a further set of changes in mental qualities, in the ways in which we train our memories and process the raw material of knowledge.[2]

What we have to observe next is the first stage of the journey of computer-based information into our culture, which is taking place more publicly in the newspaper industry than in any other area of society. There it is changing the industrial base of a medium that had already been changing its economic and financial base. It is changing the relationships between all the crafts, professions, and management cadres in what is the basic information industry of Western society.[3]

Broadening our concept of telecommunications is especially important today as this country's communication industries enter an unprecedented period of transition. . . . Telephone lines are now connected to television sets in some homes; a few commercial radio stations have broadcast data to computer enthusiasts; movies are beamed into homes by microwave or viewed on videodisc; radio programming reaches the home via cable; many TV sets have become electronic newspapers. An exciting and perplexing wave of new communication technologies and services is breaking over us.[4]

In July, 1962, the United States National Aeronautics and Space Administration (NASA) sent its first communication satellite into space. This Telstar satellite linked the United States and Europe for the pioneering television transmission. Just as with the development of radio and television technologies, military applications again helped bolster advancements in the new communication technology field. Soon to evolve were advances in satellite image, voice and data transmissions, compact computers, and high definition television (HDTV), the latter a central product of the "Star Wars" SDI development program.

The advances in communication technology proved useful in combat and weapons assessment. Whereas military spy planes had been around for decades, satellites now provided clear and accurate surveillance of military targets, weapons sites, and even weather system tracking. Satellite surveillance was utilized in the Falklands invasion and was a central factor in revising nuclear weapons pacts between the United States and the Soviets. It was via the same surveillance imagery that television viewers around the world witnessed the awesome capabilities of cruise missiles, and "smart" bombs were guided to precise targets in the Persian Gulf War after being identified earlier through satellite surveillance techniques.

The same technology also was credited in the United States' efforts to help locate Mikhail Gorbachev during the August 1991 coup attempt. Using spy satellites and telephone intercepts, the United States was able to ascertain where he was being held and stayed abreast of developments in the aborted overthrow. Once again viewers of CNN sat by their television sets and watched the early hours of the military take-over. Thanks to these telecasts, viewers in other portions of the Soviet Union were able to monitor developments in the Russian capitol and mounted a resistance. The policy of glasnost that Gorbachev promoted earlier in his administration had indirectly led to the development of new global communication links that were much more powerful than his military foes could comprehend!

Although the burgeoning technology has had profound effects on the ways in which nations communicate, it also has had a marked influence on the way we lead our daily lives, from modern transportation systems to the many new conveniences found in homes. This includes communication technologies such as facsimiles (faxes), intercontinental fiber optic cable lines, direct broadcast satellites, digitization of voice, data, and images, and computerized graphics. In the future the technology is likely to make media even more complex as we enter into the frontier of virtual reality.

The new technologies have definitely affected the news media, and this, in turn, affects the way the institution operates and the content of the messages it transmits. Specifically the new technologies have increased the speed with which news is gathered and dispersed, which in turn can be viewed as a method to help reduce costs. The danger in this new environment, however, is that news quality also has the potential to be sacrificed.

We believe there is a whole climate of technocratic thought that not only has markedly affected the U.S. media and the way it behaves, but this wave has also influenced the way academe perceives the media and constructs its educational paradigms, particularly those regarding the structure of U.S. communication education.

COMMUNICATION EDUCATION AND ITS TECHNOCRATIC THRUST

Whereas communication studies have been constructed around technologically enhanced communicating since the early part of the 20th century, the technological tools now are more numerous than ever before and may be taking a dominant role in the thrust of instruction. We have one colleague, a senior professor who is highly thought of by many in the industry, who claims that the only resource he and his students will heretofore need for their research activities is the Internet. Such a position skirts issues of information reliability in a virtually unchecked medium that has been likened to the CB radio craze two decades earlier. Even URL addresses are unreliable, with continual movement between servers. With the hardware and software of the Internet now being taxed to its limits, further breakdowns similar to the America On Line (AOL) crash seems immanent, and what does this then do for its credibility in the classroom?

As far back as 1952 a *Le Monde* survey began with the observation: "There are too many half-baked intellectuals and not enough (qualified) technicians."[5] This view is not an isolated one. Jacques Ellul observed that education is becoming too specialized (even in France, he says), creating only individuals who will be technicians with limited perspective. "The intellectual will no longer be a model, a conscience. . . education will no longer be an unpredictable and exciting adventure in human enlightenment, but an exercise in conformity and an apprenticeship to whatever gadgetry is useful in a technical world," he warns.[6]

Just one year after the *Le Monde* survey, writing in a UNESCO report on vocational education, Margaret Mead noted that: "Some education must respond, not to the present but to the future needs of society, it is necessary to forecast constantly and as far as possible in advance the evolution of vocational structures."[7] In reviewing Mead's comments, Ellul concludes that this can only be interpreted as a call for an individual to be "educated and adapted in advance to his future job as a function of anticipated technical progress."[8]

The move toward greater and more narrow-minded technical emphasis has been central to the evolution of communication education. Although writing for U.S. journalism classes used typewriters in the English Departments of the 1920s, and speaking for radio classes began appearing in Speech and Rhetoric programs in the 1930s, one can argue that other nuances of media training were of utmost importance. This was a time when the liberal arts still dominated American higher education, and it was believed that general knowledge was much more important than specific technical skills. There are U.S. television network reporters and executives, major market news-room directors, and so forth, who have nothing more than a good liberal arts education, and they make fine reporters and communication industry professionals. They know more than how to write in inverted pyramid style or how a camera works. They also know how to develop ideas and build literate presentations and even tie isolated facts together. How often have you seen a television news reporter who does not even use appropriate grammar? The star television anchor in Honolulu once read a story on tax reform, then somewhat bewildered, told the audience that he was glad he could read it again after the program ended because he was having difficulty understanding it.[9]

One of the present authors recalls the early 1970s when undergraduate students he taught in one leading U.S. communication program enrolled in an advanced film production class were more enthralled with how to use a synchronous sound camera, a recorder, a flatbed editing table, or the post-production sound studio, than with giving primary attention to the "message" they hoped to deliver through the medium. It took much encouragement to get them to see beyond the technology. And this example is not an isolated one. We have seen it repeated again and again in journalism, radio, television, film, and multimedia classes from then to the present. If anything, the problem has only worsened.

This brings us to a specific question: how is the role of high technology in the media affecting the orientations we bring to communication education today?

Common are the praises for the new technology. One study of journalists and journalism educators reported a general agreement that there will be a "plethora of benefits for students." When exposed to computer-assisted reporting techniques the group agreed that "students will acquire knowledge vital to their future jobs and beneficial to other university courses; develop statistical, analytical and computer-reporting proficiencies; enjoy an improved learning environment; and have a broader perspective of available news sources."[10] This is not to criticize U.S. communication education per se, but rather to isolate those curricula which are heavy on the "skills" course while sacrificing the liberal arts, an approach we believe to be short-sighted and counter-productive.

In some communication curricula, the study of journalism, broadcast, film, and common carrier institutional or social history takes a back seat to more recent mechanical developments and communication devices. Even the topic of cable television, that just 10 to 20 years ago was the sign of a progressive university mass media program, is absent from course catalogues today. Proponents argue that "all media" are now their focus, as the strategies explored apply to one and all, but then we still offer the traditional television production classes and supplement this with "how to do it" multimedia classes that spend the greater part of a semester on home page construction and learning HTML coding. Is media history or social impact a part of these classes? It is usually hard to find even one chapter devoted to it in the required textbooks. Is communication becoming as silent on side effects ("externalities") as economics?

Also lost in glorification of new technology is the discussion of basic communication or aesthetic theory, for the literature on communication technology almost always dwells on technological diffusion and marketing problems rather than the tried and true social science and humanities concerns. When the literature turns to political economy it is most likely to herald current Western thinking on market liberalism and privatization, providing support for transnational corporate policies and the removal of national market entry barriers in the developing world. Books such as the critically interesting *The Second Media Age* by Mark Porter, Theodore Roszak's *The Cult of Information*, and Herbert Schiller's *Information Inequity* are unfortunately outnumbered by the much more mainstream work of the technocrats, for which we have William J. Mitchell's *City of Bits*, Robert K. Heldman's *Future Telecommunications*, Neil Postman's *Technopoly*, John V. Pavlik's *New Media and the Information*

Superhighway, and the classics in the area, Alvin Toffler's *The Third Wave*, and John Naisbitt's *Megatrends*.[11] Technological determinism tends to be the dominant paradigm of our high-tech soothsayers.

Yet, at least some in the field are expressing alarm. We are told that in the newsroom, "many editors are starting to worry that too much emphasis is being placed on the technology and not enough on nurturing the more traditional, basic journalistic skills."[12] To this we would add the lack of true intellectual development in favor of technical training that caters more to fad than meaningful educational theories.

As Clifford Stoll has recently observed:

> I've never seen a memorable computer-generated chart. The speakers who amazed me scribbled their displays by hand, using blackboard or overhead projector. Of course: they knew their subjects, wanted to tell me about them, and could rattle off their main points impromptu. Their ideas carried me along, not their graphics. . . . Fancy backgrounds and multicolor borders pull my eyes away from the text. Special fonts and classy paper emphasize the designer's message. Pullout quotes and insert headlines flash the editor's point of view. (Yet) such eye candy gets in the way of the author's message. It prevents me from searching out fallacies in his logic. The typography dilutes the presentation.[13]

It is this entire culture of pro-technology and technology-makes-it-better that has permeated the communication discipline, and our continued existence as a meaningful academic discipline remains precariously in balance. It is these trends that also may be threatening the pursuit of global communication equity with a two-fold dilemma. First, our Western education systems serve as a model for many in the developing world. We are saying, this is how you teach journalism or mass media or new communication technology. We run the risk that educators in the developing world will want to emulate our programs and techniques. At best this will help stifle the development of intellectual leaders in these communities, and it even may reduce the art of journalism to one designed by heavily commercialized media in the West. Second, we run the risk that this is yet one more step in the imposition of Western thinking and Western ideals upon the world's population. Look at how sterile and one-dimensional our news reporting now is—sensational news from the West, glorification of current economic powers, coverage of developing world news only when it is catastrophic and tends to support already held views of widespread political and social instability among these people. These are likely scenarios if the rest of the world chooses to adopt our models; and they already are, through the U.S. State Department-sponsored journalism training programs in Eastern Europe, the CIA-backed programs for Latin American journalists at Boston University, and via the federally financed and U.S. military-influenced East-West Center, which particularly targets Asian populations with educational programs.

Alternatives would be to design programs on how to use media to enhance peace education, engage in proactive social journalism, or how NGOs might better utilize media to promote individual agendas, among other approaches.

HOW HIGH TECHNOLOGY AFFECTS POLITICAL DISCOURSE: TEN POINTS

Society is changing rapidly. The role of technology as a catalyst for change is undeniable. And with this change come new ways of performing traditional human tasks. The trends in communication education outlined above demonstrate how strong this influence has been on the news media. The questions that remain are how exactly will they change, and to what degree will educational institutions affect this change.

It is hard to dispute the notion that media programming practices may often promote mediocrity. The Lowest Common Denominator concept is said to dictate the design of much U.S. media programming with the emphasis being on providing the least objectionable rather than the most provocative and challenging content. It is the recognition of such a milieu that led FCC Commissioner Newton Minnow to refer to the American Television Industry as a "vast wasteland" in 1961. Many will argue that conditions have not changed markedly since that time, except for the worse.

Our fear is that one consequence of increasingly high-tech newscasting (HTN) will be that the discourse for news will in the future become even poorer than it has been in the past. This is to say that our news discourse is in danger of becoming even less complex and less rich for discourses than it has been. The culprit may be the increasingly complicated technology, which may be inadvertently directing our attention away from information functions even when it appears that it is helping to lead us to an advanced and more highly refined news production process via HTN. Here are some more precise mechanisms, as hypotheses about how complicated technology stands in the way of complex discourses:

1. *An obsession with technology helps shift attention away from the real problems.* As technology becomes more complicated, an increasing portion of the mental energy of the journalist will be spent on handling the technology, and a decreasing portion on content.

During the Vietnam War it took at least 36 hours to get film footage on the air for the major U.S. television networks. The 1966 story of CBS newsman Morley Safer offers a prime example. His report on American Marine torching and leveling of the Vietnamese village of Cam Ne, a village occupied by only women, children, and the elderly—is credited with helping change the way Vietnam was thereafter reported to the American public. Both Safer and CBS had a day and a half to ponder the potential ramifications of the report. The film awaited a flight from Saigon to Tokyo and then on to Los Angeles and New York.[14] Much to the chagrin of President Lyndon Johnson and many other Americans, CBS chose to run the highly emotional story. Today, however, such time delays would be comparatively nonexistent. We saw the new instantaneous journalism during the Persian Gulf War.[15] One of the present authors looked closely at Persian Gulf War reporting:

> With so much time to fill, it made sense to supply live coverage whenever feasible. After all, live, continual coverage was something the competition could not do given the multiplicity of its programming schedule, particularly when the war did not conveniently end within a few days. And it was in crises and disasters such as the Space Shuttle Challenger disaster that CNN had demonstrated the advantages of a twenty-four hour news service in the past. CNN regularly carried live news event coverage as news interest warranted.[16]

Such live reporting lends itself well to the nature of television. Television equipment has become extremely portable and satellite transmission technologies have reduced the costs of sending footage coast to coast as well as around the world.

We witnessed problems when the new technology was first introduced in the television newsroom. In the early 1970s, lightweight cameras in combination with mobile microwave transmitters led to the wide distribution of so-called "mini cam" technology or electronic news gathering (ENG)/electric field production (EFP). The introduction of this new form of television news recording and transmission effectively made the film camera obsolete for the industry.

It was in this milieu that ENG took over in most local U.S. television newscasts. And because of the large investments placed in the new technology, almost everything suddenly was covered by these "live," real-time cameras. Hence we had reports outside darkened buildings where hours before a school board or city council had met and later disbanded. Another example is the weather forecaster standing outside the studio delivering the day's weather report, sometimes with umbrella in hand, just to demonstrate what the weather is indeed doing at that moment. Years later the latest technology within the reach of many a U.S. television news operation would be the helicopter-mounted camera. With this the reporter would fly the aircraft, operate the camera, and typically narrate while shooting. With this technology we rarely got better news, but we did now have access to birds-eye views of stranded flood victims, close-ups of hostage situations, and an occasional police car chase. A recent example of the latter is the infamous O.J. Simpson Ford Bronco car chase as he and a friend tried to elude pursuing authorities on the Los Angeles freeway system.

The trouble with HTN is that the emphasis often falls on the technology rather than the events to be reported. The large investment placed in this technology almost guarantees that this will happen. Yet this emphasis is unwarranted. Technique should be invisible. The news story is of paramount importance. An insightful narrative is necessary, not catchy special effects. No matter how technologically advanced a newsroom might be, this is no substitute for good journalists with the critical skills to go deeper into a story and pose intriguing questions.

In our earlier book, *Global Glasnost*, we discussed the problem of "parachute journalism," where journalists fly into foreign news locations and read scripts on-camera only 30 minutes after landing.[17] Obviously this is bad journalism, and it is an insult to the people and events being reported. A journalist at the *Irish Times* recently told us how U.S. reporters often come into Ireland to report on the troubles in the North. They expect to understand the intricacies of the conflict in two or three minutes. Yet the events are not that simple. They are the result of centuries of colonial rule, land allocations, and continued political bungling. How does one learn this in three minutes, and how does HTN with its live reporting, teleprompters, nonlinear editing, and so forth, help the American public better understand what is going on in Northern Ireland? The answer is: It does not. Good journalism via good writing, good research, and a good critical perspective will help the public better understand. Sweeping helicopter shots of the lush Irish countryside may help make the visuals more appealing, and the story may be edited and on air faster than it would have been using traditional techniques, but the events are still the same and they warrant dedication and hard work if the reporter hopes to do them justice. No special effects or high-tech gimmickry is going to change things substantively. There is the danger, though, that HTN will be confused with good reporting. After all, it is not very hard to construct a shallow message when that is all the communicator sets out to do.

2. *Real-time reporting means less time for reflection.* As real-time reporting becomes more feasible there will be more real-time reporting, hence less time for reflection on the issues, let alone for investigative reporting.

Most telling is the present trend toward placing newspapers on the Internet. Rather than seeking to provide thorough coverage of the printed edition or even supplemental coverage of stories not included in the paper version (some online newspapers do occasionally provide links to earlier published stories, datafiles, etc.), most newspapers seem more concerned with improving the graphic qualities of their home page presentations and other fringe news services such as a "live," permanently mounted camera to "show" the user what exactly is happening weatherwise in that locale. Yet a poor quality video picture does not show discrete variances in temperature and nothing but the most basic weather condition summaries. Why spend thousands of bits of computer memory and minutes of transmission time to show that which in print can be described with the simple words: "snow," "rain," or "sunny?" Decisions are made to limit the availability of news text, while these organizations are wasting megabyte upon megabyte for peripheral and often frivolous graphics. Sometimes the addition of these graphic images increases the download time of this information to home and office computers by minutes per page.

We turn to two recent examples from television news observed by the authors. The first was briefly mentioned earlier. It involves Honolulu's leading news anchor who, when reading a story on tax reform, told his audience with some bewilderment that he was glad he could read it again after the program ended because he was having difficulty understanding it.[18] In the other case an anchor was reading a story about how the eruption of a volcano was wrecking havoc among the people in Ireland. Well, it turned out to be Iceland; Ireland's volcanic activity ended long before humans populated the earth. The anchor never realized his mistake. Fortunately his female co-anchor did.[19]

Researchers tell us that existing professional news practices are poorly envisioned and based on custom rather than reality. The stated purpose of journalism is commonly said to serve the public interest in the United States. However, the purpose more often is to help make the job of journalists easier or to build greater audiences.

Tuchman concludes that journalists engage in rituals when doing their jobs. Such rituals help guarantee the habitual nature of information gathering. Also made possible is the simplistic development of stories, which are descriptive in only superficial ways. The details of events are often obscured or distorted to help create standardization. As part of drama manipulation, reporters often seek conflicting sources to help balance stories. As a result, inconsequential details might be emphasized to offer color to otherwise mundane events. The use of stereotypes is also employed to help reduce the need for explanation.[20]

3. *Less mental energy to expend.* As technology takes the upper hand there will be more of a tendency to direct it toward safe attention getters, like things that are highly visible and audible (dynamic), and even less reporting of the invisible and inaudible (hidden dimensions).

From a narrative viewpoint the use of live press conferences and dignitary speeches is effective because it helps frame a conflict and aids in viewer identification of major players. This allows the principals to tell their story. Unfortunately such a move also provides the opportunity for those conducting the press briefing, or other event, to potentially manipulate the agenda. It was in such a setting that Saddam Hussein requested that the U.S. television networks carry a 90-minute address to the American people during the conflict. CNN complied. Although some faulted CNN, there may be little difference between this footage and comparable addresses from American dignitaries aired almost every day. How can we judge the degree of propaganda in one over the other? By carrying such events, the media has shifted the burden of analysis from newscaster to viewer. Events are supplied live, often with superfluous footage and events. This overwhelming amount of data is at best making it more difficult to effectively process information and may act as a camouflage obscuring the more vital news now buried beneath the overload. Viewers must carry out the editing function that journalists once employed. There is less work involved in preparation of the story, but now the consumer must spend more time wading through possibly unnecessary details.

There has long been a tendency in U.S. media to equate the more sensational with greater newsworthiness. One classic study of international news in U.S. media by Mort Rosenblum is titled, *Coups and Earthquakes: Reporting the World to America*, and it speaks well about the undue emphasis placed on natural disasters and highly unstable governments.[21] Such imagery suggests a more primitive people and lifestyle that do not have the permanence of Western institutions. They do not have the living standards and infrastructure that will enable them to minimize human loss from natural disasters nor rebound with the same efficiency and speed that we might see in the West.

It is too easy to rely on such stereotypic images. There is a concept in dramatic television, particularly sit-com writing, known as "pipe." Pipe refers to the history of each character and the implication is that somehow, through speech, dress, behavior, and situation, this pipe is communicated the moment a character steps on stage. There is no room in most American television for costly and time-consuming character development when shallow story-telling devices will suffice. This mentality carries over into news programming all too often. The script is superficial. The events are conventional. We may feel that we have seen this or similar events hundreds of times before, and we probably have!

In addition to the dangers of uncreativity and underdevelopment, we also witness the inability of the system to address any questions that don't already fit into a preordained script. Sound bytes are used out of context. Detailed examples are dropped. As Chomsky observes in *Manufacturing Consent*, non-conventional explanations and concepts require time to develop and describe, and are dismissed by newspeople as too complex for the average viewer or reader. Yet it is exactly because these are not mainstream ideas that they require further time and space for development. It is only the status quo that can resort to superficial rhetoric because the script is already well known by the general public.[22] Yet how is public discourse expanded if we keep repeating only a very limited script?

4. *Fewer new ideas will surface.* As technology takes the upper hand old conceptualizations will direct newscasting, making new perspectives less likely.

Entertainment has long played a key role in the construction of U.S. television news. In recent decades the use of social science and marketing researchers, often known as the TV news doctors, conducted extensive market analysis reports for local and national television management. Poll takers such as Frank Magid, Lou Harris, and others conducted surveys and reported on the story types viewers most wanted to see. Although perhaps not recommending that news programs cover only the most sensational, shocking, and graphic stories, many an insecure or bottom-line news director in the already volatile news industry quickly chose the route guaranteed to bring the largest audiences. With new technologies such as ENG and helicopters, the shift toward entertainment and so-called "audience involvement" techniques increased.

Another event has been the introduction of the "happy talk" television news concept. This news format tends to emphasize shorter stories, supplemental visuals of any sort, even if not contributing new information, and general entertainment qualities such as physically attractive anchors, conversational style peppered with jokes and staff camaraderie, and highly sensational and visually dramatic stories.

This folksy news format tends to be more frequent on the local news level, but the keen observer can find it in network television news too. The standards of many a local news operation are pitifully low. This is often brought about because fewer news gathering resources are available, but that is not the only reason. The new technologies have a way of encouraging "localization" in national news coverage, and as Charles Bailey points out, this often lends to trivializing the news. Bailey points to one such event where a Minneapolis television station chose to report on Reagan's return from the 1985 Geneva summit meeting with Gorbachev. Immediately upon his return Reagan went to address a joint meeting of Congress. Even though the station relied on the ABC team of Peter Jennings, Sam Donaldson, and George Will to report daily during the summit, the affiliate now preempted the network report and instead their Minneapolis-based "Eyewitness News" anchors covered the story.[23] Consequently, greater quality is sacrificed for more story familiarity and editorial control.

Informative and greater analytic journalism might seem more professional, but it also tends to make for boring news. U.S. audiences by and large apparently do not want to sit through fact-filled reports and detailed analysis. The audience for the Public Broadcast System (PBS) television's more involved and analytic "McNeil-Lehrer News Hour" (now called the "News Hour with Jim Lehrer") has regularly appealed to only one or two percent of the American population. National Public Radio (NPR) programming fares even worse. Instead, journalists have developed strategies for dramatizing the news. This generally involves highlighting drama scenarios that are implicit in many daily happenings.[24] The retelling of events by reporters is actually said to be an effort to highlight conflict, tragedy, or comedy within the story. In this environment viewers are transformed into commonplace characters in the mini-dramas, which are usually carried out in 30-, 60- or 90-second time segments.

The same thing, of course, might often be said of smaller community newspapers versus the more nationally minded elite newspapers of the major cities. Here the tendency is often to frame stories in a local context and with local color. Few challenging questions are posed on controversial issues. The sensational and human interest angles all too often take precedence over in-depth investigation and comparative discussions. National and international news is minimized or avoided entirely.

In the United States news is a business and the primary purpose is to deliver an audience as large as possible to advertisers. The programming simply serves as bait. A standardized and routinized product guarantees predictable content. This content, then, can be efficiently produced in an inherently complex production process.

Contemporary U.S. news organizations are no different than most other firms that sell products and services. Decision making is mostly conducted by a small group. In this case it is the editors and producers and, indirectly, "upper" management. Stories are dictated by their perceived audience attraction, and reporters file stories in short amounts of time which must ultimately pass the scrutiny of editors. Some reporters have beats or specialties, and others may be responsible for routine events as they occur (sometimes up to ten or twelve events per day).

5. *High costs of high technology leads to dismissal of labor.* As HTN is expensive and costs of investment have to be recovered there will be a tendency in journalism as in other fields to dismiss workers, that is, journalists, to increase "productivity." This reduces the chances for reflection even further.

Costs are a reality in the news industry, but time and time again costs appear to get in the way of good journalism. The concerns raised here seriously jeopardize the quality of U.S. journalism and call into question whether news organizations are truly serving the public interest, or if instead they are serving their own corporate and personal interests.

We see it in the newspaper business as more and more U.S. cities are left with only one daily newspaper or there is more than one but all are owned by essentially the same organization (this would include many of the arrangements in organizations today). With the escalating costs of news print and other expenses, many a newspaper can no longer survive comfortably in today's marketplace. Add to this questionable marketing strategies such as dumping out-of-town newspapers in an effort to undermine the operations of some quality news operations, a practice that Rupert Murdock newspapers are now engaging in world-wide, and Gannett has been charged with domestically, and the outlook for the industry is not all that bright.

The costs of establishing news bureaus in foreign capitals has mushroomed. The cost of maintaining a news correspondent in Tokyo, for example, is estimated in excess of $200,000 annually. Hence we see the "parachute journalism" mentioned earlier more than ever. There is little time to adequately gather stories. Even if the reporter is a highly talented journalist, and knows the language spoken in the nation of assignment, he or she must still cope with the long daily schedules of working in one time zone but filing a story in news capitals many times zones away.

As noted above, the television newsroom has turned to the professional news consultant as a way of increasing the profitability of the news program. In larger markets the local news program can increase its annual revenues by over one million dollars by increasing its audience share by a simple percentage point. This truly demonstrates the nature of the news business in the United

States. As another example, we are aware of a television station in Rochester, New York, where the local news program has long been in third place among the three network affiliates in that city. Yet that station's news operations were making greater profits than the two competitors with higher ratings. The key, according to the station owner, was to minimize the costs of its news operation, so much so that the return on its investment was highest. How, we might ask, is such obvious cost slashing for the investor's sake helping serve the interests of that community?

The bottom line is not only of importance at the local level. Several years ago all three major networks did a large-scale slashing of their operations. The news staffs complained that journalistic quality would suffer. Still, the cuts continued. In addition to cuts among reporters, editors, and so forth, the behind-the-scenes support staffs, such as research departments, were almost entirely eliminated.

This mentality of treating news as any other business has long been the tradition in U.S. television. Fred Friendly gives many examples of the tensions that existed between the long-revered CBS news department and its network executives and advertising people under Edward R. Murrow and himself when each headed CBS news.[25] The purpose was to make money, and lots of it at that.

According to Friendly, the advertising department almost always had more clout than the news department, even though the latter was performing the public service. As examples, the news department was told by management that they were expected not to interrupt ads with late-breaking news bulletins; instead, they were to wait and interrupt the entertainment program itself after the advertisements had run. Murrow and Friendly also had their share of budget battles, and this was one of the contributing factors in Murrow's ultimate departure from CBS.

Because corporations are responsible to stockholders, U.S. news operations are often strangled by short-term profit pressures, ignoring longer-term strategies for a quality news operation. This is not a unique problem in American business, for many an industry has faced this problem, from the demise of Detroit automobile manufacturing to the loss of industry dominance once enjoyed by U.S. communication giants such as Ampex and Eastman Kodak. In each case futuristic visions have been stifled by short-sighted organizational goals catering to the bottom line.

In the U.S. media managers are at times even better rewarded for investing in capital expenditures such as equipment rather than personnel. Equipment can be amortized in business tax filings; personnel costs cannot. Employers must also pay for medical benefits, unemployment insurance, retirement programs, and so forth, for personnel, but there are no additional expenses other than maintenance for equipment. In addition, many local news departments have all but been eliminated thanks to radio deregulation, as these operations proved less profitable than entertainment operations. In small- and medium-sized radio markets it is often cheaper to automate operations rather than pay for a full-time on-air staff. We know of one case in the Honolulu market where it was more expensive to hire one local on-air talent for 20 hours a week (the morning drive time, 6-10 a.m., Monday through Friday) than it was to provide programming for the remaining 148 hours via a syndicated satellite-distributed program originating in Los Angeles.

The danger in the above scenarios is that news gathering in the United States is not the primary mission of the media; selling advertising to sponsors is. Hence personnel costs have always been subject to scrutiny and possible elimination. Newspapers have been no better, given the presence of news holes, that portion of the newspaper devoted to news itself, sometimes accounting for as little as 15 to 20 percent of the entire newspaper. In the *New York Times* it is 40 percent. In a newspaper such as the *Irish Times* of Dublin, on the other hand, the news hole is 80 to 90 percent. Just as in the factory, when automation threatens jobs, so too are jobs placed in jeopardy by the technological changes affecting news gathering and dissemination. The trend is only likely to get worse. News personnel and their professional groups must pressure publishers and broadcasters to preserve jobs and cut costs elsewhere. The public must assert itself and demand better news operations and lower profit margins. The news industry may be a business, but it also is a crucial public service activity.

6. *Lower diversity leads to greater reliance on transnational news organizations.* As HTN is expensive, local correspondents (also very expensive) will increasingly be withdrawn and there will be a higher reliance on agencies and national networks. As a result there will be less diversity in reporting and less possibility for the consumer to derive more complex discourses by comparing multiple images.

The problem does not improve with print journalism. Here quality is also lacking, even among the most prestigious national newspapers. As noted above, most U.S. newspapers have news holes of only about 20 percent. Add to this the understaffing of news rooms as newspapers face budget cuts in an increasingly cost-conscious industry, and their almost exclusive reliance on U.S. and Western news agencies (as well as public relations agencies such as Hill & Knowlton and Ruder Finn) for material, and the situation is not all that much better.

To elaborate on the final point, U.S. newspapers, even the largest and most powerful, rarely use alternative news agencies such as the Inter Press Service (IPS) or others that do an excellent job of reporting on the Third World and its people. Just as television has its news doctors, so too do newspapers. Many traits of the *U.S.A Today* newspaper format came about after extensive market analysis by a well-known U.S. communication professor. The paper, of course, is criticized for its shallow and predictable formulaic stories wrapped in a graphically interesting cover. It may be eye catching, but is not intellectually satisfying for a reader seeking detailed news and controversial topics. Today there are few newspapers such as the *Christian Science Monitor* that provide in-depth reporting of socially relevant issues of the day. More often the U.S. press promotes sensationalism over reflective reporting, and dwells on life's tragedies rather than seeking out stories of hope or non-elite individual and national success.

7. Because of emphasis on so-called "objectivity," the real story is not reported at all! More real time and less diversity in newscasting lead to illusions of "objectivity," reinforcing reduction of complexity.

The whole notion of objectivity as a cornerstone for good journalism is challenged by both Schiller and Schudson, who trace its origins. They argue that objectivity evolved as part of a marketing strategy to broaden appeal and reduce costs. Objective news, in the sense of being non-controversial, they contend, was less likely to offend members of specific cultural groups. Thanks to wire services, objective news packaged in one city could then be obtained and printed at relatively low cost in another.[26]

One result of this move to make news appear objective is story fragmentation. Story descriptions are isolated with few reference points to events in the past or future. Background information may be misread as inadvertent bias, hence it is typically ignored. The strategy of breaking news into hundreds of objective fragments has organizational advantages in that it can be produced in less time and with fewer resources.

Note an observation by Blumler, Gurevitch, and Katz on the relationship between a reader and a text. They report that "readers will be socially constrained in how they approach texts and that texts will be constrained in the readings they make available."[27]

We can only see the use of techniques to enhance the illusion of reality as increasing in the years ahead. With 3-D, holograms, and virtual reality among other trends, our fascination with the so-called real continues. We saw this tendency in the arts of the nineteenth century, and it has continued through to the plastic arts of photography, film, and video, and into the age of digitized data storage and manipulation. The danger in all of these, of course, is that they do not really create reality, they simply serve as substitutes for reality. However, when presented in a technologically refined environment, these images are often mistaken for the truth and this suggests many avenues for potential manipulation by image creators.

8. *The media continue to entertain instead of inform. Technology only makes this diversion easier. News and MTV are closer than you may think!* As HTN is expensive its use for entertainment will be even more pronounced, again obscuring the complex nature of issues.

The news media has been criticized for catering to popular tastes and its emphasis on entertainment rather than information and more responsible professionalism. Examples may be found in the many local newscasts and newspapers that emphasize soft, folksy news, network television morning news programs, and video news magazines. Then there are tabloid news programs such as "Cops," "Hard Copy," "Inside Edition," "World's Scariest Police Chases," "Extra," "Rescue 911," and so forth, which give the illusion of a news or documentary format by following or recreating police beats, following rescue crews and ambulances, and doing that which looks as if it is investigative journalism, but the entertainment emphasis is unmistakable throughout. These are entertainment programs, pure and simple, and they use real or quasi-real events to enhance their credibility and bolster audiences.

The changes in the news media can be seen in television news' treatment of national political campaigns. Over the years the move has been toward shorter and shorter news stories as television journalists attempt to control the content. In presidential elections, for example, the nightly treatment of major party candidates was 45 seconds to two minutes each in the 1960s. By 1988, though, the average nightly soundbite was down to only eight seconds by each candidate.[28]

What now happens is that we rely on the journalist to tell us what happened, and when we do have the opportunity to hear and see candidates it is often reduced to short, easily recognizable sound bites. How can a well-planned campaign be reduced to clever little snippets of sound and video? Thus our memorable moments of recent presidential campaigns have been quotes like Bentsen's, "I knew Jack Kennedy. Jack Kennedy was a friend of mine. Senator, you are no Jack Kennedy," Reagan's "There he goes again . . .," and George Bush's "voodoo economics." What do these tell us about the people running for office or the great issues of the day?

The potential for irresponsible news manipulation also exists, particularly when it serves specific commercial needs and interests. By taking findings on learning from television news, we know that on a typical day, just half the viewers have superficial recall of one half the stories broadcast.[29] For such simple levels of recall, it is necessary to use aided recall procedures where people are prompted with brief, two- or three-word story labels. Even using such cues, as many as one-third of the viewers have little or no recall. The most informed third of the audience will be able to report the main points from only about one-third of the stories. Once learned, most information is also quickly forgotten, almost all within the first 24 to 48 hours after the newscast.[30]

9. *Elites are highlighted more than they were before. Even so, elites will themselves be shortchanged by not being reported fully.* As elite/politician press conferences and speeches always have some relevance, they will be increasingly overreported as safe attention getters. At the same time, as complexity decreases, elites will train in using media for their purposes. Even so, their sound bites will make them look stupid. As a result, lack of respect for elites, and a feeling of cover-up will be even more pronounced, and the elites may defeat themselves.

Elite media and news media's use of elite sources have been topics of analysis in previous research. In one work looking at historical relationships between power, social order, and communications during the central middle ages (and other later time periods), James Curran demonstrates how various pre-industrial society media—buildings, paintings, statues, coins, banners, stained glass windows, songs, medallions, and rituals—served to either help establish or reinforce classes of ruling elite during the rise of the papal government, the See of Rome.[31] Not only were priests very effective vehicles for reaching mixtures of mass audiences via the pulpit, but also the traveling friars, common after the thirteenth century, "who often combined their evangelical role with reporting 'the news' to curious listeners." So effective was the papal network of propaganda that the demise of the traditional feudal system was replaced by divine-right monarchies that secured authority from the church's mediation.[32] The papacy's cultural domination is largely attributed to its "direct control over the principal agency of mass communication, the Church," says Curran. Its success relied on the "successful manipulation of élite and mass media to transmit not merely its claims to church leadership but an ideological perspective of the world that legitimized its domination of Christendom."[33] Citing sociological theory the author notes the widely held belief that mass media help authenticize social systems in which they hold membership. He draws parallels to modern media and the medieval Church. Each has the ability to connect different groups and dispense a shared experience that promotes social harmony.

In various studies by the Glasgow Media Group, the use of elite news sources by contemporary media is examined. In one study they observe that "Interviewees are drawn from an extremely narrow section of the social and political spectrum." Later they note that "A large number of the statements quoted and referenced come from the same individuals in the narrow group that were interviewed most frequently." The study makes an observation on the perceived effect of such presentations:

> . . . news was organised and produced substantially around the views of the dominant political group in . . . society. We have shown how the views of those who disagree fundamentally with this position, or who offered alternative approaches, were downgraded and underrepresented in the news coverage. This is in stark comparison with the careful explanation and heavy emphasis given to the dominant analysis and the political policies which flowed from it.[34]

They conclude that particular world views are reinforced by journalistic practices, and it "prestructures what the news is to consist of and in a sense what the journalists themselves actually see as exciting, or as being significant in the world."[35]

Use of news elites was a concern in an analysis on American television network news stories on air crashes and again in CNN's coverage of the Gulf War. In the former, according to a study conducted by one of the present authors, it was found that such coverage may lend itself to maintenance of the "status quo." Knowingly or unknowingly, such source reliance helps deliver a clear message:

> Our analysis . . . suggests that these stories are well suited to develop and sustain simple, consensual notions about the social order. There is little in such stories which would provoke questioning of the social order. . . .[36]

A telling example of the potential manipulation of news by elite news sources can be seen in R. Gregory Nokes' telling of one case where the Reagan administration worked feverishly to promote its policy toward Libya by emphasizing Khadafi's links to terrorism. Former White House spokesman Larry Speaks acknowledged in a *New York Times* interview that a campaign existed to influence international events and mold domestic reporting, including the supply of concocted details about the Libyan government and Khadafi. In addition, some reporters raised questions about unidentified intelligence reports that the Libyan leader was planning to resume terroristic activity following the U.S. bombing in April 1996. It was also reported that the Libyan military was plotting to rise up against Khadafi. As Nokes observes, "intelligence from Libya showed the opposite . . ." Speakers countered such criticism by explaining that although unauthorized, the reports were still "authoritative." Also in early October Reagan substantiated a *Washington Post* story that a secret disinformation operation had been conducted that was designed to make Khadafi "go to bed every night wondering what we might do" to dissuade him from engaging in new terroristic activity. Reagan insisted that the crusade *did not* involve feeding fraudulent information to the U.S. press, however. Nokes then quotes Secretary of State George Shultz who, while denying any falsehoods through the media, noted that, "If there are ways in which we can make Khadafi nervous, why shouldn't we? Frankly, I don't have any problem with a little psychological warfare against Khadafi." Shultz concluded things with a Winston Churchill quote that when in war "the truth is so precious it must be attended by a bodyguard of lies." He added that "we don't have a declaration of war, but we have something pretty darn close to it."[37] In early 2002, a program to formalize the dissemination of false news stories by Washington was thwarted when revealed in a *New York Times* story.

Elites must be considered, and very possibly avoided, or at least social systems must take their power presence into account if a new communicative system is desired. Fishman warns that news organizations are prime targets for manipulation by political, bureaucratic, and business elites.[38] Tuchman further argues that systemic constraints invariably produce unfavorable coverage of groups seeking social policy changes.[39] Appeals for social policy change normally comes from fringe groups, not the status quo.

10. *Media lose control given the complexity of the issues they seek to cover, hence loss of respect for media by the public.* As media lose control, failing to reflect complexity, respect for media will decline even further. So far the media reaction to recover audiences lost to increased competition in the new media marketplace seems to be to impoverish the discourse even further, a self-defeating strategy.

Research has found that when people read stories that deviate in minor ways from standardized scripts as they perceive them, their view of stories tends to be distorted. This is done to help make stories consistent with previously held expectations. Details missing from stories will often be filled in with expected events. Persons, actions, and objects that are not part of a script will tend to be overlooked.

In this view of learning, knowledge derived from news may be strongly linked to the activation of relevant schemas. Well-structured news items can assist viewers by activating appropriate schemas and minimizing activation of irrelevant ones. If it is known that relatively few viewers have developed appropriate schemas, then an effort can be made to systematically develop them. In this way, television journalists could play a very important role in assisting the development of public knowledge about specific topics.[40]

Persons who learn new information from TV news are said to be those who already have a great deal of knowledge. They are better educated, more interested in politics, and have developed conceptual frameworks that enable them to quickly make sense of fast-paced and frequently complex stories.[41] Berry observes that news does not enjoy optimum mass success in Britain because it is written and edited for an elite audience.[42] Story structures are complicated and complex or abstract terminology is employed. Just as in the United States, pictures are frequently inconsistent with verbal content.

Yet Americans may be even more poorly equipped than many of their international peers due to the highly commercialized media system they are exposed to, lower quality educational opportunities, and so forth. Americans seem to know far less about foreign affairs. For example, a 1981 *Washington Post*-ABC national poll found that only 47 percent (less than one would expect by chance) could name which country—the United States or the Soviet Union—was a member of NATO. On another question only 37 percent correctly identified the two countries involved in the SALT talks. In another survey only 25 percent knew where El Salvador was located.[43]

Another concept of news flow is the so-called agenda-setting function of mass media. Since the early 1970s, McCombs and Shaw (1976) have published a series of studies investigating the power of media as it impacts audience members. They argue that although media may not have the power to change what people think, it can indeed influence what people think about and how they prioritize information received. The notion here is that media can call attention to specific people, events, and issues simply by providing coverage of certain issues and repressing others. Through extended coverage over days, weeks, months, and years, media has the power to assign an undue and possibly unwarranted emphasis to certain issues, people, and events. McCombs and Shaw have found strong statistical relationships between the amount of coverage issues receive during political campaigns in newspapers and the ranking of those issues by voters.[44]

In an era where the proliferation of technology is having profound impact on the way we live, scholarly interests have turned to the seventeenth- and eighteenth-century concept of the civil society. Central to these foundations are writings by John Locke, Francis Bacon, Adam Ferguson, and Jean Jacques Rousseau. Within contemporary society the concern involves the role played by non-government community actions/mobilizations, in which individuals attempt to express themselves and enact change through available channels of communication.

Civil society places emphasis on the essential experiences of individuals within societies. It helps offer explanations for "why individuals participate in voluntary associations and then accept the legitimacy of authorities external to themselves."[45]

We can take this notion one step further by closely examining Giddens' writings on the "technocratic ideology of advanced capitalism." He cites Habermas who notes a burgeoning state intervention directed toward secure economic growth and the increasingly mutual reliance on "research and technology" (*Toward a Rational Society*, pp. 50ff). This helps make the advanced capitalist order a "technocratic" one, "based upon the capacity of elites to 'manage' the economy successfully and sustain economic growth."[46]

Contemporary scholars such as Hamelink see the potential to move the civil society concept from a national to a global level.[47] The convergence of communication technologies has resulted in a multitude of communication channels now readily available to individuals. These technologies afford us the opportunity to organize on levels previously not possible for most individuals. As Frederick observes, coalitions and networks have already emerged "on the world stage: the rain forest protection movement, the human rights movement, the campaign against the arms trade, alternative news agencies, and planetary computer networks," and such campaigns are being conducted on nongovernmental organization (NGO) levels.[48]

A major purpose of our previous book was to emphasize how the news media can help advance the causes of peace, international relations, global resource protection, and promote the needs of the disadvantaged. Yet, in *Global Glasnost*, we conclude that although communication has become more relevant to global problems, these global communication efforts often become counter-productive, and we may have witnessed very little progress toward global and human journalism.[49] The question is: how can U.S. media discourse be molded to help insure a greater global consciousness and human journalistic perspective?

CONCLUSIONS

Today people are better educated, at least in a formal sense, than at any time in human history. The quest for information is central to human existence. There also are many sources for information available today than there ever have been before. Although the number of newspapers has been declining across the United States, narrowly targeted magazine publishing is on the upswing. Book publishing and broadcasting remain relatively healthy and the number of information sources has increased dramatically thanks to satellites, cable television, videotext and teletext, audio and video tapes, compact discs, and DVDs. Added to this we now have computers and the information distribution network, which merges various digital information bases via a combination of older voice and data technologies. As a result, the newest medium of information dissemination is the Internet. Although most links to the Internet are established via a personal computer and a modem, Internet access is also possible directly from one's television set by using a special conversion device such as that sold by Microsoft Corp. as a result of their acquisition of the Palo Alto-based Web TV Network. It is the Internet, of course, that has become the cornerstone of the so-called information superhighway.

Much of the current thinking about the new communication technology has been framed by the Information Super Highway and the Global Information Infrastructure concepts. Yet the Information Super Highway is not only a technological project, but also an initiative that links governments and major communication corporations at the highest levels.

The danger in such a society, of course, is that the ability of the medium to provide quality information is tenuous at best. If there is danger of information being trivialized and manipulated in the older media, what might we hope of the new media, in which webs of information are being spun all over the world by corporations and governments?

Not all information posted on the Internet is produced by governments and major corporations. The infrastructure is there because of their efforts, though, and these interests have a strong desire to encourage the commercial development of the medium. It seems that the information to date on the Internet is essentially there because it serves someone's purpose for it to be there and with the realization that the space this information occupies costs money. Whereas some data bases such as "Project Gutenberg" exist to provide electronic versions of printed works, these efforts have been largely constrained by limited funding. In addition, almost everything in the "Project Gutenberg" archive are works for which copyright protection no longer exists. Besides these efforts, many marginal groups have found the Internet to be an easily assessable medium for their literature, and this includes right-wing groups that offer recipes for making explosives, those with pornographic interests, as well as cult religion. The Internet activity of the religious cult, Heaven's Gate, is just one in a series of fringe groups who find a welcome home on the Internet.[50] An irony in this latter case is that the evidence that helped convince 39 cultists in San Diego to commit mass suicide in order to be carried to a higher level by a space ship trailing the Comet Hale-Bopp apparently came from a photograph taken by the University of Hawaii telescope atop Mauna Kea on the Island of Hawaii. It seems that someone copied the original photograph from the Observatory's World Wide Web Internet pages and then altered it by digitally copying a star from the periphery of the frame and reprinting it in its center, making it appear that there was a companion. This altered photograph was then copied and recopied numerous times.[51]

Concerns have been raised regarding the new media, of course. Comparing printed communications to the programs sent by the new media, Habermas suggested that the latter "curtail the reactions of their recipients in a peculiar way. They draw the eyes of the public under their spell . . ."[52] In *The Postmodern Condition* Lyotard cautions that the trend toward computerization means the reduction of language to the level which best encourages efficiency, or as he puts it, "performity." [53] And, even a person such as Mark Poster, who is a strong advocate of the newer technology, advises a degree of caution.[54]

The potential of the Internet is not found in everyone's construction of a personal home page for self-gratification, something about as useful as the CB radio craze of the 1970s. The latter was a use of the radio spectrum that was totally devoted to casual chatter and truck drivers warning one another of police radar traps on interstate highways. Rather the true potential of the Internet is contained in the expansion of information sources such as newspapers that may not normally be available to a wide array of readers, and information data banks for various NGOs and grassroots movements whose costs for communicating to a world-wide constituency have previously been prohibitive. As for the newspapers, many U.S. newspapers including the *New York Times*, the *Philadelphia Inquirer*, the *St. Louis Post-Dispatch*, and others are charging for day- or week-old news, and other papers even charge for the current day's newspaper. This is in sharp contrast to European newspapers, which are developing a much more liberal policy about Internet newspaper access, at least for the moment. Even if information is available via the Internet, it will also depend on national policies that may affect the cost of access. The cost is already prohibitive in China, New Zealand, a sizeable portion of Asia and much of Africa. Placing Internet access in the hands of telephone companies under the guise of a competitive marketplace may also restrict future access for many in the United States. And even in the United States today only somewhere between 55 and 60 percent of the population has a computer and can potentially access the Internet versus some 7 to 10 percent worldwide.

Whether there are further restrictions on access or not, a greater concern may be the continued deterioration of control over news practices and content by both the public as well as news professionals. With greater manipulation by government and large business, the present fears of manipulation and interference may only increase. For a nation that prides itself on a so-called freedom of the press, this liberty may be in serious jeopardy. Earlier in this chapter we told the story of Morley Safer and his history-changing film story from Vietnam. This is an example of the censorship II we refer to in this book. We can only imagine what the consequences would be for the news estate with further corporate-government control of the Internet. It might mean a potentially greater hold on information sources and a further restriction on journalists who value their quest for objectivity. Add to this the danger that public trust in journalism may be eroded by the widespread interest in technology by media institution managers who are looking to streamline news production, the ranks of news personnel, and, of course, their budgets, and we may have a serious problem that may only worsen if trends continue as they have. It is time for the journalist to take back the medium and seize control of the profession. We are not arguing a Luddite-type hold on technology in a vain attempt to hold back progress, but we do advocate a serious examination of the technology and the ways it negatively affects the news media. Greater concern must come from journalists, their professional organizations, and our educational institutions, which all have the power to orchestrate a review of the industry and an evaluation of its production standards. This is the concern we raise here, and the reason we express caution regarding the growing role of technology in news production.

NOTES

1. Joseph Decken, *The Electronic Cottage* (New York: Bantam Books, 1981), p. 1.
2. Anthony Smith, *Goodbye Gutenberg; The Newspaper Revolution of the 1980's* (Oxford: Oxford University Press, 1980), p. 1.
3. Anthony Smith, *Goodbye Gutenberg; The Newspaper Revolution of the 1980's* (Oxford: Oxford University Press, 1980), p. 23.
4. Leo A. Singleton, *Telecommunications in the Information Age* (Cambridge, MA: Ballinger, 1983), p. 1.
5. Jacques Ellul, *The Technological Society* (Trans. John Wilkerson, New York: Knopf, 1964), p. 349.
6. Ibid.

7. *UNESCO: Cultural Patterns and Technical Change*, a manual edited by Margaret Mead, 1953.
8. See note 5.
9. Spencer A. Sherman, "Letter from Hawaii," *Columbia Journalism Review*, September/October 1994, 33.
10. Kevin C. Lee and Charles Fielding, "Problems of Introducing Courses in Computer-Assisted Reporting," *Journalism Educator*, Autumn 1995, 26.
11. Mark Portner, *The Second Media Age* (Cambridge: Polity Press, 1995); Theodore Roszak, *The Cult of Information*, 2d ed. (Berkeley: University of California Press, 1994); Herbert Schiller, *Information Inequity* (New York: Routledge, 1996); William J. Mitchell, *City of Bits* (Cambridge, MA: MIT Press, 1995); Robert K. Heldman, *Future Telecommunications* (New York: McGraw-Hill, 1993); Neil Postman, *Technopoly* (New York: Alfred A. Knopf, 1992); John V. Pavlik, *New Media and the Information Superhighway* (Boston: Allyn and Bacon, 1996); Alvin Toffler, *The Third Wave* (New York: William Morrow & Co., 1980); John Naisbitt, *Megatrends* (New York: Warner Books, 1982).
12. Andrew Schneider, "The Downside of Wonderland," *Columbia Journalism Review*, 3, March/April 1993, 55.
13. Clifford Stoll, *Silicon Snake Oil* (New York: Doubleday, 1995), pp. 76-77.
14. David Halberstam, *The Powers That Be* (New York: Alfred A. Knopf, 1979).
15. Phillip B. Davidson, *Vietnam at War* (Novato, CA: Presidio Press, 1988), p. 810; William M. Hammond, "The Press in Vietnam as Agent of Defeat: A Critical Examination," *Reviews in American History* 17, June 1989, 312-323.
16. Richard C. Vincent, "CNN: Elites Talking to Elites," in *Triumph of the Image: The Media's War in the Persian Gulf. A Global Perspective*, Hamid Mowlana, George Gerbner and Herbert I. Schiller, eds. (Boulder, CO: Westview, 1992), pp. 181-201.
17. Johan Galtung and Richard C. Vincent, *Global Glasnost: Toward a New World Information and Communication Order?* (Cresskill, NJ: Hampton Press, 1992).
18. Spencer A. Sherman, "Letter from Hawaii," *Columbia Journalism Review*, September/October 1994, 33.
19 Evening news brief, KITV News, Honolulu, 5 October 1996.
20. Gaye Tuchman, *Making News: A Study in the Construction of Reality* (New York: Free Press, 1978).
21. Mort Rosenblum, *Coups and Earthquakes: Reporting the World to America* (New York: Harper Colophon Books, 1979).
22. Edward S. Herman and Noam Chomsky, *Manufacturing Consent: The Political Economy of the Mass Media* (New York: Pantheon Books, 1988), pp. 305-306 and elsewhere.

23. Charles W. Bailey, "Foreign Policy and the Provincial Press," in *The Media and Foreign Policy*, Simon Serfaty, ed. (New York: St. Martin's Press, 1990), p. 181; William Drummond, "Is Time Running Out for Network News?" *Columbia Journalism Review*, May/June 1986, p. 50.

24. See David Gergen, "Diplomacy in a Television Age: The Dangers of Teledemocracy," in *The Media and Foreign Policy*, Simon Serfaty, ed. (New York: St. Martin's Press, 1990), p. 52.

25. Fred Friendly, *Due to Circumstances Beyond Our Control* (New York: Random House, 1967).

26. Herbert I. Schiller, *Who Knows: Information in the Age of the Fortune 500* (Norwood, NJ: Ablex, 1981) and Michael Schudson, *Discovering the News: A Social History of American Newspapers* (New York: Basic Books, 1978).

27. Jay G. Blumler, Michael Gurevitch, and Elihu Katz, "Reaching Out: A Future for Gratifications Research," in *Media Gratifications Research*, in K. E. Rosengren, L. A. Wenner, & P. Palmgreen, eds. (Beverly Hills, CA: Sage, 1985), p. 264.

28. Daniel Hallin, *We Keep America On Top of the World* (New York and London: Routledge, 1993), pp. 133-152.

29. Doris Graber, *Processing the News: How People Tame the Information Tide* (New York, Longman, 1988); J.P. Robinson and M. Levy, *The Main Source: Learning from Television News* (Beverly Hills, CA: Sage, 1986).

30. Doris Graber, *Processing the News: How People Tame the Information Tide* (New York: Longman, 1988).

31. James Curran, "Communications, Power and Social Order," in *Culture, Society and the Media*, Michael Gurevitch, Tony Bennett, James Curran, and Janet Woolacott, eds. (London: Routledge, 1982), p. 209. See also: E.H. Kantorowicz, *The King's Two Bodies: A Study in Medieval Political Theology* (Princeton, NJ: Princeton University Press, 1957); W.W. Ullmann, *The Carolingian Renaissance and the Idea of Kingship* (London: Methuen, 1969); W.W. Ullmann, *Medieval Political Thought* (Harmondsworth: Penguin, 1975); W.W. Ullmann, *Principals of Government and Politics in the Middle Ages*, 4th ed. (London: Methuen, 1978).

32. Curran, pp. 202-235.

33. Ibid.

34. Glasgow University Media Group, *More Bad News* (London: Routledge & Kegan Paul, 1980), p. 11.

35. Ibid.

36. Richard C. Vincent, Bryan K. Crow, and Dennis K. Davis, "When Technology Fails," *Journalism Monographs*, 117, 1989; Richard C. Vincent, "CNN: Elites Talking to Elites," in *Triumph of the Image: The Media's War in the Persian Gulf. A Global Perspective*,

Hamid Mowlana, Herbert Schiller, and George Gerbner, eds. (Boulder, CO: Westview), pp. 181-201.

37. R. Gregory Nokes, "Libya: A Government Story," in *The Media and Foreign Policy*, Simon Serfaty, ed. (New York: St. Martin's Press, 1990), pp. 39-40; *New York Times*, 8 October 1986; *Wall Street Journal*, 25 August 1986; *Washington Post*, 2 October 1986.

38. Mark Fishman, *Manufacturing the News* (Austin: University of Texas Press, 1988).

39. Gaye Tuchman, *Making News: A Study in the Construction of Reality* (New York: Free Press, 1978).

40. Ibid.

41. Graber, 1988.

42. Berry, 1988.

43. David Gergen, "Diplomacy in a Television Age: The Dangers of Teledemocracy," in *The Media and Foreign Policy*, Simon Serfaty, ed. (New York: St. Martin's Press, 1990), p. 51.

44. M. McCombs and D. Shaw, "The Agenda-Setting Function of Mass Media," *Public Opinion Quarterly*, 36, 176-187.

45. Keith Tester, *Civil Society* (London: Routledge, 1992), p. 5.

46. Anthony Giddens, *Profiles and Critiques in Social Theory* (Berkeley: University of California Press, 1982), pp. 90-91.

47. Cees J. Hamelink, "Global Communication: Plea for Civil Action," in *Informatics in Food and Nutrition*, B. V. Hofsten, ed. (Stockholm: Royal Academy of Sciences, 1991), pp. 5-8.

48. Howard H. Frederick, *Global Communication & International Relations* (Belmont, CA: Wadsworth, 1993), p. 271.

49. Johan Galtung and Richard C. Vincent, *Global Glasnost: Toward a New International Information/Communication Order?* (Cresskill, NJ: Hampton Press, 1992).

50. "From Porn to Cults, The Internet has an Image Problem," *New York Times*, 30 March 1997, p. 1.

51. Michael Hammerschlag, "Photo Altered, UH Scientist Says," *The Honolulu Advertiser*, 20 April 1997, pp. A1 & A10.

52. Jurgen Habermas, *The Structural Transformation of the Public Sphere: An Inquiry into a Category of Bourgeois Society*, Thamas Burger, trans. (Cambridge, MA: MIT Press, 1989), pp. 170-171.

53. Jean-Francois Lyotard, *The Differed: Phrases in Dispute*, Georges van den Abbeele. trans. (Minneapolis: University of Minnesota Press, 1988).

54. Mark Poster, *The Second Media Age* (Cambridge: Polity Press, 1995), p. 25.

10

Missing Political Themes in U.S. Media Discourse

THE WORLD AS A MISSING THEME

We start this concluding chapter with a major missing theme in U.S. political discourse: *the world*. Or, to be more specific, "the Third World, which represents more than two-thirds of the world's population and area, [and] accounts for only 25 percent of the reports from the four [leading news] agencies" as pointed out by Dingaan Mpondah, writing from Zimbabwe for the Third World Network Features service of Malaysia.[1] And he continues, reporting that AP "sends from New York to Asia an average of 90,000 words a day," and takes in return only "19,000 words either from its correspondents or from the national news agencies of Asia." The geographic distribution of wire-service correspondents reflects this: 34 percent of them in the United States, 28 percent in Europe, less than 18 percent in Asia and the Pacific, 13 percent in Latin America, and 7 percent in Africa.

But the focus is not on what is written. What was the focus of the two U.S. wire services (Associated Press and United Press International) in contrast to Third World-oriented editors outside?

World Press Review publishes each year the lists of the ten major news events released by AP and UPI, contrasting them with a survey of editors "particularly attuned to the Third World."[2] Of the total of twenty issues reported by the two U.S. wire services the first year we looked into, 1988, eighteen overlap and nine appear twice. The only difference between the two lists was that AP had a focus on "jet crashes in Detroit and Denver" and UPI on "federal budget and national debt battle." The overlap is sufficient to conclude that we are dealing with a U.S. wire service culture in general.

The other remarkable point about the two lists would be that every single one of the nine overlap items is U.S.-centered. That does not mean that they are only U.S.-centered; but when there is an international implication the linkage to the United States always has to be up front. The world is seen from the United States, through U.S. spectacles, in the way it relates to the United States, not on its own terms. It is the world *für mich*, not *an sich*; some kind of virtual reality.[3]

In contrast, the six other lists could almost be accused of the opposite, of focusing too much on issues internal to countries and regions, not sufficiently on underlying linkages to other parts of the world. We notice that the United States recedes into the background, that the Third World is in the foreground, as is to be expected from "Third World-oriented editors outside the United States," and that the whole world simply looks very different. The parochialism thesis is quite well illustrated, but with the passing comment that there might also be a Third World parochialism lurking somewhere.

Let us now see whether these findings hold up when contrasted with later years, using the *World Press Review* surveys for the years 1993, 1994 and 1995.[4] In 1993 the overlap between AP and UPI was down from nine issues in 1988 to seven; but the number of foreign affairs issues was up from four of twenty to eleven of twenty. In 1994 the overlap stayed at seven issues; and foreign affairs went up to seventeen of twenty. In 1995 we are up to an overlap of nine issues again; and the number of foreign affairs issues reaches fifteen of twenty. In other words, the overlap remains high; there is that culture. But the focus on foreign affairs increases, from Cold War stability (all news are "olds") to inter-nation [ethnic] conflicts all over.

How about the other six media or news services polled, the "Third World oriented editors outside the United States"? Their issues are spread over the world, but they also include news from the United States:

> 1988: Market crash/budget deficit/economic problems;
> Irangate/scam
> 1993: U.S. APEC focus; NAFTA; World Trade Center
> bombing
> 1994: Rise of the U.S. right/end of Democratic majority
> 1995: U.S. & World Bank privatization; Oklahoma blast;
> federal budget; O.J. Simpson

The *World Press Review* commentary on these different world views:

> 1993: Derek Davies in the Far Eastern Economic Review/
> wondered:

. . . if American journalists really found a fruit-fly infestation and a baseball strike more important than guerrilla war in Afghanistan. . . . The list demonstrates just why the Third World is resentful of the West's media.

James Fallows, quoted from an *The National Interest* article:

1994: Apparently no one has figured out how to interest the American public in international trends without exaggerating, oversimplifying, or warping the reality of events to fit domestic U.S. preoccupations of the moment.

1995: . . . the AP poll of U.S. editors and broadcast news-directors seems to underscore the international image of the U.S. media as jingoistic and self-centered, playing up local items while ignoring international news that is arguably more pressing.

Thus, having made the point that the United States either misses the world or sees the rest of the world as related to the United States, let us now focus again on some key missing themes in the U.S. discourse. No attempt will be made to make a summary of the content of this book and the examples mentioned. Nor will we make a systemic comparison on the basis of contrasting U.S. media with media in other countries, and not only with Third World-focused media. But some general remarks can be made about themes that are particularly conspicuous by their absence, beyond missing theme number one: the world.[5]

KEY MISSING THEMES IN US MAINSTREAM DISCOURSE

Let us first look at the mainstream discourse typical of major media, and then at a counter-trend discourse, using as an example U.S.

peace studies. The latter is a rather modest discourse and can be described fairly easily; for the former we need some kind of systematic entry. And the simplest entry in a discourse of how U.S. media relate to international events would be in terms of power, and more precisely in terms of the four basic types of power—military, economic, political, and cultural power—using many of the examples of missing themes from chapter 2.

Discussing military power the United States misses a very basic point in contemporary discourse by not focusing on military doctrine, instead always focusing on military hardware capabilities with some side glances at motivations. A first distinction made in any analysis of military doctrine would be in terms of "aggressive/non-aggressive." The United States, just as others, sees itself as fundamentally non-aggressive. This might itself be worth discussing, in light of more than 200 U.S. military interventions abroad.[6]

The next distinction, given that the military tend to see themselves as non-aggressive, would be whether the country *looks* non-aggressive to others, particularly to "the other side." This can be phrased in terms of "provocative/non-provocative" doctrines, which is another way of stating "offensive defense/defensive defense." Very slowly this type of distinction is entering U.S. discourse, but the basic problem is that other countries are not seen as having the right to judge the United States according to looks.

Again, the point is not whether there is agreement or disagreement on this important issue, but whether the issue is available for public discussion at all. In making it unavailable the United States might simply miss the boat. If others disarm or transarm to defensive defense[7] the United States might find itself in the position of being the last dinosaur, as it once was one of the last countries with slavery intact, and today is one of the last countries with colonialism (the other "last countries" were not the United States, although the United States came fairly close—Brazil/Portugal and France).

And finally, in that connection, attention to non-military power and active non-violence in general. Obtaining the release of Jews in Berlin, who were headed for Auschwitz in early 1943; ending the British rule in India (spelling the end of colonialism everywhere); desegregating the U.S. South; playing a major role ending the Indochina war; overthrowing Marcos, not to mention ending the Cold War are rather major achievements.[8] Not to possess the discourse to discuss nonviolence is intellectually deficient. And yet the deficit persists.

Discussing economic power, a rather important distinction is covered by the "exchange/in-change" division between the external economic effects of exchange with other countries in terms of surplus or deficit, and the internal economic effects of that exchange in terms of whether changes inside a country are basically positive or negative. Assuming that the United States is interested in improving its own economic position, a single-minded focus on trade surplus/trade deficit at the expense of necessary internal changes inside the United States could make the United States slip more deeply into recession.

Conceivably the combination of devaluation of the dollar with a heavy export load on products with a low degree of processing might one day correct the trade deficit. But at the same time the capacity of the country for innovative, sophisticated, enduring and competitive approaches, in the world market and inside the United States, might have been seriously curtailed. Import duty is the easy way out as exemplified by the heavy steel import tariffs imposed in early 2002. And import duty itself constitutes a danger to world peace, because in the longer run that makes either for continued accumulation of a trade deficit again, or for a lasting degradation of the economy to Third World conditions. How the United States will react militarily to this frustration is for anybody to guess. And it does not help that the U.S. discourse on alternative economic systems is so poor; it exists only in terms of the tired dichotomy capitalism/socialism.

Discussing political power, the failure of the United States to build the United Nations into the discourse, except as something to be ridiculed, marginalized, used, perhaps even crippled,[9] might also make the United States miss the boat. The UN will eventually come out of its crisis; possibly through some sort of decoupling from the United States, and not by U.S. withdrawal or bullying, but rather by the UN increasing its distance. The United States might then discover that a world community of relatively equal partners is taking shape all the time, and to be on top may mean to be outside. If the country has an offensive military doctrine, a stockpile of long-range weapons, quantitative economic doctrines, and a deteriorating economic condition in terms of quality of production, all is set for a rather dangerous scenario, not only for the world but also for the United States.

Discussing the cultural power underlying the previous three, there are points relating *taboos* to *myths*. A taboo protects a myth known to be vulnerable by serving as a stop sign. If the myth is solid there is no problem talking about it; only the weak myth gives rise to taboos, showing up as a discourse reduction to zero.

Examples:

Americans as a chosen people. A well-disseminated Manifest Destiny myth, present in most military encounters involving the

United States since the nineteenth century. A discourse relating this cultural item to U.S. military, economic, and political behavior has yet to surface in the mainstream media, however.

The United States as a democracy. A highly vulnerable myth when scrutinized. Consequently, taboos against discussing (sometimes even reporting) the weak voter participation in U.S. elections, the narrow range of choice, the way in which crucial issues are kept outside the democratic debate (covert action, the whole Iran-gate complex except for the problem "did the President know"), and so forth.

The United States as a problem, not as a solution. Reports from abroad, including public opinion polls in which the United States is seen more as a problem than as a solution, are accompanied by great disbelief; how can people be that stupid and/or ideological. The focus is on "will the Russians cheat," "will the Sandinistas cheat," "will Saddam Hussein cheat," not on a question that can be answered affirmatively with higher probability: "will the Americans cheat."

The killing engaged in by U.S. covert action. Interestingly, even the Christic Institute focused on *illegal* covert action and ARDIS (the Association for Responsible Dissent, created by ex-CIA agents) also focused on precisely that, *responsible* dissent. However, the statement, attributed to ARDIS, that more than six million people have been killed by U.S. covert action since the end of the Second World War, was not made available in U.S. media.[10] This already indicates why people wanting to do something qualify their target as "illegal, covert," and themselves as "responsible."

The killing of Native Americans. Everybody knows about it; few talk about it. One of the biggest genocides in human history, and at least partly intended, took place in North America and Hawai'i, eliminating wholly or partly, one way or the other, nations in the way of settlement; personified by Sitting Bull and Queen Liliuokolani.[11] This set a pattern for U.S. behavior toward other people. That other people, and the survivors of genocide in particular, might have some views on the subject; that the United States would prefer to forget and place a taboo on the issue, is obvious.

But sometimes frankness and honesty pay off better than concealment, as can be seen so clearly in the Japanese efforts to cover up that which happened in the Second World War (the "textbook issue," Korean "comfort women" forced into prostitution). This issue is important not only for human rights, and the territorial rights of Native Americans (including Hawaiians); but also because what happened set a pattern for U.S. behavior in other countries, for instance in the Pacific (Guam, American Samoa) converting "natives" into minorities, and then treating them as "minority problems."

Revolution as a normal social process. U.S. ambivalence in connection with "revolution" is proverbial: on the one hand a glorification of The American Revolution, on the other hand the denial of the right of most other peoples in the world to have a revolution (unless they revolt against enemies of the United States). The American Revolution was not that revolutionary, but it was a reaction to intolerable conditions (whether the conditions were "no taxation without representation," "the demarcation line," both, neither, something else). Other countries also have intolerable national or international conditions, and will continue trying to do something about it regardless of how the United States reacts or what it writes. But there are taboos against comparing revolutions elsewhere with the American Revolution, thereby denying them legitimacy.

The linkage between capitalism and social evils. The evils are discussed as eco-disasters, crime, corruption, materialism, individualism, excessive competitiveness, social inequality, dissolution of the social fabric, and so on; seen in their own right, not as emanating from capitalism, which is not so good. Of course one should also discuss "the linkage between socialism and social evils," but that is no counter-argument. First, two wrongs do not make one right. Second, that problem is not the key problem of the United States. The capitalism-social evils linkage discourse has a leftist tinge to it, and the plea would be for that element of leftism to enter mainstream U.S. public discourse. Anyone leaving it out does so at considerable risk to the country and its people, as important remedies for the ills may take the form of modifying capitalism.

The particular position of the Jewish-American element in the U.S. social system; and of Israel in the U.S. world system. Any taboo in this connection will only lead to a much higher level of anti-Semitism once the taboo is broken than if such issues as AIPAC influence over U.S. foreign policy, Jewish-American influence over media and academic life, and Israeli influence over the United States are brought out in the open and discussed. In Israel this taboo has been broken, also before the Palestinian uprising and the accords. The point is not only the sacred nature and the "moral high stand" of Israel, but also the ability of Israel to steer U.S. foreign policy. The same argument applies: with this taboo anti-Israel sentiment will erupt when the taboo is finally broken (and taboos are very attractive), and at a considerably higher level than the trickle resulting from minor taboo infractions.

MISSING THEMES IN A COUNTER-TREND DISCOURSE

Let us now turn our attention to a counter-trend discourse, certainly of minor significance compared to what has just been said, and have a look at the discourses opened by U.S. peace studies. One little example will make the basic point. An important organization in U.S. peace studies was the Institute for Global Conflict and Cooperation, the IGCC of the University of California system headquartered in University of California San Diego, La Jolla, California. The name of the Institute is already a 2-point discourse and not a bad summary of what peace studies is or should be about: *conflict* and *cooperation.* There is a negative aspect, something dangerous that should somehow be controlled; and there is a positive aspect, something promising that should be encouraged. In other words, a discourse is opened, inviting explorations to establish discourses within discourses and so on.

However, the point made here is more modest: *Only the first discourse point is developed.* Everything about conflict was spelled out in great detail. An analytical discourse was established for conflict, but very little for cooperation as such, except in the sense of cooperation to avert conflict.[12] Why? Probably because the meta-script is more about conflict than cooperation.[13]

So there are missing themes also in U.S. peace studies. More particularly, we would recognize five such missing themes, based on some experience with this particular field in that particular country. But saying this is also belaboring the obvious: no discourse is complete, there will always be missing themes.

First, as just mentioned: a general failure to come to grips with positive peace in the sense of cooperation between equal partners. The reason is obvious: the general absence in the United States of theories of equity and equality, beyond a theory of equality of opportunity, as something to be built into a structure, so that the outcome is equitable. In other words, equity as absence of exploitation, which is not discussed either, there being no theory of exploitation. "International equity" is more easily said than done when one country is a super-power and most others are not. But without an equity discourse it cannot even be said, much less done.

Thus, cooperation on an equal basis would presuppose, in the military field, that the parties are equally strong or operating within a defensive military doctrine, based on short-range weapons systems. Economically the assumption would be a high level of self-reliance, and on top of that exchange on an equitable basis, not cheating, sharing positive and negative "side-effects" equally.

Politically the assumption would be democratic world assemblies operating according to the "one country, one vote" principle, weighted voting according to military and economic power making equality impossible. And culturally the assumption would be that no country sees itself as more chosen, more annointed, with more rights and duties to "assume leadership" than others. Since none of the above applies to the United States it may not be so easy, even for U.S. researchers with a strong peace commitment, to develop images of cooperation on an equitable basis. In fact, very few such images seem to thrive on U.S. soil.

Second, and very much related to the first point: absence of an adequate discourse for a peaceful world. A peaceful world is hardly possible without a high level of cooperation, in other words positive peace, and that in turn is not possible without patterns of equality and equity backed up by solid theory and practice. With no image of equity the temptation to yield to hierarchic *pax americana*-type models, with the United States playing a "leading role," will prevail over solid, well-reasoned peace discourse. Such ideas are already built into the culture of which U.S. peace researchers are a part and protected by solid taboos. The choice is usually put in terms of "hierarchy" versus "anarchy," or "global responsibility" versus "isolationism"; not in terms of equality versus inequality, equity versus exploitation. Without that third discourse U.S. peace research degenerates to security studies, biological aggressiveness or not studies, and so forth. And, as mentioned above, studies of negative peace, how to make people or countries less aggressive, tend to be better developed than studies of positive, cooperative, peace.

Third, a rather important actor in the world system, the United States, is missing from so many U.S. articles and books on peace studies. From the outside it is rather obvious that the United States was not born as a good world citizen in the world community of countries; the rather violent history of the country, both on the inside (labor relations, African-Americans, Native Americans) and the outside (interventions) bear ample testimony to this. Some marxists have a ready answer why this is so: capitalism. Inadequate, but better than the many who deny any violent inclination in the United States.

The problem with the marxist answer is that capitalism came after, not before, violence in U.S. history, which existed from the very beginning to eliminate those who stood in the way, Native Americans, other nations and ideologies, and so forth. If the marxist discourse is inadequate and should be played down, not for political but for intellectual reasons, then there should be a solid search for an *alternative, critical discourse* within which a theory about the country could emerge. That happens in several fields in the United States, such as in history and economics, but not much in peace studies (nor in communication studies). Instead other peoples' conflicts are studied. And the formula "ethnic conflict" comes in very handy at this point. It points in the intra-county direction (meaning that the United States at most plays a marginal role), and points to other nations, the term "ethnic" usually being applied to somebody else (like in "let's go out having some ethnic food tonight"). The understanding of the forces outside the conflict theater, where "ethnics" are killing each other, is low and in addition unexplored, like in the discourses for Yugoslavia and Somalia indicated in chapter 2. That discourse also makes it possible for the superpowers, such as the United States and the European Union, to appear as the disinterested third parties who kindly offer their services for mediation (maybe with a little "muscle").

Fourth, we are also missing a more holistic approach to peace studies. The global aspect of peace studies is relatively well taken care of, among other reasons because so many nationalities can be found on any campus in the United States. There is inter-disciplinarity in the sense of people from different disciplines cooperating.

But there is not much holism, the rhetoric notwithstanding. A simple reason for this would be that career patterns are still within well-established disciplines. A peace researcher will be evaluated according to the field of the Ph.D. degree, and can only deviate from this at his or her own considerable risk. This may also be the case in three other inter-disciplinary, to a large extent holistic, areas perhaps better established than peace studies: women's studies, development studies, and environmental studies. The great advances made in these fields, exploring the discourses surrounding gender and nature, are among the strongest U.S. contributions to peace studies. Why?

Probably because the issues are not necessarily international. Women's studies challenge patriarchic more than patriotic values; technical development/environmental studies can be shared by many. But honest peace studies attempt to clarify the relation of the United States to others, not easily done without challenging "U.S. exceptionalism."

Fifth, very little research is done in the field of cultural power, this being where taboos of the most solid nature are located. Basic tenets of U.S. civil religion, such as being chosen, being above others, being born for leadership, are not brought into the open and evaluated in terms of their peace productive or peace counter-productive relevance. Consequently, little attention is paid to the United Nations in U.S. peace studies in particular, and in U.S. social science and U.S. media in general. The UN is based on the assumption that all are equal (except in security matters), an assumption which does not go well with the U.S. self-image.

In short, the discourse of U.S. peace studies is not very different from mainstream U.S. discourse. There are such nuances in the military field as more emphasis on disarmament, not only "arms control," but not much emphasis on alternative military doctrines as an intellectual rationale for alternative security policies. And nothing so far can be used as a basis for equitable economic cooperation between economic giants (albeit sometimes with shaky legs, standing on clay) and economic dwarfs. The United States plays the first role in South America, and both roles relative to countries on the Western Rim of the Pacific Ocean, now transforming the world economic system. So, what are we going to do about it?

U.S. GLASNOST

The conclusion from everything said so far in this book is rather clear. It is not only in the world interest but also in the U.S. national interest that the U.S. public discourse, not only in the media but also in political circles, undergoes a dramatic transformation. The range of important perspectives and available options not covered is simply too broad, as if every issue that impinges on U.S. media is forwarded to some big factory for quick transformation, cutting corners, blunting edges, making the issues unrecognizable. But if not properly debated, options are not seen, and options not seen are options not available. The United States is hurt, and, being a major world actor, the world is also hurt. And the people are hurt, being fed conflicts as entertainment script poured into poor discourses with heavily biased analysis.[14]

Is the question "only" how to do it? Let us look at the country of origin for the title of this book: Gorbachev's Soviet Union. The total story of the Soviet *glasnost* has by no means been told, but a short list of significant factors would include:

1. The Soviet Union labored under Censorship I conditions.
2. The result was not only a highly distorted discourse, but also an almost complete lack of credibility for whatever was communicated in public space. Private space became rich, creative, expressive, just as in Nazi-occupied Europe during World War II.
3. The initiative to change points (1) and (2) came from above: a nonviolent revolution spearheaded by Gorbachev.

4. The Soviet Union had in recent decades obtained a quite
   high level of education and sophistication, including at
   the top.

The key factor here, the factor of intervention, is number (3).
But this was not a sufficient condition. The Soviet people had been
trained to live under Censorship I conditions, certainly leading to a
total lack of media credibility, but also to the idea that initiatives
come from above. The forces that had introduced Censorship I were
also seen as capable of removing, or at least dramatically reducing,
censorship. Indeed, the very same forces at the top of society that
had commanded absence of clearness and frankness could now
demand the presence of those formerly so scarce commodities. Of
course, this invariably led to the problem that a broader discourse,
and a deeper discourse, requires more of the readers/
listeners/viewers. But that was also to a large extent taken care of
because of the increase in general education.

In short, Gorbachev was a necessary, but by no means a
sufficient, factor. He could only have operated in a context of the
other three, and other factors other analysts of the situation might
bring to our attention. The question is to what extent this model also
could apply to the United States, saying from the very beginning that
the Soviet story is only a heuristic device to explore a discourse
about discourse transformation.

The United States is not really suffering from Censorship I,
but smarting under Censorship II conditions. Partly for that reason
there is no basic lack of credibility. Precisely because what is
presented in the media in general does not originate in a command
from above it is assumed to be uncensored. And that is the problem.

The repair needed for a discourse transformation would have
to take place inside the heads of countless editors, columnists,
journalists, educators, and a public used to narrow discourses, not
only inside the head of one very powerful person at the center of the
system. It is all reminiscent of Voltaire's famous statement about the
advantage of monarchy: "in a democracy you have to train everybody
in order to get good politics; in a monarchy one pupil is sufficient"
(with Voltaire as a teacher, one might presume?). Clearly, nothing
like this is true for the United States today.

The U.S. conditions for a transformation are the opposite of
the conditions for *glasnost* in the Soviet Union. The Soviet Union not
only tolerated but needed a vertical approach to the problem; the
United States would need a horizontal approach. Censorship II sits
in the minds of countless people; somehow they have to remove it
together.

A new president with a new discourse would not automatically be listened to, except to point out how he does not fit into mainstream discourse. A good example of this from recent U.S. history would be President Jimmy Carter, whose moralistic, often compassionate, highly human rights-oriented discourse did not sit well with the media. A transformation in the White House is neither necessary nor sufficient for discourse transformation.

However, before leaving the comparison completely: how about the educational factor? The United States is also a country with a high percentage of the population in and with higher education, and with centers of sophistication such as New York, the Boston area, Chicago, the San Francisco and Los Angeles areas, and some others. The United States is also an educational superpower.

But education might work in very different ways in the two countries. The Soviet Union had intellectuals in the traditional European sense—people who are individualistic, self-assertive, and are being read, interviewed, and listened to in the media. An *akademik* in the Soviet Union counted, and not only when his name was Sakharov. Books, newspaper columns, interviews would be on everybody's lips. This is not the case in the United States, as argued in chapter 6. Marginalization of intellectuals in campus ghettos and discipline ghettos has worked: few would be quoted nationally, and certainly not those with very controversial messages (like Noam Chomsky, Herbert Schiller, I. F. Stone, and so forth). Apparently, a country feeding on junk food will also feed on junk intellectuals, the columnists, rather than drawing on the thousands of real intellectuals.

Where would the opening be for a discourse transformation in the case of the United States if there is no real sense of credibility crisis? The answer would probably have to dwell on the latter point first. Crises will accumulate, no problem with that. True, Black Monday 1987 came and went without any basic change in the discourse demanded from economists, presumably the experts in the matter. But such crises may be more dramatic in the future, and there may be a demand for alternative forms of understanding that could lead to ways out of the crises. The assumption that such demands would necessarily come from center/left (social democrat or green) quarters is rather naive; it could just as well come from a right-wing (ultra-conservative, even brown/black) orientation.

There is an important difference, however. If a reader is particularly interested in seeing the present from the point of view of the past, then right-wing media are recommended. They will present the present as seen by established forces, the forces of the past. But if the focus is on the future, then the left-wing media are better. They will generally have better contact with the discontented and underprivileged, and be more willing to give them a voice. Among them the new emerging forces will be located. A person only exposed to right-wing media will have an interesting life, full of surprises, because he has not been introduced to these forces. His image will be that they are evil, lurking under the horizon, and hence very dangerous. And a person only exposed to left-wing media may have a tendency to overestimate these forces and to underestimate the staying power of the establishment.

But there will be a demand. And if the supply is not forthcoming the population will create its own media, some type of underground press marginalized by the mainstream media, flowering not only to the left but also to the right (but by definition not in the middle), and all over the country.

The problem is that any discourse transformation would have to be brought into the major media, the heavy TV and radio networks, including the public TV/radio system, which is certainly broader, more elaborate, but not necessarily deeper in the sense of bringing up new dimensions, and that is what matters. Attention to the basic issues will have to break through the walls between marginalized and mainstream media, and the walls between jesting columns/cartoons and the front and editorial pages. Three approaches could now be contemplated, all of them problematic.

First, building on demand/supply: readers/listeners/viewers demanding a more adequate discourse, threatening punishment in the form of boycott, promising rewards in buying, listening, and viewing more should a more adequate discourse emerge. Demonstrations by irate viewers circling the CNN building fifteen times would be well reported by ABC, NBC, and CBS, and vice versa. Whether this would lead to any transformation is an open question. And letters to the OpEd page would probably have very little impact, as letters critical of the medium itself do not tend to be printed often, just as the Action for Childrens' Television (ACT)-led campaign to improve children's programming never received wide coverage by the news departments of the three major U.S. television networks.

Call-in programs on the radio might be more useful, but generally enjoy less credibility than the news media. Time is scarce and not devoted to discourse discussions, but to quick questions and answers within the discourse already set. Moreover, talk radio in the United States has become a haven for extreme right-wing hatred discourse, possibly an abuse of freedom of expression.

Second, educating journalists and editors. The tortuous road toward this goal would inevitably pass through the many Schools of Journalism and Departments of Communication. However, not only is the road long, it is also tortuous in the sense that it is not obvious that the tremendous labor that might be spent in trying to influence curricula, writing new books on U.S. media and so on would easily find their ways to the hearts and minds of the target recipients, the journalists/editors. At best this would be a long-term project. And the general tendency is for those teaching the craft of journalism and communication methods to be empirical and technologically deterministic, not critical and not constructive; "this is how it has always been done," perpetuating biases.

Third, there is the possibility of renewal coming from the media themselves. One of them starts, inspired by counter-trend media; the others follow in order not to lose customers. Would the best approach be to open a new network, a new station, a new paper or have the transformation take place within existing ones? The argument would probably end in favor of the latter, because anything new would need much time to become a model imitated by the others. But minority ownership of media does also hold some potential.

The success of the first really national newspaper in the United States, *USA Today*, is certainly not due to any innovation where discourse is concerned, but probably precisely due to the lack of discourse transformation. All over the United States people can feel comfortable with the paper, feel at home not only because their own state is always mentioned—and the glorious, glaring weather maps certainly cover everything under the sky, and the sports section is so comprehensive—but also because nothing controversial is written without being accompanied by mainstream counterpoints.[15]

What, concretely, could one then demand or at least hope for from U.S. media? We would say the following: *be honest*, have discourse transformation itself as a major and explicit focus. Invite people into the media not only to discuss the pros and cons of actions to be taken in connection with any issue, but also to discuss how to discuss the issue. A couple of years devoted to this in a major part of the U.S. media might pay off.

Let the networks compete in having the best panel, once a week, of intellectuals, politicians, and just people, not more than four at a time, and have them discuss how to discuss! This format was sometimes seen during the Persian Gulf War as the media debated coverage strategies. In such dialogues questions to be asked would include: What is missing, what is consistently left out? Let them review programs, with the viewers reviewing the programs, critically, openly. And, let at least 50 percent of the participants belong to groups carrying subjugated discourses in their minds and hearts—women, blacks, minorities of all kinds.

Much attention should also be paid to the major syndicated columnists, about half a dozen in number. Their ways of framing the conceptual pie and deliberating on the issues can be read all over the country. There is some political variety, and that variety is sometimes put inside the same paper (in Europe a much broader variety would be available, but in different papers).

And yet it is remarkable that such a large country with 250 million inhabitants shall be serviced, for its views on very basic matters particularly in foreign affairs, essentially by half a dozen columnists. In a sense it is understandable. The United States has a broad spectrum of engagements all around the world, and it cannot be easy for the editor of a paper in, say, up-state Nebraska to have a clear idea of where to stand on Somalia, Rwanda, Haiti. The predictable arrival of a well-researched column by fax from a syndicated columnist's office must be a blessing even if the editor prefers not to admit it. Economic reasons might also dictate a certain receptivity to the columnist's view: cheap and predictable.

What did we say about the Soviet Union when six people or so in the Politburo had that power over the minds of 290 million? But did they? Under Censorship I they were probably not believed anyhow; people picked up their own media interpretations. And this may also be the key to the solution of the U.S. problem: *use local people much more for commentary.* The United States has universities in abundance, with many professors eager to access public space, and having much to offer. This might also be much better in generating local debate than using an inaccessible columnist from afar.

To that final point should only be added one argument that might sound slightly self-serving: the U.S. media might do well to remember that there is also a rather big "minority" outside the U.S. borders—foreigners, those who live in the remaining well above 180 countries around the world. They/we also have a stake in this discourse. Given the major role of the United States in the world it does matter to all how U.S. media discuss or do not discuss the issues of the world. The United States is not alone in the world. Those who try to broaden and deepen the U.S. discourse will not be alone. They might even be applauded.

NOTES

1. "The Top 10 Stories of 1988", *World Press Review*, February 1989.
2. Ibid.
3. Virtual reality = constructed reality. Of course, all reality is also constructed, so it becomes a question of degree. For the concept in general, see Howard Rheingold, *Virtual Reality* (London: 1991) and Benjamin Woolley, *Virtual Worlds* (Oxford: Blackwell, 1992).

4. As usual, reported in *World Press Review* in the February issue of the following year.
5. For an effort to explore missing themes in a U.S. presidential campaign, see Johan Galtung, "US Political Discourse and US Media", in *Gazette* 43, 1989, 195-204.
6. *Instances of Use of United States Armed Forces Abroad, 1798-1945* prepared by the Congressional Research Service, Library of Congress, includes 168 cases (not counting wars of conquest against Native Americans), bringing the total to date (early 2002) well above 200, probably around 215. William Blum, in *Killing Hope: U.S. Military and CIA Interventions Since World War II* (Monroe, ME: Common Courage Press, 1995), lists 55 cases of U.S. interventionism around the world after World War II; a question being to what extent this is "Use of United States Armed Forces Abroad." Anyhow, 168 + 55 = 223, a lower estimate being 215.
7. Or abolish the military forces; about 30 countries (mainly small ones) have no army at all.
8. See *Peace by Peaceful Means*, part II, chapter 5, "Nonviolent Conflict Transformations," pp. 114-126.
9. For instance by withholding the U.S. contribution to the UN, the same way the U.S. Senate can cripple a foreign policy desired by the Executive by refusing to vote the funding necessary (obvious examples: the search for alternative funding, ultimately leading to Iran/contra, by the Reagan administration; or the idea of taxing international monetary transactions/transport by the Boutros Boutros-Ghali administration).
10. See *The Guardian Weekly*, 30 December 1987, article by Coleman McCarthy, "Excesses of the CIA": "With the group estimating that at least six million people have died as a consequence of U.S. covert operations since World War II one question rushes in from the cold. Why not go beyond the banning of all covert actions to abolishing the CIA altogether?"
11. Some of the best books are by David Stannard: *Before the Horror* (Honolulu: University of Hawai'i Press, 1989, about the Hawaiians) and *The American Holocaust* (New York: Oxford University Press, 1993, about the Americas).
12. Have a look at the themes for the 1988 Summer Seminar: "the history of the arms race; the causes of war; proliferation; the psychology of the arms race; how a nuclear war might start; deterrent theory; views on arms control; current arms negotiation; U.S. and Soviet decision making for national security; ally relations and European security; new technologies; ethical and moral issues; antinuclear activism; where we go from here."

On the other hand, six years later, and five years after the Cold War officially ended, the *IGCC Newsletter* (vol. X, no. 1 Spring 1994)—in addition to "Arms Control and Security in the Middle East," "U.S. Leadership in the Asia-Pacific region," "North East Asian Cooperation Dialogue" (without North Korea), and "Enforcement of International Environmental Agreements"— contains a feature, "Negotiating with an Adversary" (pp. 6-8), with quite useful advice about negotiations, even if the language is adversarial.

13. As the saying goes, "Winning is not everything; winning is the only thing!", exemplified by the powerful scripts of sports, business, and war. Thus, typical photos of a U.S. congressman in the secretary's office would display the politician in sports clothes or a military uniform, not the politician engaging in cooperative brain-storming to arrive at, together with others, some new form of cooperation. A winner, for sure, a leader; not a wimp.

14. President Traina of Clark University in Massachusetts expresses this point as follows: "Television has also had a profound effect. . . . The students are accustomed to being entertained. They are not accustomed to sustained analysis and attention. They don't read well. They don't write well." They do, however, have a visual acuity that Traina sometimes envies. "But visual literacy cannot supplant reading and writing," Traina believes. "Both remain essential intellectual tools." From "Presidents See their Roles as Unique and Essential," *Sunday Telegram,* Worcester, MA, April 2, 1995.

15. Consider its current nickname: MacPaper. The promise is to deliver a product as homogeneous and sterile as you will get at a McDonald's restaurant.

Author Index

Subject Index

A

ABC (American Broadcasting Company—*see* Capital Cities/ABC Inc.)
Abraham, 62
abstract terminology, 218
academics (*see* scholarly community)
Academy of Sciences, 142
access to information (*see* freedom of speech)
accidents, 180
Action for Children's Television (ACT), 240
actor, 161, 163-164, 182-183, 194
additivity hypothesis, 164
Adenauer, 144
adequacy, 100, 117, 119, 157
adolescent, 192
advertising, 209, 211-212
aesthetic theory, 201
Afghanistan, 21, 80
Africa, 10, 72, 221, 227
African American, 76, 126, 194 235

age, 158
agenda setting, 75, 144, 153, 218, 225
aggression, 168, 230
agriculture, 89
aided, 71
AIDS (Acquired Immunity Deficiency Syndrome), 136
AIPAC (American Israeli Public Affairs Committee), 233
airplane, 165
akademik, 239
Albanian, 73, 108, 121
Alla'h, 155
alphabet (Morse), 14, 149
Alta, Norway, 30
Alto-based Web TV Network, 220
ambiguity, 137
ambulances, 214
America On Line (AOL), *see* AOL-Time Warner
American Medical Association (AMA), 35
American Revolution, 233
American Samoa, 233
America-philia, 50-51

Lightning Source UK Ltd.
Milton Keynes UK
UKHW011833100521
383490UK00001B/8

9 781572 731868